GCSE ENGLISH LITERATURE

Ian Barr
Chief Examiner GCSE English

and

David Bazen
Chief Examiner GCSE English Literature

Letts Educational
Aldine Place
London W12 8AW
Tel: 0181 740 2266
Fax: 0181 743 8451
e-mail: mail@lettsed.co.uk

Every effort has been made to trace copyright holders and obtain their permission for the use of copyright material. The authors and publishers will gladly receive information enabling them to rectify any error or omission in subsequent editions.

First published 1997

Text: Ian Barr and David Bazen 1997
Design: BPP (Letts Educational) Ltd 1997

All our Rights Reserved. No part of this publication may be reproduced, stored in a retrieval system, or transmitted, in any form or by any means, electronic, mechanical, photocopying, recording or otherwise, without the prior permission of Letts Educational.

British Library Cataloguing in Publication Data
A CIP record for this book is available from the British Library.

ISBN 1 85758 579 8

Printed in Great Britain by The Nuffield Press Limited, Abingdon, Oxon OX14 1RL

Letts Educational is the trading name of BPP (Letts Educational) Ltd

Contents

Section 1	**Starting points**	*1*
	Introduction	1
	Syllabus analysis	5
	Studying and revising	14
Section 2	**English Literature skills**	*18*
	1 Making comparisons in essays	18
	2 Historical, social and cultural background	27
Section 3	**Prose**	*40*
	3 Responding to prose: novels	40
	4 Responding to prose: short stories	56
Section 4	**Drama**	*64*
	5 Responding to drama: twentieth-century plays	64
	6 Responding to drama: pre-1900 plays	93
	7 Responding to Shakespeare	115
Section 5	**Poetry**	*131*
	8 Responding to poetry	131
Section 6	**Coursework**	*145*
	Coursework skills	145
Section 7	**The examination**	*153*
	Examination questions	153
	Glossary	161
	Index	165

Section 1 Starting points

Introduction

How to use this book

This book is divided into seven sections, which will provide you with a basis for working towards your examination.

The first section gives you general advice on how to revise and prepare for your examination. Use this section to make sure that you understand everything you need to cover, including the specific requirements of your syllabus. Find out (from your teacher) which syllabus you are studying. Although the approaches suggested in this book are relevant to all syllabuses, there are options within each syllabus. You must make sure you know which option you are preparing for. You will find details of your syllabus in the syllabus analysis section on pages 5–13.

The middle sections contain detailed advice on writing and revising essays. The first two chapters focus on skills that you will need to display in your essays; the remaining chapters focus on how to approach prose, drama and poetry.

The last two sections look at coursework and then at the examination itself, taking you through sample questions, or tasks, and sample answers.

Introduction to GCSE English Literature

Literature is part of our heritage. Characters created in novels, short stories and plays come alive for us, while descriptions of places in literature enable us to see our own surroundings in ways we never appreciated before. Plots are sometimes told in ways which, by their very intricacy, fascinate us. Perhaps poetry sharpens these feelings in us.

To have no knowledge of literature is to have a gap in our knowledge; it is as important to have some understanding of literature as it is to know arithmetic or to understand the basic principles of science.

English Literature is not a National Curriculum subject, although you will be aware that English contains a great deal of work based on literature. In most schools, English literature is studied as a natural part of English lessons and the opportunity to enter for the GCSE in English Literature is seen by the school simply as a part of your English course assessment. In other schools, you may choose to study English Literature as part of the option system, having made a personal, positive decision to study literature in particular.

Changes to the study of GCSE English Literature

Under the new syllabuses, all GCSE English Literature courses require you to study the three genres of prose, drama and poetry. For each genre, you must study one text of 'sufficient substance and quality' published before 1900 and one text of high quality

Introduction

published after 1900. These regulations are meant to ensure that you do not study just modern literature, but that you begin to be acquainted with some of the fine writing published in previous centuries. This has been interpreted to mean that you must study six texts in all:

- two plays, one published before 1900 and one after;
- two sets of poetry, one published before 1900 and one after;
- two novels (or selections of short stories), one published before 1900 and one after.

Nowhere in all of this is Shakespeare mentioned. For English Literature, it is not necessary to study Shakespeare unless your examination board requires it. However, the most obvious choice of a dramatist before 1900 is Shakespeare, so most English Literature students will study Shakespeare.

When you study poetry, you should cover a reasonable number of poems. This will help your understanding of poetry in general, as well as fulfil the syllabus requirements. There are various ways of grouping poetry: by poet, by theme (e.g. 'love' or 'war'), by form (e.g. ballad or sonnet), or by type or approach (e.g. humour or satire).

Other requirements have also been introduced, such as the comparison of different texts. See 'Assessment Objectives' on page 3 for a breakdown of how you will be assessed.

Tiering

All GCSE examinations are tiered and you should discuss with your teacher which tier you should enter for.

The Higher Tier will give you access to grades A★ to D, while the Foundation Tier will give you access to grades C to G. Clearly there needs to be careful consideration at the time of entry, especially if your teacher believes you could achieve a grade C.

GCSE English Literature and English

GCSE English Literature is both a study in itself as well as an integral part of your English course. National Curriculum (GCSE) English requires a number of different types of reading, including media and non-fiction sources like travel books and biographies, as well as literature. The National Curriculum Orders (or requirements) for English specify literature 'from the English literary heritage in previous centuries', as well as major works from the early twentieth century and 'high quality' contemporary literature. Some of your reading for GCSE English will include works from this list, which is reprinted below.

- two plays by Shakespeare;
- drama by major playwrights, e.g. *Christopher Marlowe, J.B. Priestley, George Bernard Shaw, R.B. Sheridan*;
- two works of fiction of high quality by major writers, published before 1900, drawn from those by Jane Austen, Charlotte Brontë, Emily Brontë, John Bunyan, Wilkie Collins, Arthur Conan Doyle, Daniel Defoe, Charles Dickens, George Eliot, Henry Fielding, Elizabeth Gaskell, Thomas Hardy, Henry James, Mary Shelley, Robert Louis Stevenson, Jonathan Swift, Anthony Trollope, H.G. Wells;
- two works of fiction of high quality by major writers with well established critical reputations, whose works were published after 1900, e.g. *William Golding, Graham Greene, James Joyce, D.H. Lawrence, Muriel Spark*;
- poems of high quality by four major poets, whose works were published before 1900, drawn from those by Matthew Arnold, Elizabeth Barrett Browning, William Blake, Emily Brontë, Robert Browning, Robert Burns, Lord Byron, Geoffrey Chaucer, John Clare, Samuel Taylor Coleridge, John Donne, John Dryden, Thomas Gray, George Herbert, Robert Herrick, Gerard

> Manley Hopkins, John Keats, Andrew Marvell, John Milton, Alexander Pope, Christina Rosetti, Shakespeare (sonnets), Percy Bysshe Shelley, Edmund Spenser, Alfred Lord Tennyson, Henry Vaughan, William Wordsworth, Sir Thomas Wyatt;
>
> - poems of high quality by four major poets with well established critical reputations, whose works were published after 1900, e.g. *T.S. Eliot, Thomas Hardy, Seamus Heaney, Ted Hughes, Philip Larkin, R.S. Thomas, W.B. Yeats.*
>
> *Material from the National Curriculum is Crown copyright and is reproduced by permission of the Controller of HMSO.*

Remember, this list comes from the National Curriculum Orders for *English*. The examining boards acknowledge that the study of English and English Literature are closely related, and therefore there is considerable overlap between the two courses. Having said that, the requirements for *literature* are not determined by the National Curriculum. GCSE English Literature courses can therefore include a wide range of literature in the English language, including works by American authors. This has resulted in the rather odd situation where Shakespeare must be studied for English but not necessarily for English Literature, and American writers can be studied for English Literature but not for English!

You may be able to use some coursework assignments for both English and English Literature, so long as each piece fulfils the criteria for both syllabuses. Consult your teacher and your syllabus to find out how your coursework might 'overlap'.

Assessment Objectives

You should always obtain a copy of the syllabus for the subjects you are studying from the relevant examining board. The syllabus sets out what you are expected to learn from your course. For English Literature, of course, both you and your teacher will be concerned with the set books. But you should also look carefully at the Assessment Objectives, which describe how your achievement will be judged, in terms of your coursework and the examination.

Here are the Assessment Objectives for GCSE English Literature as set out in one of the syllabuses. You should be able to demonstrate your ability to:

❶ *respond to texts critically, sensitively and in detail, selecting appropriate ways to convey response, and using textual evidence as appropriate.*

You could turn this objective into a checklist for yourself both before writing – at the planning and drafting stage – and after you have finished. Responding 'critically' means you are able to say why one thing is important and another is not, why one character's action is justified while another's is not, or why one thing has been expressed in a certain way while another is expressed differently. You should show yourself to be 'sensitive', showing understanding and empathy, and showing awareness of the ways in which the writer has chosen to arrange things. You should also show a good knowledge of the text, by selecting illustrations, references and quotations appropriately.

❷ *explore how language, structure and forms contribute to the meaning of texts, considering different approaches to texts and alternative interpretations.*

This objective highlights how important it is to look at the way a writer has constructed a novel, poem or play. The way that the writing is expressed (this includes the choice of vocabulary, the order of events, what is said by characters, what is said about characters, and so on) plays an important part in the way we understand what we read, and it enables us to work out what the author may have intended. You should show how the way in which the writing is arranged and expressed affects the reader or the audience. In fact, there are usually different ways of looking at what is read; you should also show that you are aware of alternative views to your own. You can demonstrate this through discussion or reading. Some expressions that you might use are 'perhaps' or 'maybe' or 'alternatively'.

❸ *explore relationships and comparisons between texts, selecting and evaluating relevant material, and show an understanding of literary tradition and an appreciation of social and historical influences and cultural contexts.*

This objective picks out a skill that is given particular emphasis in the new GCSE courses. You need to show that you understand how things are connected or related, and you should make comparisons to show similarities and differences. It is also important that you are aware of the 'literary tradition'. The texts that we read have a background in English literature because writers are readers, too! A text you read may be like other types of writing, for example the Gothic novel or love poetry. We may even be able to say how one type of writing gave rise to another at a later date. This is what is meant by 'literary tradition'. As you read and study, you should also recognise that texts come from particular times and societies. These factors influenced the way the text was written, so it helps to know something of a writer and the times or conditions in which he or she lived. Beliefs held strongly by a society at one time may be of little or no concern two hundred years later, but your awareness of this will help you to study more successfully. Your ability to make comparisons and to show an understanding of social, historical and literary contexts must be conveyed in writing, so it is of the utmost importance that you practise the skill of writing well.

These Assessment Objectives are the 'rules of the game'. Examination questions must give candidates opportunities to demonstrate these skills. In the whole 'examination', i.e. in the written paper plus coursework, you will have to demonstrate all of these skills.

Examiner's tip

Look carefully at what you are expected to do. Check that you cover all aspects of the course, but put particular emphasis on:
- how writers achieve effects;
- relationships and comparisons;
- carefully constructed essays.

You, the reader

Throughout this book we hope to give you useful advice and there is only one additional message that we want to put here. Give yourself time to enjoy literature. Some of you will say that you naturally read fast while others of you will say that you find it takes you a very long time to read a book. Whichever sort of reader you are, you still need time to read and reflect on what you have read. If you ever feel you haven't quite understood a twist in the plot then go back and make sure. If you enjoy a poem then go back and read it again; poetry is worth re-visiting over and over again. If you find that one of the plays you are studying is on the television or at a local theatre then take time out and go and watch it.

Life is lived at a fairly hectic pace and literature is a study which allows you to have a new perspective on things. So take some time, enjoy your study of English literature and good luck!

Syllabus analysis

Understanding your syllabus requirements

Examiner's tip

- Check with your teacher to find out not only which syllabus you are studying, but also which options and which set texts.
- Make sure that you also check how any possible overlap of your English and English Literature coursework will be managed.

Find out from your teacher which syllabus you are studying. There are choices in all of the syllabuses. Although there may be some compulsory sections, your teacher will have decided which texts you are to study. Several boards produce their own anthologies, containing many or all of the set texts. You will study some texts for the examination and others for coursework. Make sure that you know the complete list of texts that you will be studying and that you understand which will be used for the examination and which for coursework. This is important, as it may affect the way you use your texts; for instance, you might annotate your coursework texts differently from the examination texts.

Remember that some of your coursework assignments can be used for both English Literature and English. In any 'overlapping' assignment, the piece must meet the criteria for both syllabuses. Just how the overlap is managed is not the decision of the examination board, but of your teacher. Some teachers will plan to overlap as many assignments as possible while others may decide to keep the two subjects separate.

You will find an analysis of *your* syllabus on one of pages 6–13. This will sum up the general requirements for the examination paper and coursework, as well as details of the set texts. The address of the examination board is also provided; you should always obtain a copy of the complete syllabus through the board. Consult the syllabus for full details of your course and make sure you are aware of any recent changes in the requirements. As the examination approaches, you may wish to obtain some past papers from the board. If you are a private candidate not attached to a school or college, you may wish to find a centre where you can take the examination.

Note

When you are preparing coursework make sure you ask your teacher which pieces can be submitted for both English and English Literature. All syllabuses allow this overlap and your teacher will almost certainly suggest that you exploit the possibility; with some syllabuses the overlap can be total.

Syllabus analysis

London Examinations (part of EdExcel)

Stewart House, 32 Russell Square, London WC1B 5DN Tel: 0171 331 4000

Option 1 or 2

Coursework

3 units, free choice of texts:
- Unit 1 pre-1900 drama
- Unit 2 pre-1900 prose (Option 1) or post-1900 prose (Option 2)
- Unit 3 post-1900 poetry

30% of total marks

Examination (open book)

2 hours 30 minutes

70% of total marks

- **Section A**: 1 question on pre-1900 poetry

    Set texts
    Poems by Wordworth and Rossetti (in the board's *Anthology*)

- **Section B**: 1 question on post-1900 prose (Option 1) *or*
    1 question on pre-1900 prose (Option 2)

Set texts (Option 1)	**Set texts (Option 2)**
To Kill a Mockingbird (Lee)	*Silas Marner* (Eliot)
Roll of Thunder, Hear My Cry (Taylor)	*Great Expectations* (Dickens)
The Wheel of Surya (Gavin)	*Jane Eyre* (Charlotte Brontë)
Ethan Frome (Wharton)	*Far from the Madding Crowd* (Hardy)
Of Mice and Men (Steinbeck)	*The Picture of Dorian Gray* (Wilde)
Nineteen Eighty-Four (Orwell)	*Pride and Prejudice* (Austen)

- **Section C**: 1 question on post-1900 drama

    Set texts
    Educating Rita (Russell)
    Equus (Shaffer)
    Journey's End (Sherriff)
    An Inspector Calls (Priestley)
    A View from the Bridge (Miller)
    The Glass Menagerie (Williams)

Midland Examining Group (MEG)

Syndicate Buildings, 1 Hills Road, Cambridge CB1 2EU Tel: 01223 553311

Option 1 or 2

Coursework
3 units, free choice of texts:
>   post-1900 prose or pre-1900 prose, depending on choice of examination text
>   pre-1900 poetry
>   pre-1900 drama

30% of total marks

Examination (open book)
2 hours 30 minutes
70% of total marks

- **Section A**: 1 question on post-1900 drama

Set texts (List 1)	Set texts (List 2)
Billy Liar (Waterhouse)	*Hobson's Choice* (Brighouse)
Pygmalion (Shaw)	*Educating Rita* (Russell)
When We Are Married (Priestley)	*Absent Friends* (Ayckbourn)
The Crucible (Miller)	*A View from the Bridge* (Miller)
	An Inspector Calls (Priestley)

- **Section B**: 1 question on pre-1900 prose or post-1900 prose

Set texts (Option 1)	Set texts (Option 2)
The Withered Arm and Other Wessex Tales (Hardy – Heinemann edition)	*The New Windmill Book of Nineteenth-Century Short Stories* (ed. Hamlin, Hall and Browne)
Pride and Prejudice (Austen)	*The Warden* (Trollope)
Dr Jekyll and Mr Hyde (Stevenson)	*The Mayor of Casterbridge* (Hardy)
Huckleberry Finn (Twain)	*Great Expectations* (Dickens)
	Roll of Thunder, Hear My Cry (Taylor)
	Animal Farm (Orwell)
	Of Mice and Men (Steinbeck)
	To Kill a Mockingbird (Lee)
	Lord of the Flies (Golding)

- **Section C**: 1 question on post-1900 poetry

Set texts (Option 1)	Set texts (Option 2)
Selected poems from: *Touched with Fire* (ed. Hydes) *MEG Anthology*	Poems of Plath and Heaney in *Poems* 2 (ed. Markus and Jordan) Selected poems from *MEG Anthology*

Northern Examinations and Assessment Board (NEAB)

Devas Street, Manchester M15 6EX Tel: 0161 953 1180

Coursework

3 assignments, free choice of texts:
   Shakespeare (pre-1900 drama)
   post-1900 drama
   wide reading (pre-1900 prose)

30% of total marks

Examination (open book)

2 hours
70% of total marks

- **Section A**: 1 question on post-1900 prose

    Set texts
    NEAB Anthology
    The Lord of the Flies (Golding)
    The Go-between (Hartley)
    I'm the King of the Castle (Hill)
    A Kestrel for a Knave (Hines)
    To Kill a Mockingbird (Lee)
    My Oedipus Complex and Other Stories (O'Connor)
    Animal Farm (Orwell)
    Salt on the Snow (Smith)
    Of Mice and Men (Steinbeck)
    Daz 4 Zoe (Swindells)
    Roll of Thunder, Hear My Cry (Taylor)
    Talking in Whispers (Watson)

- **Section B**: 1 question on pre- and post-1900 poetry

    Set texts
    Selected poems from:
    NEAB Anthology
    A Choice of Poets (ed. Hewett)
    New Dragon Book of Verse (ed. Harrison and Stuart-Clark)
    Visible Voices (ed. Jones)

Northern Ireland Council for the Curriculum, Examinations and Assessment (NICCEA)

Clarendon Dock, 29 Clarendon Road, Belfast BT1 3BG Tel: 01232 261200

Coursework

3 units, free choice of texts:
   pre-1900 prose
   pre-1900 poetry
   post-1900 poetry

30% of total marks

Examination (open book)

2 hours 30 minutes
70% of total marks

- **Section A**: 1 question on Shakespeare
   Set texts
   The Merchant of Venice
   Macbeth

- **Section B**: 1 question on post-1900 drama
   Set texts
   Juno and the Paycock (O'Casey)
   Pygmalion (Shaw)
   An Inspector Calls (Priestley)
   All My Sons (Miller)
   Philadelphia Here I Come! (Friel)

- **Section C**: 1 question on post-1900 prose
   Set texts
   The Old Jest (Johnson)
   Animal Farm (Orwell)
   Of Mice and Men (Steinbeck)
   To Kill a Mockingbird (Lee)
   A Town Like Alice (Shute)

Southern Examining Group (SEG)

Stag Hill House, Guildford, Surrey GU2 5XJ Tel: 01483 506506

Version 1

Coursework

3 assignments, free choice of texts:
- pre- or post-1900 drama
- pre- or post-1900 poetry
- pre- or post-1900 prose

Note: In each case, the period and text chosen for coursework must not have been studied for the examination.

30% of total marks

Examination (closed book)

2 hours 15 minutes
70% of total marks

- **Section A:** 1 question on pre-1900 drama or post-1900 drama (whichever was **not** studied for coursework)

Set texts (pre-1900 drama)	**Set texts (post-1900 drama)**
Romeo and Juliet (Shakespeare)	*An Inspector Calls* (Priestley)
Macbeth (Shakespeare)	*The Crucible* (Miller)
The Importance of Being Earnest (Wilde)	*The Long and the Short and the Tall* (Hall)

- **Section B:** 1 question on pre-1900 poetry or post-1900 poetry (whichever was **not** studied for coursework)

Set texts (pre-1900 poetry)	**Set texts (post-1900 poetry)**
Selected poems from: *The Works of Elizabeth Barrett Browning*, *The Works of Alfred Lord Tennyson*, *The Works of Christina Rossetti* (all available in Wordsworth Editions)	Poems by Heaney, Hughes, Thomas from *19th and 20th Century Verse* (ed. Woodhead) Poems by Kipling, Owen, Rosenberg, Sassoon from *Up the Line to Death* (ed. Gardner) Poems by Clarke, Lochhead, Nichols from *Six Women Poets* (ed. Kinsman)

- **Section C:** 1 question on pre-1900 prose or post-1900 prose (whichever was **not** studied for coursework)

Set texts (pre-1900 prose)	**Set texts (post-1900 prose)**
Great Expectations (Dickens)	*Of Mice and Men* (Steinbeck)
The Mayor of Casterbridge (Hardy)	*To Kill a Mockingbird* (Lee)
Selected stories from *The New Windmill Book of Nineteenth Century Short Stories* (ed. Hamlin, Hall and Browne)	Selected stories from *Short Stories of Our Time* (ed. Barnes)

Version 2

Coursework

3 assignments, free choice of texts:
  pre- or post-1900 drama
  pre- or post-1900 poetry
  pre- or post-1900 prose

Note: In each case, the period and text chosen for coursework must **not** have been studied for the examination.

30% of total marks

Examination (open book)

2 hours 15 minutes
70% of total marks

- **Section A:** 1 question on pre-1900 drama or post-1900 drama (whichever was **not** studied for coursework)

Set texts (pre-1900 drama)	Set texts (post-1900 drama)
Twelfth Night (Shakespeare)	*Pygmalion* (Shaw)
Macbeth (Shakespeare)	*Hobson's Choice* (Harold Brighouse)
She Stoops to Conquer (Goldsmith)	*An Inspector Calls* (Priestley)

- **Section B:** 1 question on pre-1900 poetry or post-1900 poetry (whichever was **not** studied for coursework)

Set texts (pre-1900 poetry)	Set texts (post-1900 poetry)
The General Prologue (Chaucer)	Poems by Noyes, Hardy and Masefield from *The Oxford Book of Narrative Verse* (ed. Opie)
Selected sections from *Poems from Other Centuries* (ed. Tissier)	Poems by Frost and Thomas from *A Choice of Poets* (ed. Hewett)
Poems by Cowper, Tennyson, Rossetti from *The Oxford Book of Narrative Verse* (ed. Opie)	Selected poems from *War Poems* (ed. Martin)
Poems by Blake and Wordworth from *A Choice of Poets* (ed. Hewett)	Selected poems from *Axed Between the Ears* (ed. Kitchen)
Selected poems from *War Poems* (ed. Martin)	

- **Section C:** 1 question on pre-1900 prose or post-1900 prose (whichever was **not** studied for coursework)

Set texts (pre-1900 prose)	Set texts (post-1900 prose)
Pride and Prejudice (Austen)	*Lord of the Flies* (Golding)
Wuthering Heights (Emily Brontë)	*Of Mice and Men* (Steinbeck)
Far from the Madding Crowd (Hardy)	*Roll of Thunder, Hear My Cry* (Taylor)

Welsh Joint Education Committee (WJEC)

245 Western Avenue, Llandaff, Cardiff CF5 2YX Tel: 01222 265000

Syllabus A

Coursework

4 assignments, free choice of texts:
- pre-1900 poetry
- post-1900 poetry
- pre- or post-1900 drama
- pre- or post-1900 prose

Note: For drama and prose, the period and text chosen for coursework must **not** have been studied for the examination.

30% of total marks

Examination (open book)

2 hours 30 minutes

70% of total marks

- **Section A:** 2 questions on pre-1900 prose or post-1900 prose (whichever was **not** studied for coursework)

  Set texts (pre-1900 prose)
  Hard Times (Dickens)
  Silas Marner (Eliot)

  Set texts (post-1900 prose)
  I Know Why the Caged Bird Sings (Angelou)
  Paddy Clarke Ha Ha Ha (Doyle)
  To Kill a Mockingbird (Lee)
  Of Mice and Men (Steinbeck)
  A Welsh Childhood (Ellis)

- **Section B:** 2 questions on pre-1900 drama or post-1900 drama (whichever was **not** studied for coursework)

  Set texts (pre-1900 drama)
  The Merchant of Venice (Shakespeare)
  Macbeth (Shakespeare)
  The Tempest (Shakespeare)

  Set texts (post-1900 drama)
  My Mother Said I Never Should (Keatley)
  A View from the Bridge (Miller)
  Abigail's Party (Leigh)
  An Inspector Calls (Priestley)

- **Section C:** 1 question on an unseen poem

Syllabus B

Coursework

4 assignments, free choice of texts:
- pre-1900 poetry
- pre-1900 prose
- pre-1900 drama or post-1900 drama
- wider reading (any genre, pre- or post-1900)

Note: For drama, the period and text chosen for coursework must **not** have been studied for the examination. Texts from the *Anthology* on which the written paper is based may not be used as the main focus for the 'wider reading' assignment.

30% of total marks

Examination (open book)

2 hours 30 minutes
70% of total marks

- **Section A:** 2 questions on post-1900 prose

    Set texts
    Selected short stories from the board's *Anthology*

- **Section B:** 2 questions on post-1900 poetry

    Set texts
    Poetry section from the board's *Anthology*

- **Section C:** 1 question on pre-1900 drama or post-1900 drama (whichever was **not** studied for coursework)

Set texts (pre-1900 drama)	**Set texts (post-1900 drama)**
The Merchant of Venice (Shakespeare)	*My Mother Said I Never Should* (Keatley)
Macbeth (Shakespeare)	*A View from the Bridge* (Miller)
The Tempest (Shakespeare)	*Abigail's Party* (Leigh)
	An Inspector Calls (Priestley)

Studying and revising

Revising for the examination

Plan your reading

The first step in revising is to plan your reading programme. You know how fast or how slow you read; your planning should take this into account. You know how your reading must fit in with work you have to do for other subjects. Decide whether you want to read in solid chunks of time (perhaps a couple of hours), or whether you would prefer to read for shorter periods of time (say half an hour), but more frequently.

Some examination boards require you to take the set texts into the examination room; others will expect you to work without the texts. If you are allowed to take your texts in with you, make sure that you know exactly where to look in the text for important points that you may want to include in an answer.

> **Examiner's tip**
> An open book examination is no case for not reading the text. Keep one of your texts with you at all times so that you can use any spare time constructively.

Annotate your texts

Different schools and examining boards have different policies with regard to **annotation** (marking up a text with your own notes). Make sure that you know exactly what is allowed by your examining board: your board might allow the texts to be annotated, or it might require you to use 'clean copies' during the exam. Whatever the case, it is very useful to annotate texts while you are studying them.

You should make brief marginal notes to do with the language, the plot, the characters, the setting and the themes. Also highlight or underline quotations which you regard as significant or useful. However, simply annotating everything is not the answer. At the beginning of your revision, it is extremely useful to review your annotations.

- Make sure that your notes really are relevant, to the point and not repetitive.
- You might think about re-writing your notes using a variety of coloured pens, so that each is clearly relevant to the different headings of plot, character, etc.
- Check through your quotations to make sure that you have not picked out too many. Only highlight the best ones, which illustrate the different aspects of the text.
- You might also want to use different colours for the quotations you highlight, so that each quotation's relevance to plot, character, etc, is immediately clear.

> **Examiner's tip**
> Annotations can be an enormous help, but you must still know where to look in the text or you will waste time. Remember also that too many annotations will muddle you.

Review your essays

In preparing for this examination, you will have written a number of essays and had them marked and commented on by your teacher. These are very important as undoubtedly your teacher will have modelled the questions on the type which might come up in an examination.

- Read your essays through, noting your teacher's comments.
- Summarise each essay in note form, incorporating the comments. How you make your notes is up to you; there is no right or wrong way to make notes. What you end up with, though, should look like a detailed essay plan.

Planning a revision schedule

- Don't be satisfied with your first effort to make this essay plan, but refine it until it is as succinct and clear as possible.
- Spend time learning these notes. Along with your annotations, your essays and essay plans will help you to revise a text.

Review your own notes

During the two years of your course, you will have written notes as you went along. Depending on your school's policy, these notes might be in a file or an exercise book. They are unlikely to be in a systematic order because of the way in which they were compiled. So the first thing you should do when checking through your notes is to put them in order. You might want to start by going through your notes with highlighter pens, identifying which notes are relevant to different aspects of the set texts. Then extract all the notes on one aspect and group them together. Then refine your notes – if you like, make notes on your notes!

Preparation complete!

Check that you are ready for the basis of your revision:
- your set texts are annotated clearly;
- your notes on your essays are in the form of detailed essay plans;
- your course notes are systematically ordered and refined.

Examiner's tip

Always prepare your own notes and don't try to use those prepared by other people. Notes are personal and the very process of writing them will help you to remember them.

Examiner's tip

You might have decided to use literature guides to some of your set texts, such as the *Letts Explore* series. These books can be very useful in your revision, but think of these books as an addition to your armoury, not as your only weapon.

Examiner's tip

Keep a careful watch on your work, completing each aspect as you are required. Avoid getting behind on your coursework. Once you start work on examination texts, use annotation and notes to help you. All of these things will help you to revise effectively before the final examination.

Examiner's tip

When planning your revision, start with the set text which you like least. You need to be doubly sure of this text, so that you don't let yourself down.

Planning a revision schedule

Your final reading programme should start four months before the examination. During the first week of the Easter holidays, you should plan a revision schedule for all your subjects, not just English Literature. As time goes on, you will find that you cannot always keep to it, but that is no reason for despair. Try to build some slack time into your schedule, just in case. For English Literature, try to follow a revision schedule like the one planned below.

Revision schedule

Four months before the exam

Allocate five hours every week to reading one or more of your set texts. During this first month of revision, you should read each of your set texts at least once and you might read one or two of them more often, especially the poetry and drama, which might include Shakespeare. Remember to allow enough time in your schedule to read any prose works properly, especially novels.

Three months before the exam

Allow yourself two weeks to work on all aspects of your preparation: annotation, reviewing your essays and sorting your own course notes.

Then allocate one week to your least favourite text, or, if you love them all, the text you find most difficult.
- *Re-read the text.*
- *Read through all your annotations and notes*, spending time to learn your notes carefully.

Studying and revising

- *Set yourself an examination-style question on the text.* You may be able to get a past paper that will provide you with a question, you could ask your teacher to set one, or you might be able to create one based on the questions you have been set during your course. You will find more advice on practising examination questions in the last section of this book.

Allow yourself the same amount of time you will have in the actual examination to write your answer. For example, say your examination is two hours long and you will have to answer three questions. Assuming that you will spend the same length of time on each answer, you should allow yourself 40 minutes to plan and write each one.

When you have written your answer, read it through carefully and make a personal judgement of its worth. In a quiet half-hour, think through whether or not there are things that you feel your answer may have missed out, whether you have expressed your answer well, and even whether, given another go, you would approach it in a completely different way.

It is important that you set yourself timed tasks as part of your revision – it will help you to manage your time better and this is an essential feature of success in examinations.

Repeat this same process with another of your texts each week until you have set and answered questions on all your examination texts.

 **xaminer's tip**

As well as using this schedule, do not forget that your teacher will almost certainly be revising with you in class. Adapt your schedule so that your personal revision and your class revision fit together.

Six weeks before the exam

Spend one week working with all your texts and concentrating on the quotations of prime importance that you have selected. Remember that, even if you are allowed to take annotated texts into the examination, you must know where the quotations occur so that you don't waste time. If you are not allowed to use annotated texts, you will need to do some learning.

Set yourself more timed essays, perhaps one on each of your texts and review them afterwards. Again, stick to the required time when writing your answers.

Four weeks before the exam

With only one month to go, carefully review where you are. Only you will know whether you should re-read one of your set texts because you are still unsure. Only you will know whether you feel you have learned your notes on one text better than another, or whether you need more practice in timed essay-writing.

Choose the 'key' episodes from each of your set texts. For instance, if you are studying *Macbeth*, you might pick the scenes with the witches and the banquet scene. For *The Mayor of Casterbridge*, you might pick Weydon Priors Fair, Farfrae's fair compared with Henchard's and the skimmity ride. Make your own choices and re-read the episodes. Then sit back for a while and think about why you have chosen those particular episodes.

The final two weeks before the exam

At this point, you may be into the examination period and your immediate concerns will be the examinations coming up the next day. Find a little time, perhaps every other day, to spend with your notes for English Literature, just to read them through and learn a few quotations.

In the last week:
- read and re-read your notes;
- skim-read parts of your texts – your key episodes – again;
- look at past papers and all the examination questions which you have practised in class and on your own.

You will now be completely prepared, or as ready as you ever can be, so good luck!

xaminer's tip

If you have followed the above schedule, or something similar, you should feel confident that you have done everything possible, but *don't be over-confident.*

Examination technique

❶ Take care to read the *rubric*, the instructions on the front of the examination paper. Make sure you follow the rubric carefully.

❷ Give yourself time to read the whole paper, to decide which questions to answer and plan your essays. To spot a question and begin writing without really thinking could be a recipe for disaster.

❸ Remember that you don't get more marks just for writing an essay which is longer than everyone else's. The *quality* of the content is what really matters.

❹ Try not to use too many quotations in your answers. Although it is important to use quotations, some students believe that if they have marked or learned quotations, then these should all go into the answer, whether or not they are relevant. Five or six short, pertinent quotations are probably as many as you need in any answer.

❺ It is natural to hope that essay questions that you have already practised will come up in the actual examination. However, don't try to twist the examination question to fit an answer that you have prepared. It is very important that your answer is relevant to the precise question set on the paper.

❻ Make sure that you manage your time. It is important to finish the paper – you will almost certainly get a better overall mark for three consistent answers rather than two brilliant answers and one not done at all.

❼ Finally, as in all examinations, take care with your handwriting. Remember that an examiner has to read your paper in order to mark it; it is very frustrating for the examiner if he or she can't read what you have written.

Section 2 **English Literature skills**

Chapter 1
Making comparisons in essays

Getting started

An important part of GCSE English Literature is the ability to compare either complete pieces of writing or aspects of writing. You will find this idea explicitly written into examination syllabuses. It is a good idea to check where in the syllabus making comparisons will be tested, but you will usually find that it is most important in poetry. It is usually covered both in coursework and in the examination.

In this chapter we are going to look at making comparisons and identifying relationships in literature. This will cover the following forms of writing found in GCSE coursework and in English Literature examinations.

Poetry is most often the subject for comparisons. This is because most poetry (or, at least, that commonly studied for GCSE) contains many different thoughts in a comparatively short space. Poems are full of ideas, thoughts and feelings, and poems with the same ideas or 'themes' can be compared easily. There are many common themes: nature, war, love and death, amongst others.

A second area for comparison in poetry is the way in which poems are written. Because poetry is packed with many thoughts in a short space, poets use numerous ways to get their messages across to the reader. They make comparisons (**similes**), they write about one thing in terms of another (**metaphor**), they make connections with and between sounds (**alliteration, assonance**), they group surprising and contradictory things together (**oxymoron**), they are interested in **rhythm** and sometimes in **rhyme**, they express moods and feelings and choose suitable words (**vocabulary**) to fit them.

Drama presents us with characters in special circumstances. Through the behaviour of characters on stage (or on film, video or television) we see a story unfolding. We react to the characters (they are nice, good, horrible, evil, cunning, clever and so on). We also begin to see that the writer is testing out features of human behaviour or showing us how tragic events can overtake people, or what happens when people are tempted to do something wrong. And all these are presented in dramatic ways. So, it is possible to compare characters, themes, ideas, reactions and the way these are all arranged and presented.

Prose (novels and short stories) gives the writer more space and time to work with than poetry. A story, or connecting stories, may unfold at some length. But a novel or short story must hold our attention if we are to read it and enjoy it. So, as well as comparing characters, the development of plot(s), ideas or reactions, we can also look at the way these things are presented and how authors try to affect their readers.

1.1 Comparisons in poetry

In this section we are going to look at two examples of comparing poems. These will be followed by suggestions of work for yourself.

The two poems below are on the theme of love. They were both written in the seventeenth century by the poets Andrew Marvell and Aphra Behn.

To His Coy Mistress

Had we but World enough, and Time
This coyness, Lady, were no crime,
We would sit down, and think which way
To walk, and pass our long Loves Day.
Thou by the Indian Ganges side
Should'st Rubies find: I by the Tide
Of Humber would complain. I would
Love you ten years before the Flood:
And you should, if you please, refuse
Till the Conversion of the Jews.
My vegetable Love should grow
Vaster than Empires, and more slow.
An hundred years should go to praise
Thine Eyes, and on thy Forehead gaze.
Two hundred to adore each Breast:
But thirty thousand to the rest.
An Age at least to every part,
And the last Age should show your Heart.
For, Lady, you deserve this State;
Nor would I love at lower rate.

But at my back I always hear
Times winged Charriot hurrying near:
And yonder all before us lye
Deserts of vast Eternity.
Thy Beauty shall no more be found;
Nor, in thy marble Vault, shall sound
My echoing song: then Worms shall try
That long preserv'd Virginity:
And your quaint Honour turn to dust;
And into ashes all my Lust.
The Grave's a fine and private place,
But none, I think, do there embrace.

Now therefore, while the youthful hew
Sits on thy skin like morning dew,
And while thy willing Soul transpires
At every pore with instant Fires,
Now let us sport us while we may;
And now, like am'rous birds of prey,
Rather at once our Time devour,
Than languish in his slow-chapt pow'r.
Let us roll all our Strength, and all
Our Sweetness, up into one Ball:
And tear our Pleasures with rough strife,
Thorough the Iron gates of Life.
Thus, though we cannot make our Sun
Stand still, yet we will make him run.

Andrew Marvell

Chapter 1 Making comparisons in essays

> **Song: The Willing Mistress**
>
> Amyntas led me to a Grove,
> Where all the Trees did shade us;
> The Sun it self, though it had Strove,
> It could not have betray'd us:
>
> The place secur'd from humane Eyes,
> No other fear allows,
> But when the Winds that gently rise,
> Doe Kiss the yeilding Boughs.
>
> Down there we satt upon the Moss,
> And did begin to play
> A Thousand Amorous Tricks, to pass
> The heat of all the day.
> A many Kisses he did give:
> And I return'd the same
> Which made me willing to receive
> That which I dare not name.
>
> His Charming Eyes no aid requir'd
> To tell their softning Tale;
> On her that was already fir'd
> 'Twas Easy to prevaile.
> He did but Kiss and Clasp me round
> Whilst those his thoughts Exprest:
> And lay'd me gently on the Ground;
> Ah who can guess the rest?
>
> *Aphra Behn*

To begin with read the poems through several times. It is often a good idea to read poetry aloud to yourself (or even into a tape recorder) as this may well make you more sensitive to sounds and rhythms. You will see that one poem is the words of a man, and the other the words of a woman. That is the first obvious difference. Secondly, their points of view are different. The man in Andrew Marvell's poem complains that the woman he loves is playing with his affections, keeps him at a distance and rejects him. The woman in Aphra Behn's poem is the opposite. She has given herself to her lover already and is clearly happy about it. We can see a difference of speaker, of attitude and of mood. Notice that both poets have chosen to put the words into the mouth of a speaker; each poem is a monologue.

Having established basic differences we can consider these poems in detail. Marvell's poem is in three sections and each has a connecting theme. Behn's has four verses and the story develops in each. Yes, there is story but there are strong feelings too. In Marvell's poem the speaker is annoyed, thinks time is short and so is pleading with his lady. In Behn's the woman is happy, enjoying the memory of what happened and delighting in her love. These ideas affect the reader. We may well share the speaker's frustration in *To His Coy Mistress*; there are many memorable phrases here and they may even raise a smile.

> An hundred years should go to praise
> Thine Eyes, and on thy Forehead gaze.
> Two hundred to adore each Breast:
> But thirty thousand to the rest.

In Behn's poem the woman speaking is enjoying herself at the reader's expense: she is telling us things, but also keeping something back from us.

> A many Kisses he did give:
> And I return'd the same
> Which made me willing to receive
> That which I dare not name.

Very different from these last poems are the two which follow by Wilfred Owen and Henry Reed. The theme of the poems is war.

Dulce et Decorum Est

Bent double, like old beggars under sacks,
Knock-kneed, coughing like hags, we cursed through sludge,
Till on the haunting flares we turned our backs,
And towards our distant rest began to trudge.
Men marched asleep. Many had lost their boots,
But limped on, blood-shod. All went lame, all blind;
Drunk with fatigue; deaf even to the hoots
Of gas-shells dropping softly behind.

Gas! GAS! Quick, boys! – An ecstasy of fumbling,
Fitting the clumsy helmets just in time,
But someone still was yelling out and stumbling
And floundering like a man in fire or lime. –
Dim through the misty panes and thick green light,
As under a green sea, I saw him drowning.

In all my dreams before my helpless sight
He plunges at me, guttering, choking, drowning.

If in some smothering dreams, you too could pace
Behind the wagon that we flung him in,
And watch the white eyes writhing in his face,
His hanging face, like a devil's sick of sin;
If you could hear, at every jolt, the blood
Come gargling from the froth-corrupted lungs,
Bitter as the cud
Of vile, incurable sores on innocent tongues, –
My friend, you would not tell with such high zest
To children ardent for some desperate glory,
The old Lie: *Dulce et decorum est*
Pro patria mori.

Wilfred Owen

The first thing that must be said is that these poems are similar. Each in its own way is decrying what happens in warfare. The poems come from different generations: Owen's is written from his own experiences during the First World War (1914–1918); Reed was called up to join the army in 1941, two years after the beginning of the Second World War (1939–1945). One poem is about the battlefield; the other about military training. The first is a heartfelt plea against military propaganda, and the glorifying of war; the second shows the futility of much that men were expected to do in fighting for their country.

Let us look at the way these poems 'work'. Owen writes directly about what he actually sees. There are no glorious deeds, charges, battles or victories, but only the brutal reality of human suffering. This is where he starts – 'Bent double…Knock-kneed, coughing like hags'. He continues writing with precision and detail about tiredness and exhaustion; he coins the phrase 'Drunk with fatigue'. But this is not all; there is a gas attack and these men, already worn out, have to fit on their masks quickly or they will be poisoned. One man does not succeed, and it is his tragic end which inspires this poem. Owen cannot forget him:

> In all my dreams before my helpless sight
> He plunges at me, guttering, choking, drowning.

This is the incident and these are the ways in which the poet chooses to offer it to us. But the poem does not stop there – Owen has something else to say. He makes an appeal to us: if we had experienced this and realised what actually happened, then we would no longer tell lies about the glory of dying for our country.

Naming of Parts

To-day we have naming of parts. Yesterday
We had daily cleaning. And tomorrow morning,
We shall have what to do after firing. But today,
Today we have naming of parts. Japonica
Glistens like coral in all of the neighbouring gardens
    And to-day we have naming of parts.

This is the lower sling swivel. And this
Is the upper sling swivel, whose use you will see,
When you are given your slings. And this is the piling swivel,
Which in your case you have not got. The branches
Hold in the gardens their silent, eloquent gestures,
    Which in our case we have not got.

This is the safety-catch, which is always released
With an easy flick of the thumb. And please do not let me
See anyone using his finger. You can do it quite easy
If you have any strength in your thumb. The blossoms
Are fragile and motionless, never letting anyone see
    Any of them using their finger.

And this you can see is the bolt. The purpose of this
Is to open the breech, as you see. We can slide it
Rapidly backwards and forwards: we call this
Easing the spring. And rapidly backwards and forwards
The early bees are assaulting and fumbling the flowers:
    They call it easing the Spring.

They call it easing the Spring: it is perfectly easy
If you have any strength in your thumb: like the bolt,
And the breech, and the cocking piece, and the point of balance,
Which in our case we have not got; and the almond blossom
Silent in all of the gardens and the bees going backwards and forwards,
For to-day we have naming of parts.

Henry Reed

Owen was a soldier in 'the war to end all wars'. A generation later Reed was enlisted too. He writes here about military training, not war as such. He calls the activity 'naming of parts', which perhaps suggests something like 'knowledge without purpose'. His is a gentler poem with a very clear pattern. In each stanza there is detail from the instruction Reed receives, and then a reference to the world around. So, in stanza two, there is much about 'swivels', even the 'piling swivel/Which...you have not got', and then there are gardens and branches with 'silent, eloquent gestures'. The poem moves forward in this pattern, in a quiet and methodical rhythm, gently pointing to the futility of the whole exercise.

From these two examples we see how poems may be compared. The advantage of doing this is that reading one poem helps us to understand the other. Comparisons involve both similarities and differences in what is said and in the way poets say it.

Now try the following tasks:

- Read *The Soldier* (by Rupert Brooke) and *The Charge of the Light Brigade* (by Alfred Lord Tennyson). Compare the ways in which the two poets present war.
- Compare the way in which Gerard Manley Hopkins writes about nature in *God's Grandeur* with William Wordsworth's *I Wandered Lonely As a Cloud*.
- What interests you about the two poems that have telephones in them: *The Telephone Call* (by Fleur Adcock) and *Telephone Conversation* (by Wole Soyinka)?

Examiner's tip

Always read poems several times. Think carefully about the subject matter, the way ideas are expressed and the choice of words.

1.2 Comparisons in drama

In this section we shall consider comparisons within a single play as well as between plays. Both plays and novels have characters, and for many people characters and stories are the things which interest them most. You have only to listen to a great actor or actress talking of the roles he or she has played to understand the fascination that we all have with others; who they are, what they are, why they are and how they change. We ask whether a character is good or bad, noble or villainous, admirable or despicable, amusing or pitiable.

Comparing characters within a play

If we are to make comparisons, pairing characters within a play is a useful approach. In *Macbeth* (by William Shakespeare) we see the decline of a man from greatness to villainy. Who is Macbeth's opposite? The answer has to be Macduff. Our task, therefore, might be to compare these two. We might think about it as follows.

The play starts with Macbeth: he has been successful in battle, he has saved his country by extraordinary deeds of courage and everyone admires him. His king is ready and willing to promote him and so Macbeth may look forward to a happy life. Indeed, the strange women whom he meets, who have the ability to forecast the future, promise him just this. But it all goes wrong for him. He will not wait for good fortune, but wants to seize it for himself. He thinks of murder, which he has never considered before. And if he has any doubts about this (and he does) then his wife has the determination and power to overcome them. Once he is king, Macbeth feels threatened and tries to achieve security for himself by perpetrating further murders. He also decides to consult the strange women again. His rash belief in their riddle-like promises leads him to foolish arrogance, which is his undoing.

Macduff is entirely different. He becomes more important as the play progresses. It is he who discovers Duncan's murdered body and from the first seems wary of explanations that are offered to account for this event. We notice what he doesn't do – attend Macbeth's coronation at Scone or accept the invitation to the banquet to celebrate it. We learn that in his house (amongst others) Macbeth has a spy. Once Macbeth has learnt that Macduff has fled to England to join Malcolm, then Lady Macduff, her children and servants become his next victims. Macduff, who learns of this dreadful news while he is in England, feels it 'like a man' but determines on revenge. His cause is right; he fights for himself and for his country but, unlike Macbeth, he has no personal ambition. He it is who meets Macbeth in single combat and, once he has revealed that he was 'from his mother's womb/ Untimely ripped', he kills Macbeth and establishes peace in Scotland with the accession of Malcolm.

Comparing characters between plays

In simple terms Macbeth is a villain. So a different approach would be needed in order to compare him with other villains in Shakespeare's plays: Iago in *Othello*, Edmund in *King Lear*, Claudius in *Hamlet*, or Tybalt in *Romeo and Juliet*.

The essential questions to ask when approaching characters in this way are:
- What does each character say and do?
- What do others say about him or her?
- What are his/her motives?
- How much do we know about his/her inner feelings?
- What are our own reactions?

Comparing themes between plays

As well as characters, we might compare what plays have to say to us about social or human issues. Among the plays which are offered for GCSE are *An Inspector Calls* (by J.B. Priestley), *A Taste of Honey* (by Shelagh Delaney) *Hobson's Choice* (by Harold Brighouse), and *Educating Rita* (by Willy Russell). Each play presents us with a particular problem and a way of approaching it.

In *An Inspector Calls* the members of a family have to consider their degree of responsibility for the death of a girl known to each of them separately. The play goes on to ask the wider question of what level of responsibility each of us in society has for others.

A Taste of Honey concerns a young girl, her relationship with her mother, her boyfriend (who becomes the father of her child) and another male friend who helps her. What view of young people growing up does this present? Or what view of family life? Or what view of prejudice and tolerance?

Hobson's Choice is set in the last century, but its themes are still very important today. The destructive power of alcohol, 'the demon drink', although not the central theme of the play, is a powerful one. The main issue, however, is the role of men and women. Who should be dominant? What happens when a powerful man and a determined woman clash? What happens when a timid man makes good, led by his determined wife?

In *Educating Rita* the problems and advantages of education surface. What we learn, how we learn, how we are changed by what we learn and the effect this has on our personal relationships: these are the issues which exercise our minds. In these four plays, then, there are many opportunities for comparisons and contrasts, using the various themes and ideas.

Now try the following tasks:

- Compare two heroes or heroines in plays by Shakespeare.
- What views of love are to be found in *Romeo and Juliet* and *A Taste of Honey*?
- Compare Sybil Birling in *An Inspector Calls* with Lady Macbeth.
- What views about women are to be found in *Hobson's Choice* and *Educating Rita*?
- Consider the presentation of war in *Journey's End* by R.C.Sherriff and *The Long, the Short and the Tall* by Willis Hall.

Examiner's tip

- When studying a play watch a production.
- If this is not possible, then always think of the text you read in terms of how it would be performed and presented.
- Never ignore 'stage directions': they may tell you as much as dialogue.

Plays as productions

In all these examples plays have been thought of as texts. But plays are more than simply written words. Plays are written to be performed, and performance is crucial. If you are studying plays try to see a production, and, if possible, more than one. Performances can be seen in theatres, cinemas, on video and on television. No one production will be the same as another. If the medium changes, then the play will be presented differently. In a production, what you see and hear helps you respond to the text of the play.

1.3 Comparisons in prose

The possibilities for comparative work on novels and short stories are almost endless; some of these tasks are listed below.

- Character comparison in the same novel, e.g. the characters of Henchard and Farfrae in *The Mayor of Casterbridge*.
- Character comparison in two novels by the same author, or by different authors, e.g. Pip in *Great Expectations* and *Jane Eyre*.
- Comparison of two novels by the same writer or by writers working at a similar period of time.
- Comparative treatment of a theme in two novels, e.g. love in *Great Expectations* and *Wuthering Heights*.
- Comparison of two works from a particular type of literature – historical fiction, gothic novels, detective fiction, science fiction, e.g. *Brave New World* and *Nineteen Eighty-Four*.
- The way in which a story is told in two novels, contrasting first person narrative with third person narration.

- The different ways in which setting, description and mood are used in two or more novels.
- The different ways in which stories develop and reach a conclusion – this could include considering the endings in novels.
- Comparison of novels which deal with social issues – education, poverty, wealth, justice, racism, e.g. *To Kill a Mockingbird* and *Roll of Thunder, Hear My Cry*.
- Comparison of novels which make a personal and individual appeal.
- Comparison of relationships between men and women in two novels.
- Study of two novels presenting life in different times, cultures or countries.

Putting this into practice

- Prejudice plays an important part in both *The Merchant of Venice* (Shakespeare) and *To Kill a Mockingbird* (Harper Lee). Compare the various types of prejudice found and say how you react to them.

The notes below show how you might plan an answer to this question.

Prejudice in *The Merchant of Venice*

- The prejudice is racial and religious.
- Shylock is Jewish by race and creed and is despised by the Venetian merchants and citizens, who are Christian.
- They keep away from him as much as possible.
- Antonio and Bassanio only get involved with Shylock when it suits them.
- Shylock 'helps' them because it suits him personally and because he sees a chance to pay them back for all the abuse he has suffered.
- Shylock also treats others badly, e.g. his servants and his daughter. She robs him and runs off with a gentile (i.e. non-Jew) and a Christian.
- When the opportunity comes for revenge, Shylock wants to take it – it means more to him than money, reputation or appeals for mercy.
- Shylock becomes a victim when he cannot legally carry out what is forfeit to him. He loses everything.

Prejudice in *To Kill a Mockingbird*

- The prejudice is racial and is also to do with handicap.
- Black people in general, along with Tom Robinson and Boo Radley, are the victims of prejudice.
- Atticus Finch does not join in the prejudice around him and passes his values on to his two children, Jem and Scout.
- Jem and Scout regard Boo Radley as an oddity: they are frightened of him but intrigued at the same time. They play games – dares, acting – to cope with their feelings.
- They gradually become aware of the charges against Tom Robinson and how this is affecting the place where they live. Their father tries to protect them but they become aware of what is said about him ('nigger-lover'). They are drawn into the trial.
- When Tom is found guilty it is a clear example of prejudice.
- Atticus is hated by Bob Ewell for making the truth clear, and Ewell seeks revenge.
- Tom Robinson dies in tragic circumstances, but Boo Radley emerges as a hero when he saves the lives of Jem and Scout.
- The prejudice is so deep-seated that when Jem and Scout go to a black church with Calpurnia they arouse feelings of suspicion and distrust in the congregation. Later black adults defer to them as (superior) white children.

Chapter 1 Making comparisons in essays

Bringing these ideas together

- Shylock is a victim but not the sort of character we like: we rarely feel any sympathy for him, except (perhaps) when Jessica runs away or when Portia pronounces the final judgement. Tom Robinson, however, is a good man, caught up in a hopeless set of circumstances from which he cannot emerge. His is a truly tragic story.
- While Tom Robinson's case brings out wonderful qualities in Atticus, Shylock is entirely alone.
- Boo Radley becomes a hero and Jem and Scout recognise his true qualities. There is no equivalent of this in *The Merchant of Venice*.
- The 'heroes' in *The Merchant of Venice* never repent of their prejudice, indeed they benefit from it. Their victim is worse off at the end of the play than he was at the beginning.
- Shakespeare uses contemporary feelings about Jews in his play without questioning whether they are right or wrong.
- Harper Lee writes to expose the racism inherent in American society (at the time of the book). She clearly sees racism as wrong but powerful: it takes great courage to resist. Each work reflects its own age and time. There is now something uncomfortable about watching *The Merchant of Venice*, but it is saved by its historical setting and the fact that it is impressively written by Shakespeare.

Examiner's tip

- Make sure you draw the comparison point by point and illustrate it by reference to the text.
- Never tell the story and leave the examiner to draw conclusions.

Chapter 2
Historical, social and cultural background

Getting started

Many people have been to weddings. From their experience they could tell you about the sorts of things that happen. They could explain the terms 'bride', 'bridegroom', 'best man', and 'bridesmaid'. They could almost certainly tell you what brides are supposed to wear and to carry, about receptions (or 'wedding breakfasts') about toasts and speeches and about the 'honeymoon'. In other words, people who have grown up in this country know the traditions of weddings.

In St Matthew's Gospel, in the Bible, is a story about the kingdom of heaven. It refers to customs at a wedding. Read it for yourself.

> Jesus told this parable to his disciples: 'The kingdom of heaven will be like this: Ten bridesmaids took their lamps and went to meet the bridegroom. Five of them were foolish and five were sensible: the foolish ones did take their lamps, but they brought no oil, whereas the sensible ones took flasks of oil as well as their lamps. The bridegroom was late, and they all grew drowsy and fell asleep. But at midnight there was a cry, "The bridegroom is here! Go out and meet him." At this, all those bridesmaids woke up and trimmed their lamps, and the foolish ones said to the sensible ones, "Give us some of your oil: our lamps are going out." But they replied, "There may not be enough for us and for you; you had better go to those who sell it and buy some for yourselves." They had gone off to buy it when the bridegroom arrived. Those who were ready went in with him to the wedding hall and the door was closed. The other bridesmaids arrived later. "Lord, Lord," they said "open the door for us." But he replied, "I tell you solemnly, I do not know you." So stay awake, because you do not know either the day or the hour.'
>
> *Jerusalem Bible:* Matthew 25, 1-13

You do not have to read very far into this story (written down about 85 AD) to find wedding customs very different from those with which we are familiar. Here it is the job of the bridesmaids to wait for the bridegroom. In a different age and with different customs, planning and timing were not as precise as they are now: so the bridesmaids were uncertain about the time the bridegroom would come. They had to wait, with oil lamps ready, until he arrived. Their task then was to escort the bridegroom to the bride and accompany them both to the place where the wedding would take place.

Now that you have read this explanation you are able to do two things. First, to understand what is happening in the story itself. Secondly, make sense of the meaning of the story, based upon knowledge of the customs of which the writer was familiar.

These ideas are the basis for using historical, social and cultural background to what we read. Everyone studying GCSE English Literature (as well as National Curriculum English) has to read novels, plays and poetry written before 1900. Reading literature by British writers before the year 1900 will usually fulfil the requirements of National Curriculum English, which refers to 'reading in the literary heritage', and those of some examination boards, who refer to studying 'literary tradition' in their English Literature syllabuses. What is involved is reading major works by established authors. In coursework it is possible to discuss themes or ideas which have been written about across the centuries, e.g. 'love' in poetry or 'social conditions' in novels.

It won't be long before 1900 is a hundred years away, and in a hundred years many things happen. So, if we are to read literature which is one, two, three or four hundred years old, then we need background information to help us understand what is going on. Of course, this doesn't just apply to things written before 1900. All novels and stories from places, times and cultures different from our own need this kind of study. If we have no background information then we may be perplexed or, worse, come to conclusions that are quite inappropriate. In this chapter we shall be looking at examples of social and cultural themes drawn from literature of the past and discussing how to cope with them. Most GCSE courses expect you to show understanding of social and cultural background in your coursework. However, some examinations questions also cover this issue, so be clear exactly where you will be expected to show evidence of what you understand.

2.1 Marriage: a social and cultural theme

Here is the ending of a short story entitled *The Election*, written by Mary Russell Mitford (1787–1855).

> Time wore on; Rose had refused half the offers of gentility in the town and neighbourhood; her heart appeared to be invulnerable. Her less affluent and less brilliant friend was generally understood (and as Rose, on hearing the report, did not contradict it, the rumour passed for certainty) to be engaged to a nephew of her mother's, Sir William Frampton, a young gentleman of splendid fortune, who had lately passed much time at his fair place in the neighbourhood.
>
> Time wore on; and Rose was now nineteen, when an event occurred which threatened a grievous interruption to her happiness. The Earl of B's member died; his nephew, Sir William Frampton, supported by his uncle's powerful interest, offered himself for the borough; an independent candidate started at the same time; and Mr Danby felt himself compelled, by his vaunted consistency, to insist on his daughter's renouncing her visits to the rectory, at least until after the termination of the election. Rose wept and pleaded, pleaded and wept, in vain. Her father was obdurate; and she, after writing a most affectionate note to Mary Cardonnel, retired to her own bedroom in very bad spirits, and, perhaps, for the first time in her life, in very bad humour.
>
> About half an hour afterwards, Sir William Frampton and Mr Cardonnel called at the red house.
>
> 'We are come, Mr Danby,' said the rector, 'to solicit your interest.'
>
> 'Nay, nay, my good friend,' returned the reformer, 'you know that my interest is promised, and that I cannot with any consistency – '
>
> 'To solicit your interest with Rose – ' resumed his reverence.
>
> 'With Rose!' interrupted Mr Danby.

2.1 Marriage: a social and cultural theme

'Ay – for the gift of her heart and hand – that being, I believe, the suffrage which my good nephew here is most anxious to secure,' rejoined Mr Cardonnel.

'With Rose,' again ejaculated Mr Danby: 'why, I thought that your daughter – '

'The gipsy has not told you, then!' replied the rector. 'Why, William and she have been playing the parts of Romeo and Juliet for these six months past.'

'My Rose!' again exclaimed Mr Danby. 'Why, Rose! Rose! I say!' and the astonished father rushed out of the room, and returned the next minute, holding the blushing girl by the arm. 'Rose do you love this young man?'

'Oh, papa!' said Rose.

'Will you marry him?'

'Oh, papa!'

'Do you wish me to tell him that you will not marry him?

To this question Rose returned no answer; she only blushed the deeper and looked down with a half smile. 'Take her then,' resumed Mr Danby; 'I see the girl loves you. I can't vote for you, though, for I've promised, and, you know, my good sir, that an honest man's word – '

'I don't want your vote, my dear sir,' interrupted Sir William Frampton; 'I don't ask for your vote, although the loss of it may cost me my seat, and my uncle his borough. This is the election that I care about, the only election worth caring about. Is it not, my own sweet Rose? – the election, of which the object lasts for life, and the result is happiness. That's the election worth caring about. Is it not, mine own Rose!'

And Rose blushed an affirmative; and Mr Danby shook his intended son-in-law's hand, until he almost wrung it off, repeating at every moment, 'I can't vote for you, for a man must be consistent, but you're the best fellow in the world, and you shall have my Rose. And Rose will be a great lady,' continued the delighted father; 'My little Rose will be a great lady after all!'

The story concerns two families, the Danbys and the Cardonnels. In the extract, we can see that the two fathers do not approve of each other; nor does Mr Danby approve of the young man, Sir William Frampton, who is seeking election as an MP. What is clear from the extract is something of the marriage customs of the day. Daughters were required to marry only with the agreement of their fathers; sometimes they were required to marry on the instructions of their fathers. The circumstances in which young men and women might meet in 'polite society' were strictly controlled. There is reference here to the fact that Rose and Sir William met at the Cardonnel's rectory where they would not, of course, have been left alone. In order for their relationship to proceed into marriage, Mr Danby's permission was essential. Without it there would be criticism from people in their circle of friends and acquaintances; their disapproval would be felt very strongly. Furthermore, to marry without consent would most likely leave a young woman without any income from her father and she might be disinherited under the terms of his will. The social conventions surrounding marriage were very strong indeed.

A much fuller treatment of this aspect of life, which has changed so much in the twentieth century, is to be found in Jane Austen's *Pride and Prejudice*. The Bennet family have two related problems. First, Mr and Mrs Bennet have five daughters and no sons. Secondly, the Bennet property is 'entailed' which means that on the death of Mr Bennet it will pass to a relative of the family, Mr Collins. Mrs Bennet is concerned to solve these difficulties: there is but one solution – marriage for her daughters. Marriage brings status, security and respectability; without it the Bennet girls have no prospects except of becoming penniless old maids. It is, therefore, not just a question of her own feelings when Mr Collins proposes marriage to Elizabeth.

> 'Almost as soon as I entered the house I singled you out as the companion of my future life. But before I am run away with by my feelings on this subject, perhaps it will be advisable for me to state my reasons for marrying – and moreover for coming into Hertfordshire with the design of selecting a wife, as I certainly did.'
>
> The idea of Mr Collins, with all his solemn composure, being run away with by his feelings, made Elizabeth so near laughing that she could not use the short pause he allowed in any attempt to stop him farther, and he continued:
>
> 'My reasons for marrying are, first, that I think it a right thing for every clergyman in easy circumstances (like myself) to set the example of matrimony in his parish. Secondly, that I am convinced it will add very greatly to my happiness; and thirdly – which perhaps I ought to have mentioned earlier, that it is the particular advice and recommendation of the very noble lady whom I have the honour of calling patroness. Twice she has condescended to give me her opinion (unasked too!) on this subject; and it was but the very Saturday night before I left Hunsford – between our pools at quadrille, while Mrs Jenkinson was arranging Miss de Bourgh's foot-stool, that she said "Mr Collins, you must marry. A clergyman like you must marry. – Choose properly, choose a gentlewoman for *my* sake; and for your *own*, let her be an active, useful sort of person, not brought up high, but able to make a small income go a good way. This is my advice. Find such a woman as soon as you can, bring her to Hunsford, and I will visit her." Allow me, by the way, to observe, my fair cousin, that I do not reckon the notice and kindness of Lady Catherine de Bourgh as among the least of the advantages in my power to offer. You will find her manners beyond any thing I can describe; and your wit and vivacity I think must be acceptable to her, especially when tempered with the silence and respect which her rank will inevitably excite. Thus much for my general intention in favour of matrimony; it remains to be told why my views were directed to Longbourn instead of my own neighbourhood, where I assure you there are very many amiable young women. But the fact is, that being, as I am, to inherit this estate after the death of your honoured father, (who, however, may live many years longer,) I could not satisfy myself without resolving to choose a wife from among his daughters, that the loss to them might be as little as possible, when the melancholy event takes place – which, however, as I have already said, may not be for several years. This has been my motive, my fair cousin, and I flatter myself it will not sink me in your esteem. And now nothing remains for me but to assure you in the most animated language of the violence of my affection. To fortune I am perfectly indifferent, and shall make no demand of that nature on your father, since I am well aware that it could not be complied with; and that one thousand pounds in the 4 per cents which will not be yours till after your mother's decease, is all that you may ever be entitled to. On that head, therefore, I shall be uniformly silent; and you may assure yourself that no ungenerous reproach shall ever pass my lips when we are married.'
>
> It was absolutely necessary to interrupt him now.
>
> 'You are too hasty, Sir,' she cried. 'You forget that I have made no answer. Let me do it without further loss of time. Accept my thanks for the compliment you are paying me. I am very sensible of the honour of your proposals, but it is impossible for me to do otherwise than decline them.'

A great deal has changed since Jane Austen's time as regards marriage, family life and relationships between men and women. The formality between people, the particular situation that women found themselves in, the position of wives – all these were different from the conventions and practices that apply now. An understanding of past conventions will help us to appreciate the situations in novels and stories.

2.2 Religion: a historical and cultural theme

Anyone who has studied British history knows that the Christian religion has been a major influence on the life of our country. Particularly influential has been the translation of the Bible, made in 1611, and called the *Authorised Version*. Its language, its stories and its ideas have influenced countless numbers of people. It is not surprising to find references to the Bible and to biblical stories throughout literature.

In Chapter 4 of *Great Expectations* by Charles Dickens, Pip and his brother-in-law, Joe Gargery, go to church on Christmas Day. Pip, who tells the story, says that Joe sets off for church 'in a full suit of Sunday penitentials'. No one would have gone to church improperly dressed: 'Sunday best' was required. In church the 'banns were read' and the clergyman says 'Ye are now to declare it'. After church, 'Mr Wopsle, the clerk at the church' comes to Christmas dinner at Pip's home. The conversation over the meal turns to sermons and Mr Wopsle is critical of the clergyman. He suggests that pork, the meat being consumed on that Christmas day, would make a good subject for a sermon and reminds all the guests that 'Swine were the companions of the prodigal'.

These are small details from one chapter, but they illustrate the point. Dickens, a popular writer producing his book in serial instalments, wrote for the general public. He is not referring here to unusual or unknown experiences. Everyone in Victorian England who read this story knew about church-going, about Sunday best, about the Bible and about the story in St Luke's gospel of the Prodigal Son. You could read the story of the Prodigal Son, preferably in the *Authorised Version*, for yourself: St Luke, chapter 15, verse 11 to the end.

Perhaps an example from a twentieth-century novel would help too. In *Animal Farm* George Orwell writes of an animal revolution, which overthrows the farmer and expels all humans from the former Manor Farm. The animals who achieve this set down the rules which are to govern life on the farm; these are called 'the Seven Commandments'. Why does Orwell choose this term? Because going back to the Bible we find the 'Ten Commandments' – rules laid down showing how we should behave.

2.3 Death: a social and cultural theme

At different times and in different places the customs surrounding death and mourning have varied greatly. Until fairly recently, when cremation has become quite common, burial was the usual Christian way of dealing with a body. Many plays and films have scenes at the graveside, often using the words 'earth to earth, ashes to ashes, dust to dust' and referring to 'sure and certain hope of the resurrection to eternal life'. These words come from the Burial Service used in the Church of England since the mid-sixteenth century.

There have always been social customs accompanying death. In the nineteenth century there were particular conventions for dealing with a body, for the decoration of a house, for the funeral arrangements and for the clothes to be worn. For the death of national figures, newspapers had thick black borders around them. In Chapter 35 of *Great Expectations* Pip tells us of his sister's funeral: as he arrives at the forge from London his description indicates something of the customs of the time.

> At last I came within sight of the house, and saw that Trabb and Co. had put in a funereal execution and taken possession. Two dismally absurd persons, each ostentatiously exhibiting a crutch done up in a black bandage – as if that instrument could possible communicate any comfort to anybody – were posted at the front door; and in one of them I recognised a postboy discharged from the Boar for turning a young couple into a sawpit on their bridal morning, in consequence of intoxication rendering it necessary for him to ride his horse

> clasped round the neck with both arms. All the children of the village, and most of the women, were admiring these sable warders and the closed windows of the house and forge; and as I came up, one of the two warders (the postboy) knocked at the door – implying that I was far too much exhausted by grief, to have strength remaining to knock for myself.
>
> Another sable warder (a carpenter, who had once eaten two geese for a wager) opened the door, and showed me into the best parlour. Here, Mr Trabb had taken unto himself the best table, and had got all the leaves up, and was holding a kind of black Bazaar, with the aid of a quantity of black pins. At the moment of my arrival, he had just finished putting somebody's hat into black long-clothes, like an African baby; so he held out his hand for mine. But I, misled by the action, and confused by the occasion, shook hands with him with every testimony of warm affection.
>
> Poor dear Joe, entangled in a little black cloak tied in a large bow under his chin, was seated apart at the upper end of the room; where, as chief mourner, he had evidently been stationed by Trabb. When I bent down and said to him, 'Dear Joe, how are you?' he said, 'Pip, old chap, you know'd her when she were a fine figure of a –' and clasped my hand and said no more.
>
> Biddy, looking very neat and modest in her black dress, went quietly here and there, and was very helpful. When I had spoken to Biddy, as I thought it not a time for talking, I went and sat down near Joe, and there began to wonder in what part of the house it – she – my sister – was. The air of the parlour being faint with the smell of sweet cake, I looked about for the table of refreshments; it was scarcely visible until one had got accustomed to the gloom, but there was a cut-up plum cake upon it, and there were cut-up oranges, and sandwiches, and biscuits, and two decanters that I knew very well as ornaments, but had never seen used in all my life: one full of port, and one of sherry. Standing at this table, I became conscious of the servile Pumblechook in a black cloak and several yards of hatband, who was alternately stuffing himself, and making obsequious movements to catch my attention. The moment he succeeded, he came over to me (breathing sherry and crumbs), and said in a subdued voice, 'May I, dear sir?' and did. I then descried Mr and Mrs Hubble; the last-named in a decent speechless paroxysm in a corner. We were all going to 'follow', and were all in the course of being tied up separately (by Trabb) into ridiculous bundles.

In these three themes we see some of the customs and attitudes that lie behind a great deal of literature. As times change and we get further from the period when a book was written we need to attune ourselves to the thinking and the customs which lie behind much of what is written: without doing so we may miss a great deal.

2.4 More themes to look at

Occupations

Let's look first at some of the characters in pre-1900 novels and ask what their occupations are and how they would have carried these out at the time. What do you know, for example, about a nineteenth-century blacksmith (Joe Gargery in *Great Expectations*), or farmer (Michael Henchard in *The Mayor of Casterbridge*), or clergyman (Mr Collins in *Pride and Prejudice*, and Mr Harding, Dr Grantly and Bishop Proudie in the *Barchester* novels by Anthony Trollope), or lawyer (Mr Jaggers in *Great Expectations*) or landowner and baronet (Sir Thomas Bartram in *Mansfield Park*)?

2.4 More themes to look at

Formal speech

One important aspect of character is the way in which people speak and address each other. Below is an extract from the beginning of *Mansfield Park* by Jane Austen.

Mrs Norris was often observing to the others, that she could not get her poor sister and her family out of her head, and that much as they had all done for her, she seemed to be wanting to do more: and at length she could not but own it to be her wish, that poor Mrs Price should be relieved from the charge and expense of one child entirely out of her great number. 'What if they were among them to undertake the care of her eldest daughter, a girl now nine years old, of an age to require more attention than her poor mother could possibly give? The trouble and expense of it to them, would be nothing compared with the benevolence of the action.' Lady Bertram agreed with her instantly. 'I think we cannot do better,' said she, 'let us send for the child.'

Sir Thomas could not give so instantaneous and unqualified a consent. He debated and hesitated – it was a serious charge – a girl so brought up must be adequately provided for, or there would be cruelty instead of kindness in taking her from her family. He thought of his own four children – of his two sons – of cousins in love, etc – but no sooner had he deliberately begun to state his objections, than Mrs Norris interrupted him with a reply to them all whether stated or not.

'My dear Sir Thomas, I perfectly comprehend you, and do justice to the generosity and delicacy of your notions, which indeed are quite of a piece with your general conduct; and I entirely agree with you in the main as to the propriety of doing everything one could by way of providing for a child one had in a manner taken into one's own hands; and I am sure I should be the last person in the world to withhold my mite upon such an occasion. Having no children of my own, who should I look to in any little matter I may ever have to bestow, but the children of my sisters? – and I am sure Mr Norris is too just – but you know I am a woman of few words and professions. Do not let us be frightened from a good deed by a trifle. Give a girl an education, and introduce her properly into the world, and ten to one she has the means of settling well, without farther expense to anybody. A niece of ours, Sir Thomas, I may say, or, at least of *yours*, would not grow up in this neighbourhood without many advantages. I don't say she would be so handsome as her cousins. I dare say she would not; but she would be introduced into the society of this country under such very favourable circumstances as, in all human probability, would get her a creditable establishment. You are thinking of your sons – but do not you know that of all things upon earth *that* is the least likely to happen, brought up, as they would be, always together like brothers and sisters? It is morally impossible. I never knew an instance of it. It is, in fact, the only sure way of providing against the connexion. Suppose her a pretty girl, and seen by Tom or Edmund for the first time seven years hence, and I dare say there would be mischief. The very idea of her having been suffered to grow up at a distance from us all in poverty and neglect, would be enough to make either of the dear sweet-tempered boys in love with her. But breed her up with them from this time, and suppose her even to have the beauty of an angel, and she will never be more to either than a sister.'

'There is a great deal of truth in what you say,' replied Sir Thomas, 'and far be it from me to throw any fanciful impediment in the way of a plan which would be so consistent with the relative situations of each. I only meant to observe, that it ought not to be lightly engaged in, and that to make it really serviceable to Mrs Price, and creditable to ourselves, we must secure to the child, or consider ourselves engaged to secure to her hereafter, as circumstances may arise, the provision of a gentlewoman, if no such establishment should offer as you are so sanguine in expecting.'

'I thoroughly understand you' cried Mrs Norris; 'you are everything that is generous and considerate, and I am sure we shall never disagree on this point. Whatever I can do, as you well know, I am always ready enough to do for the good of those I love; and, though I could never feel for this little girl the hundredth part of the regard I bear your own dear children, nor consider her, in any respect, so much my own, I should hate myself if I were capable of neglecting

> her. Is not she a sister's child? And could I bear to see her want, while I had a bit of bread to give her? My dear Sir Thomas, with all my faults I have a warm heart: and, poor as I am, would rather deny myself the necessaries of life, than do an ungenerous thing. So, if you are not against it, I will write to my poor sister tomorrow, and make the proposal; and, as soon as matters are settled, *I* will engage to get the child to Mansfield; *you* shall have no trouble about it. My own trouble, you know, I never regard. I will send Nanny to London on purpose, and she may have a bed at her cousin, the sadler's, and the child be appointed to meet her there. They may easily get her from Portsmouth to town by the coach, under the care of any creditable person that may chance to be going. I dare say there is always some reputable tradesman's wife or other going up.'

Notice the way the characters speak to each other, especially when they talk to a husband or a wife, or when they know each other well. You will see that Mrs Norris calls her brother-in-law 'Sir Thomas'; that she refers to her own sister as 'Mrs Price'; that Sir Thomas calls her 'Mrs Norris'.

Class distinctions

Class distinctions in the nineteenth century were very important and were closely observed. The use of titles helped to emphasise differences of class and you will notice characters working hard to observe the rules of polite society. Servants have strictly controlled modes of behaviour. Both male and female servants are referred to by their surnames. Dukes are called 'Your Grace' (as are archbishops), bishops and earls are called 'My Lord' and their wives 'My Lady'.

The whole idea of being a gentleman, or being a lady, was very important indeed. Ladies and gentlemen did not work for their living: they had land and other property, they had family money. But they did need 'occupations'. For women these included reading, embroidery, walking, visiting, conversation, the management of family affairs, extended visits to friends and acquaintances and, if they owned several properties, spending time in both town (London or possibly Bath) and country. Gentlemen managed their property, went riding, hunting, shooting and fishing (all this was termed 'sport'). Of course, if they got bored they did things they shouldn't: they gambled, drank too much or took mistresses.

The limitations on upper- and middle-class women were immense. In effect they had only two choices: either to marry or to remain with their parents. If they really did need to earn money they could become governesses or write poetry or novels. This is reflected in the lives and writings of the Brontë sisters, but even as writers they hid their female identity, calling themselves 'Currer, Ellis and Acton Bell'.

Those who did not come from the aristocracy or the gentry (including eventually the self-made men of the middle class) could be termed 'working class'. Their lives lacked both variety and opportunity. It would be true to say that once they had started working, which they did at a very early age, they would have expected to continue working as long as their health permitted. For many such who appear as characters in literature they worked on the land; with the coming of the Industrial Revolution many people migrated to the new industrial centres in the Midlands and the North. Others, of course, lived in the slum conditions of London. Life expectancy was not long for many of them; families were often large (although many children died soon after birth) and staying alive was often their greatest challenge. Some writers (Dickens, for example) set out to show the degradation of these people's lives: their writing was part of the pressure in society for reform. You will find much in the writing of Thomas Hardy that reflects the life of the agricultural labourer; Charlotte Brontë's *Shirley* gives a picture of workers ignored by a mill-owner concerned with his own financial security; J. B. Priestley, in plays such as *When We Are Married* and *An Inspector Calls*, reflect the beliefs and behaviour of the successful middle-class industrial bosses. The life of the Nottinghamshire coal-miner is to be found in the writings of D. H. Lawrence; look, for example, at the short story, *The Odour of Chrysanthemums* or the novel, *Sons and Lovers*.

2.4 More themes to look at

Historical events

Actual historical events sometimes play an important part in particular novels or plays. Shakespeare wrote many 'history' plays based on the lives of the kings of England. *Richard III* ends with the Battle of Bosworth Field (1485), *Henry V* includes the Battle of Agincourt (1415). Writing in the nineteenth century Charles Dickens uses the French Revolution (which began in 1789) as the setting for *A Tale of Two Cities*, while the American writer Mark Twain uses his experiences in the Mississippi and the practice of slavery in *The Adventures of Tom Sawyer* (1876) and *The Adventures of Huckleberry Finn* (1884). When we turn to the twentieth century we find literature which reflects the two world wars, which draws on the Russian Revolution of 1917 and the establishment of Communism, or which takes up past historical events. The life and death of Sir Thomas More is the subject of *A Man for All Seasons* (Robert Bolt) and the Salem witchcraft trials of 1692 the subject of *The Crucible* (Arthur Miller).

Honour and etiquette

We have already referred to social customs; a further aspect of these concerns notions of respectability, of honour and of other ways in which the behaviour of men and women were regulated. In the early nineteenth century a young woman, falling in love, could not directly declare her feelings: to do so would have lowered her in the eyes of her lover, let alone everybody else. So, in *Emma,* the eponymous heroine cannot declare her love for Mr Knightley; she must wait for him. And in *Pride and Prejudice* Jane Bennet waits desperately for Mr Bingley to speak to her. In the same novel, Lydia Bennet breaks all the accepted codes of behaviour by running off with Mr Wickham. Her family have two concerns about this: first, that she should be found and married to Wickham as soon as possible; secondly, that such disgrace will be brought upon the whole family that no one will ever make an offer of marriage to any of Lydia's sisters.

The Importance of Being Earnest, written in 1895, is Oscar Wilde's most famous and probably his best play. It is a highly amusing work which satirises the conventions and behaviour of people in polite Victorian society. It is one of the most entertaining ways of coming to understand the conventions of behaviour and social etiquette prevalent a hundred years ago.

Here are some examples from the play. It would be a good idea to read the play in full and pick out others for yourself.

- When Jack wants to propose marriage to Gwendolen Fairfax he waits until he is on his own with her, but she warns him that her mother may surprise them by suddenly coming back into the room. Although it is clear that Gwendolen wants to marry Jack she insists on a formal proposal. She also mentions that you cannot always take proposals seriously because 'Men often propose for practice', and she admits that her brother Gerald does just that.

- When Gwendolen's mother, Lady Bracknell, finds Jack and Gwendolen together, she is surprised and takes command of the situation. She reminds her daughter that when she gets engaged to be married she will be informed of the fact by her mother or by her father. 'An engagement' she declares, 'should come on a young girl as a surprise, pleasant or unpleasant as the case may be.'

- Lady Bracknell is, however, prepared to consider Mr Worthing. She asks him questions about himself such as, 'Do you smoke?', 'How old are you?', 'What is your income?' and 'You have a house, I suppose?' Lady Bracknell is impressed with Jack's money and the three houses that he owns. However, when she discovers that Jack does not know his parents and that he was 'found' in the left luggage office at Victoria Station in London, she decides that marriage is out of the question unless he can take her advice 'to produce at any rate one parent, of either sex, before the season is quite over.'

This is all very amusing stuff. It works by exaggerating the behaviour of people in this part of society. But it would not be funny unless it reflected many assumptions and conventions that existed at the time as well as the way that people actually behaved.

The treatment of children

The treatment of children by adults reflects the values of the times in which novels were written or set. Dickens wrote many novels to protest at Victorian values and practices. He wrote frequently about the lot of orphans: perhaps most fully in *Oliver Twist*. The novel opens in the workhouse when Oliver 'asks for more'; it goes on to look at the conditions he lives and works in when he is placed with an undertaker. We then learn how he becomes involved in petty crime when he runs away to London and is recruited by the Artful Dodger for Fagin's gang. In *Great Expectations* the young Pip is 'brought up by hand' by his unfeeling sister, Mrs Joe Gargery, as well as being bullied by the pompous Pumblechook. Education is carried out by Mr Gradgrind (a very suggestive name) in *Hard Times*. Charles Kingsley in *The Water Babies* tells a story of Tom, the chimney sweep, who escapes from his bullying employer, Mr Grimes, and while making his escape falls into a river where he becomes transformed into a water baby.

Letters

Letters often play an important part in novels of the pre-1900 period. In themselves they show us how much time there was for ladies and gentlemen of leisure to keep up correspondence. They also have a role in plot, allowing characters to confide their feelings and opinions to friends and family. From an historical point of view they show us how different communications were in former times. Modern devices, such as mobile telephones, fax machines and E-mail, would have been unimaginable.

Racial prejudice: a contemporary theme

In the twentieth century details of social and historical background continue to help us understand and respond to what we read. Racial prejudice is often reflected in novels, either as the main theme (for example in *Roll of Thunder, Hear My Cry* and its sequels by Mildred Taylor) or as an episode in a novel such as *Of Mice and Men* by John Steinbeck, where the treatment of Crooks by his fellow workers and by Curley's wife is entirely explained by his position as a black man. Chinua Achebe is a Nigerian author who, in *Things Fall Apart*, writes about the clash between African and European cultures and beliefs. There are novels which reflect the dealings of white men with indigenous peoples during the period of the British Empire. *A Passage to India* by E.M. Forster and the play, *Conduct Unbecoming* by Barry England both reflect the assumption that when something goes wrong or a crime is committed, the white man must be innocent.

   This is not a complete list by any means. It does show though the many different ways in which the prevailing social and historical context influences the literature that we read and study.

Examiner's tip
- Do not be over-anxious about social, historical and cultural issues: get them into perspective. They should be looked at to help your understanding.
- By referring to them you will demonstrate a fuller understanding of, and response to, literature.
- GCSE English Literature is about texts and responses to texts: it is not about knowledge of texts.

Some other twentieth-century themes

War has played a significant part in the story of the twentieth century. It is not surprising, therefore, that it appears as a great issue in literature. The First World War (1914–1918) saw a great deal of poetic writing. The poets who are most often read and remembered these days are those who protested against the brutality and futility of the war. The most notable is Wilfred Owen. But the Second World War (1939–1945) produced its poets too: the poems of Henry Reed and Keith Douglas are often included in school anthologies. Again, the approach of such writers is often to reflect the suffering of war or to comment on strange aspects of human behaviour. Poetry in the twentieth century rarely glorifies the patriotic idea of dying for your country.

   Political themes are also to be found in modern literature. The writing of George Orwell comes readily to mind here and two of his novels are particularly worth mentioning. *Animal Farm* uses the idea of animals overthrowing their human master and setting out to run their own farm. *Nineteen Eighty-Four* places its hero, Winston Smith, in a futuristic society where every aspect of life is controlled by the all-powerful state represented by 'Big Brother'. Both these novels explore the struggle for power and domination of one human being by another. Both novels are profoundly pessimistic.

2.4 More themes to look at

Another novel which is less 'political' but concerned with social trends is Aldous Huxley's *Brave New World*. We may say of much of this sort of writing that it uses an imaginary world as comment on the society in which the writers lived. You can find similar approaches in Robert Westall's *Supertrack 5* and P. D. James' *The Children of Men*.

The study of 'historical, social and cultural' dimensions of literature may be interpreted as awareness of particular types of writing with imaginary features of time, place and ways of life. 'Science fiction' writing has flourished and remains very popular, particularly among young readers. Detective fiction, which has an established tradition going back to Arthur Conan Doyle and G. K. Chesterton, is another type of writing worthy of study.

Finally, in this brief survey we should perhaps refer to 'Aga sagas', a title given to much popular writing by female novelists in the past ten years or so. Their novels are often set in affluent, middle-class homes and neighbourhoods and explore the crises faced on the personal rather than the grand scale. Writers of this type of novel include Joanna Trollope, Mary Wesley and Marika Cobbold.

Putting this into practice

Here is an examination question based on an extract from Thomas Hardy's short story 'The Son's Veto' (to be found in *The Withered Arm and other Wessex Tales*).

- Bearing in mind the time when the story is set, why is it so difficult for Mrs Twycott to accept Sam's proposal of marriage?

MEG (specimen)

> Soon, however, she gave way to the temptation of going with him again, and on this occasion their conversation was distinctly tender, and Sam said he never should forget her, notwithstanding that she had served him rather badly at one time. After much hesitation he told her of a plan it was in his power to carry out, and one he should like to take in hand, since he did not care for London work: it was to set up as a master greengrocer down at Aldbrickham, the county-town of their native place. He knew of an opening – a shop kept by aged people who wished to retire.
>
> 'And why don't you do it, then, Sam?' she asked with a slight heartsinking.
>
> 'Because I'm not sure if – you'd join me. I know you wouldn't – couldn't! Such a lady as ye've been so long, you couldn't be a wife to a man like me.'
>
> 'I hardly suppose I could!' she assented, also frightened at the idea.
>
> 'If you could,' he said eagerly, 'you'd only have to sit in the back parlour and look through the glass partition when I was away sometimes – just to keep an eye on things. The lameness wouldn't hinder that ... I'd keep you as genteel as ever I could, dear Sophy – if I might think of it!' he pleaded.
>
> 'Sam, I'll be frank,' she said, putting her hand on his. 'If it were only myself I would do it, and gladly, though everything I possess would be lost to me by marrying again.'
>
> 'I don't mind that! It's more independent.'
>
> 'That's good of you, dear Sam. But there's something else. I have a son... I almost fancy when I am miserable sometimes that he is not really mine, but one I hold in trust for my late husband. He seems to belong so little to me personally, so entirely to his dead father. He is so much educated and I so little that I do not feel dignified enough to be his mother ... Well, he would have to be told.'
>
> 'Yes. Unquestionably.' Sam saw her thought and her fear. 'Still, you can do as you like, Sophy – Mrs Twycott.' he added. 'It is not you who are the child, but he.'
>
> 'Ah, you don't know! Sam, if I could, I would marry you, some day. But you must wait a while, and let me think.'

Chapter 2 Historical, social and cultural background

> It was enough for him, and he was blithe at their parting. Not so she. To tell Randolph seemed impossible. She could wait till he had gone up to Oxford, when what she did would affect his life but little. But would he ever tolerate the idea? And if not, could she defy him?
>
> She had not told him a word when the yearly cricket-match came on at Lord's between the public schools, though Sam had already gone back to Aldbrickham. Mrs Twycott felt stronger than usual: she went to the match with Randolph, and was able to leave her chair and walk about occasionally. The bright idea occurred to her that she could casually broach the subject while moving round among the spectators, when the boy's spirits were high with interest in the game, and would weigh domestic matters as feathers in the scale beside the day's victory. They promenaded under the lurid July sun, this pair, so wide apart, yet so near, and Sophy saw the large proportion of boys like her own, in their broad white collars and dwarf hats, and all around the rows of great coaches under which was jumbled the débris of luxurious luncheons; bones, pie-crusts, champagne-bottles, glasses, plates, napkins, and the family silver; while on the coaches sat the proud fathers and mothers; but never a poor mother like her. If Randolph had not appertained to these, had not centred all his interests in them, had not cared exclusively for the class they belonged to, how happy would things have been! A great huzza at some small performance with the bat burst from the multitude of relatives, and Randolph jumped wildly into the air to see what had happened. Sophy fetched up the sentence that had been already shaped; but she could not get it out. The occasion was, perhaps, an inappropriate one. The contrast between her story and the display of fashion to which Randolph had grown to regard himself as akin would be fatal. She awaited a better time.
>
> It was on an evening when they were alone in their plain suburban residence, where life was not blue but brown, that she ultimately broke silence, qualifying her announcement of a probable second marriage by assuring him that it would not take place for a long time to come, when he would be living quite independently of her.
>
> The boy thought the idea a very reasonable one, and asked if she had chosen anybody? She hesitated: and he seemed to have a misgiving. He hoped his stepfather would be a gentleman? he said.
>
> 'Not what you call a gentleman,' she answered timidly. 'He'll be much as I was before I knew your father;' and by degrees she acquainted him with the whole. The youth's face remained fixed for a moment; then he flushed, leant on the table, and burst into passionate tears.
>
> His mother went up to him, kissed all of his face that she could get at, and patted his back as if he were still the baby he once had been, crying herself the while. When he had somewhat recovered from his paroxysm he went hastily to his own room and fastened the door.

To answer the question we need to remember the circumstances in which Sophy Twycott married. She had been a parlour maid in the Reverend Mr Twycott's house and had nursed his first wife in her final illness. After her death Mr Twycott had proposed marriage to Sophy. She 'did not exactly love him' and he 'knew perfectly well that he had committed social suicide by this step, despite Sophy's spotless character'. However, they married, moved away from Aldbrickham and settled in south London. After fourteen years of marriage Mr Twycott died leaving a widow and a son.

In the extract we can see the situation in which Sophy Twycott finds herself. She has met her old admirer Sam Hobson. After renewing their acquaintance, Sam asks her to marry him. He is very deferential in tone because he knows that Mrs Twycott is a class above him: marrying him would lower her status. He tries to get round this by indicating that he wishes to start a business of his own which would involve running a shop. He makes it clear that he would not expect her to do any work, except a genteel amount of observation when he had to go out. Notice, too, how uncertain he is of how to address her: is she 'Sophy' or 'Mrs Twycott'? Sophy Twycott would be perfectly happy to marry Sam: indeed she might be truly happy for the first time in her life. But she is hesitant. Not because she would lose the property she lives in or her income, although that is from her late husband's will. No, it is to do with her son, Randolph, who 'with his aristocratic school-knowledge, his grammars and his aversions', no longer loves his mother or relates to her. She knows really that he would never approve of her marrying a shopkeeper.

Hardy paints the picture of Randolph in this extract by the details that he provides: Randolph is at public school, he is attending the cricket match at Lord's, he is waiting to 'go up to Oxford'. His mother knows she has an impossible task and so she hopes to slip the details of her hoped-for marriage past Randolph when he is least likely to notice it. But the occasion at Lord's proves fruitless: she tries later on one evening when they are alone together. Notice that 'marriage' is spoken of first, not marriage to someone; the boy even asks if she has anyone in mind. When there is hesitation the boy becomes suspicious and asks the fatal question – would his stepfather be a gentleman? The answer, of course, is no! Sam Hobson's qualities as a person are irrelevant to Randolph. His mother would be marrying beneath her. He is totally distraught, cannot be consoled and removes himself from his mother's company. She cannot possibly marry Sam.

Of course, a stronger-minded woman than Sophy Twycott could have defied her son. But she is well used to the class distinctions of the society in which she lives. Indeed she has been all too aware of them during her husband's life-time and her son's childhood. As we are constantly reminded in the story, her manner of speech gives away her social origins. Now, as a widow, she is entirely dependent on the provisions made for her, as well as for her son, in the will of her husband. Of course, he made these provisions without ever consulting her. And now she is as much controlled by her son as she was by her husband. She is to remain lonely and unhappy because her son can go no further in his thoughts than the effect that the marriage would have upon him. Like his father before him he is destined to be a clergyman of the established Church; that brings rank and privilege and social status. None of that must be compromised by his mother.

So Sophy Twycott's life is a sad and tragic one. She is caught up in circumstances which she feels powerless to overcome. As readers of the story we would be heartless indeed to attribute what happens merely to Sophy's character: there is much more to say.

Section 3 Prose

Chapter 3
Responding to prose: novels

Getting started

Probably the first story you ever heard began with the words, 'Once upon a time' and ended 'happily ever after'. Everybody likes a good story. Whether you are at school, at college or at work, you will notice that people get really interested in what someone is saying when there is a good story to be told. If you think, too, about leisure time it is obvious that people spend a considerable amount of time on stories. These might be in the form of films, of television plays, serials or 'soaps'. Fewer people go to plays these days, but the excitement of a live performance is something very special. What all these things have in common is a 'story'.

Many of the things mentioned above include the experience of being in an audience or of watching. But reading a novel isn't like that: it is an individual experience. You can choose your own pace for reading; you can go back and read again, or, if you are impatient, jump forward to find out what happens. You can select a novel for yourself because it is of a type that interests you – crime, mystery, romance – or because it is by a certain author and you want to read as much as possible of what he/she has written – or because it has certain ideas that are being explored or considered.

In this chapter we shall be considering ways to approach the study of novels. In order to satisfy GCSE and National Curriculum requirements to study works from before 1900 as well as those of the twentieth century, we shall look at some of the changes that have taken place in the writing of the novel over time.

3.1 Plot

Basically the **plot** of a novel is the story that is being told. This 'story' may be a simple one or it may be complex, involving many different, but related strands. Below is a summary of the plot in two well-known novels.

- A popular twentieth-century novel, often set for GCSE, is *Of Mice and Men* by John Steinbeck. It is the story of two itinerant workers, George Milton and Lennie Small. The plot can be summarised as follows: George and Lennie each find a new job on a ranch; when they arrive they meet the boss and the other workers; they start working. People are often suspicious of two men together, especially because George, the smaller of the two, speaks for and protects Lennie, the larger man. On the ranch Curley, the boss's son, takes a dislike to Lennie; eventually there is a fight. Curley's wife is the only woman on the ranch and George warns Lennie to keep away from her. One Sunday afternoon Lennie and Curley's wife are in the barn; Lennie gets frightened and he kills Curley's wife while trying to stop her shouting. Lennie runs away. When George finds him he shoots him rather than let the lynch mob get him.

- If you compare these events with those in Charles Dickens' *Great Expectations* you will immediately see the differences. Dickens writes about the life of Philip Pirrip (Pip) from boyhood, through adolescence to adulthood. Pip is an orphan living on the Kent marshes. He becomes an apprentice to his blacksmith brother-in-law, Joe Gargery, but through good fortune acquires a private income and is able to lead the life of a gentleman. Pip's story is interwoven with two other main stories. There is the story of Miss Havisham, the strange owner of Satis House, who has preserved everything as it was on the day she was jilted by her fiancé. Her adopted daughter, Estella, lives with her and is brought up to take revenge on men for Miss Havisham. Then there is the story of the convict who appears in the first chapter and is helped by Pip. This man, Abel Magwitch, plays a major role in the third section of the novel. These three stories connect with each other, and the plot here is much more complex than that in *Of Mice and Men*.

The order of events in the plot

It is not only length and complexity that may affect the structure of the plot. The order in which events are dealt with can also play a large part in the way we approach a novel.

The most straightforward way to tell a story is to begin at the beginning and go on to the end, relating one event after another as they happen. However, novelists don't always like this format. They often begin with an important event and only later on give us the background we need. Alternatively they may reveal, little by little, important events from the past. Sometimes stories may begin with the 'conclusion' and then past details which lead up to it are filled in.

In the two novels we have looked at so far these points may be illustrated as follows.

- In *Of Mice and Men* there are important details about George and Lennie's past lives – how they came to travel together, what their relationship is like – that only come out after they have arrived at the ranch. The same could be said of the details about the problems George and Lennie experience in a town called Weed.

- In *Great Expectations* the story of Pip's life begins when he is seven or eight years old and moves forward from that point. But the details of other characters' lives are filled in later. Good examples of this are Magwitch and Compeyson's 'business' arrangements and Miss Havisham's wedding day.

Narration

One further area to think about is the role of the narrator. Novels, as we know them, really began to be written in the late-eighteenth century. Many events and characters were dealt with in the story and the story-teller (narrator or writer) knew everything about everybody. This is the tradition of the **omniscient third-person narrator**. The alternative to this is when a character in a novel tells the story about himself/herself. This kind of novel is known as a **first-person narrative**. A writer may choose to do this to present a particular point of view or to give a particular slant on events.

- In *Of Mice and Men*, John Steinbeck is the omniscient narrator.

- In *Great Expectations* Pip tells his own story, looking back upon his childhood and seeing how events have happened. The story is a first-person narrative.

- A further variation is to be found in a modern novel, *Daz 4 Zoe* by Robert Swindells, where there are two narratives, each by one of the two major characters.

Examiner's tip

- Make sure you understand the twists and turns of a narrative. In studying a text use a diagram, or carefully organised notes, to show what happens and how events are related.
- When the story is told by a character (or characters), consider how this affects the way the reader thinks and feels.

3.2 Characters

The things that happen in stories, the things that make up the plot, concern people; these people are called **characters**. We react to them and the things that happen to them. We

Chapter 3 Responding to prose: novels

find ourselves liking or hating, loving or despising the characters we read about. Sometimes we even wonder what happens to them after the novel has finished.

One of the things that examination candidates are expected to be able to do is to analyse character. This involves working out what are the strengths and weaknesses of a character, his or her particular 'characteristics'. Such studies are often termed 'character studies' and learning how to do them is an important skill.

The steps that you can take are:

1. List the events in which a particular character is involved.
2. Work out how this character behaves.
3. Look for explanations of this behaviour – some may be given by the writer, some may be implied or you may simply have to make your own judgement.
4. Use any opinions about a character expressed in the book by others or by the author.
5. Identify your own opinions and feelings.
6. Come to a final judgement and make sure you can back it up by reference to the text.

Building up a character study: Michael Henchard

Thomas Hardy is a writer who creates strong characters, none more vividly portrayed perhaps than Michael Henchard in *The Mayor of Casterbridge*. The opening of the novel is a strong and powerful one. Michael, with his wife Susan and their daughter, goes to the Fair at Weydon-Priors. There, in the furmity tent, Michael gets drunk by drinking 'furmity' laced with rum.

> Neither of our pedestrians had much heart for these things, and they looked around for a refreshment tent among the many which dotted the down. Two, which stood nearest to them in the ochreous haze of expiring sunlight, seemed almost equally inviting. One was formed of new, milk-hued canvas, and bore red flags on its summit; it announced 'Good Home-brewed Beer, Ale, and Cyder'. The other was less new; a little iron stove-pipe came out of it at the back, and in front appeared the placard, 'Good Furmity Sold Hear'. The man mentally weighed the two inscriptions, and inclined to the former tent.
>
> 'No – no – the other one,' said the woman. 'I always like furmity; and so does Elizabeth-Jane; and so will you. It is nourishing after a long hard day.'
>
> 'I've never tasted it,' said the man. However, he gave way to her representations, and they entered the furmity booth forthwith.
>
> A rather numerous company appeared within, seated at the long narrow tables that ran down the tent on each side. At the upper end stood a stove, containing a charcoal fire, over which hung a large, three-legged crock. sufficiently polished round the rim to show that it was made of bell-metal. A haggish creature of about fifty presided, in a white apron, which, as it threw an air of respectability over her as far as it extended, was made so wide as to reach nearly round her waist. She slowly stirred the contents of the pot. The dull scrape of her large spoon was audible throughout the tent as she thus kept from burning the mixture of corn in the grain, flour, milk, raisins, currants, and what not, that composed the antiquated slop in which she dealt. Vessels holding the separate ingredients stood on a white-clothed table of boards and trestles close by.
>
> The young man and woman ordered a basin each of the mixture, steaming hot, and sat down to consume it at leisure. This was very well so far, for furmity, as the woman had said, was nourishing, and as proper a food as could be obtained within the four seas; though, to those not accustomed to it, the grains of wheat, swollen as large as lemon-pips, which floated on its surface, might have a deterrent effect at first.
>
> But there was more in that tent than met the cursory glance; and the man, with the instinct of a perverse character, scented it quickly. After a mincing attack on his bowl, he watched the hag's proceedings from the corner of his eye, and saw the game she played. He winked to her, and passed up his basin in reply to her nod; when she took a bottle from under the table, slily measured out a quantity of its contents, and tipped the same into the man's furmity. The liquor poured in was rum. The man as slily sent back money in payment.

He found the concoction, thus strongly laced, much more to his satisfaction than it had been in its natural state. His wife had observed the proceeding with much uneasiness; but he persuaded her to have hers laced also, and she agreed to a milder allowance after some misgiving.

The man finished his basin, and called for another, the rum being signalled for in yet stronger proportion. The effect of it was soon apparent in his manner, and his wife but too sadly perceived that in strenuously steering off the rocks of the licensed liquor-tent she had only got into maelstrom depths here amongst the smugglers.

The child began to prattle impatiently, and the wife more than once said to her husband, 'Michael, how about our lodging? You know we may have trouble in getting it if we don't go soon.'

But he turned a deaf ear to those bird-like chirpings. He talked loud to the company. The child's black eyes, after slow, round, ruminating gazes at the candles when they were lighted, fell together; then they opened, then shut again, and she slept.

At the end of the first basin the man had risen to serenity; at the second he was jovial; at the third, argumentative; at the fourth, the qualities signified by the shape of his face, the occasional clench of his mouth, and the fiery spark of his dark eye, began to tell in his conduct; he was overbearing – even brilliantly quarrelsome.

The conversation took a high turn, as it often does on such occasions. The ruin of good men by bad wives, and, more particularly, the frustration of many a promising youth's high aims and hopes, and the extinction of his energies, by an early imprudent marriage, was the theme.

'I did for myself that way thoroughly,' said the trusser, with a contemplative bitterness that was well-nigh resentful. 'I married at eighteen, like the fool that I was; and this is the consequence o't.' He pointed at himself and family with a wave of the hand intended to bring out the penuriousness of the exhibition.

The young woman his wife, who seemed accustomed to such remarks, acted as if she did not hear them, and continued her intermittent private words on tender trifles to the sleeping and waking child, who was just big enough to be placed for a moment on the bench beside her when she wished to ease her arms. The man continued –

'I haven't more than fifteen shillings in the world, and yet I am a good experienced hand in my line. I'd challenge England to beat me in the fodder business; and if I were a free man again, I'd be worth a thousand pound before I'd done o't. But a fellow never knows these little things till all chance of acting upon 'em is past.'

The auctioneer selling the old horses in the field outside could be heard saying, 'Now this is the last lot – now who'll take the last lot for a song? Shall I say forty shillings? 'Tis a very promising brood-mare, a trifle over five years old, and nothing the matter with the hoss at all, except that she's a little holler in the back and had her left eye knocked out by the kick of another, her own sister, coming along the road.'

'For my own part I don't see why men who have got wives, and don't want 'em shouldn't get rid of 'em as these gipsy fellows do their old horses,' said the man in the tent. 'Why shouldn't they put 'em up and sell 'em by auction to men who are in want of such articles? Hey? Why, begad, I'd sell mine this minute if anybody would buy her!'

'There's them that would do that,' some of the guests replied, looking at the woman, who was by no means ill-favoured.

'True,' said a smoking gentleman, whose coat had the fine polish about the collar, elbows, seams, and shoulder-blades that long-continued friction with grimy surfaces will produce, and which is usually more desired on furniture than on clothes. From his appearance he had possibly been in former time groom or coachman to some neighbouring county family. 'I've had my breedings in as good circles, I may say, as any man,' he added, 'and I know true cultivation, or nobody do; and I can declare she's got it – in the bone, mind ye, I say – as much as any

> female in the fair – though it may want a little bringing out.' Then, crossing his legs, he resumed his pipe with a nicely-adjusted gaze at a point in the air.
>
> The fuddled young husband stared for a few seconds at this unexpected praise of his wife, half in doubt of the wisdom of his own attitude towards the possessor of such qualities. But he speedily lapsed into his former conviction, and said harshly –
>
> 'Well, then, now is your chance; I am open to an offer for this gem o' creation.'
>
> She turned to her husband and murmured, 'Michael, you have talked this nonsense in public places before. A joke is a joke, but you may make it once too often, mind!'
>
> 'I know I've said it before; I meant it. All I want is a buyer.'

If you look at this passage you will see what Michael Henchard does:
- He is already in a bad mood and drinks to make himself feel better.
- He won't listen to his wife's (sensible) suggestions about lodgings.
- As he goes on drinking he changes and becomes very 'quarrelsome'.
- When the talk turns to selling horses and changing wives, he is ready to join in, prompted by praise of his own wife.
- He is sarcastic about her.
- He puts his wife up for sale.

These events give us a first glimpse of Henchard, the central character in the book. Using these events as evidence we can come to some preliminary conclusions about him:

> *Michael Henchard is a man unhappy with himself. He has married young and now has a young child, but he and his wife do not get on well. In the early pages of the book we have discovered that Henchard and his wife were not talking to each other; clearly theirs was not a happy marriage. When they go to the Fair she steers him away from the beer tent but he has the opportunity for 'strong drink' when his furmity is laced with rum. In the furmity tent his wife offers good advice that they must find somewhere to stay, but he ignores her. His obstinacy is there for all to see. He stubbornly goes on drinking. When the conversation turns to 'wives' and Susan is praised, Henchard offers her for sale. He shows little respect for, or concern about, his wife: he refers to her sarcastically as 'this gem o' creation'. He ignores her appeals to stop what he is doing, revealing how little feeling he has for her. It is also clear that this is not the first time he has humiliated his wife in public. We can see that once this headstrong man has begun on a course of action, nothing will stop him.*

Here then is the beginning of a character study built on one episode. As the novel develops we see other examples of Michael's obstinacy and stubbornness. A good example is the way he comes to turn against Donald Farfrae. But he has his good points too, for he repents of the auctioning and selling of his wife and tries to lead a good life. He deals justly with Farfrae when they are fighting and generously to Lucetta when he has it in his power to ruin her. If you are studying this novel, here is a character about whom much may be said.

The extract above shows how Hardy begins to give us a picture of a character about whom we are going to learn a great deal throughout the novel. It is not, obviously, just at one particular point in a novel that we look at character. When we finish reading it is important to see how a character is portrayed throughout the whole novel. This may seem a daunting task, especially with a long novel. The following broad points should guide you.

- Consider the changes that occur.
- Look for important moments ('turning points').
- How does the character concerned think about his/her way of life?
- How do others think about him/her?
- Does the character suffer – justly or unjustly?
- What effect does suffering or misfortune have?
- Is there any clear pattern of change?

Another character study: Pip

Pip, in *Great Expectations*, is the main character as well as the story-teller. In order to consider his character, look at the turning points in the novel. Amongst them you might like to include:
- meeting the convict in the church graveyard;
- going to play at Satis House;
- becoming apprentice to Joe;
- learning of his good fortune and the anonymous benefactor;
- going to London and living with Herbert Pocket;
- visiting Satis House and being in love with Estella;
- the return of Magwitch;
- the deaths of Magwitch and Miss Havisham;
- meeting Estella again.

If you consider these events you will see how Pip changes. Broadly speaking you could make out a case for saying that as a young man his sights are raised to the point where he does not wish to become a blacksmith like Joe. This is as a result of his going to Satis House. He becomes a snob. He is lucky to receive a fortune from an unknown source. This enables him to lead the life of a gentleman in London, but at first this means spending money rather than being a good person. He has to come to terms with himself when he finds out that a 'convict' has been his benefactor. His involvement with Magwitch helps to change him into a better person. He realises how badly he has treated Joe, his true and loving friend.

Major and minor characters

The characters we have been looking at are examples of **major characters** in two novels. But in any book there are also other characters who do not have so large a part or who are not so important. These **minor characters** are worth studying in themselves; but we can also look at the way in which they contribute to the main story or the key events in the lives of the main character(s).

The approach to take with minor characters is much the same as with main characters.
- Be clear about what happens to them in the episodes in which they appear.
- Work out the qualities or faults that they have.
- Know how they fit into the plot.
- Consider how they affect the main character.
- Identify key episodes.

In the two classical novels we have used in this section we could say that the inhabitants of Casterbridge and Henchard's workers, such as Jopp and Whittle, are minor characters in Hardy's novel. In *Great Expectations* we might want to nominate Pumblechook Wopsle, Trabb, Trabb's boy and the Pockets as minor characters.

Role-play: putting yourself in the character's place

The emphasis so far has been on analysing characters from all the clues and evidence included in a novel. We have concentrated, too, on novels written before 1900 because of the importance of that date in GCSE courses. Another way of thinking and writing about character is to imagine that the character concerned has a life outside the events in the novel. You will find 're-creative' approaches of this kind in many GCSE examinations as well as in the coursework set by teachers. Tasks of this kind often start like this:

Chapter 3 Responding to prose: novels

- Imagine you are…
- You are…
- Suppose that…

The instructions are then followed by a situation that could occur either during the course of the novel or after it has finished. The point of this 're-creative' task is to show how a character might behave or think or feel. Whatever is invented must be consistent with the character as written about in the book itself.

A favourite task here is to get a character to look back on his/her feelings after important events have taken place. These thoughts could come as diary entries or as a letter or simply as a written version of thoughts that would have occurred. Many GCSE candidates have undertaken this sort of task after reading John Steinbeck's *Of Mice and Men*. They are asked to put themselves in the role of George after the death of Lennie and are asked to look back, or 'reflect', on what has happened, say how they felt and why they behaved as they did. Below is what one GCSE candidate wrote in her coursework in response to the following task.

- Imagine you are George two months later. Describe your experiences and also your memories of the ranch.

> I'm lonely now. It's been two months since Lennie got killed, and I really miss him. I left the ranch soon after that night. When we went back to the ranch after I'd shot Lennie, I talked with Slim for hours. He was a good bloke, Slim, the sort of person you could confide in, who'd understand you. And he was respected too. Even Curley had some respect for Slim. I remember after Lennie had done Curley's hand in, Slim said 'I think you got your hand caught in a machine' to Curley. He was good and kind, Slim, trying to protect Lennie like that.
>
> I talked with Slim for a long time. He told me it was best, that it was like Candy's dog, except that I was brave enough to go through with it myself. I mean, Candy, he didn't shoot his dog himself. He hadn't got the guts to do it. Sometimes I wonder how I did it, then I start examining everything, trying to convince myself that it was the only thing to be done. That was what Slim kept telling me.
>
> 'Never you mind', he said, 'A guy got to sometimes.' Sometimes I want to shout and scream and hurl things about, but most times I try to forget. But, hell, it's useless. You can't forget somethin' like that.
>
> That night I left, I couldn't stay 'till the morning. I couldn't face Curley or Carlson, not even Candy after that. They wouldn't have understood. It wasn't their fault, they just weren't capable of understanding. Carlson killed Candy's dog, but it belonged to Candy. Lennie belonged to me, and I killed him. It's different, but nobody seems to understand, 'cept Slim.
>
> I remember me 'n' Lennie had a little fantasy, about living 'offa the fatta the land'. It nearly came true. But that fantasy, it's been me 'n' Lennie, see. Without Lennie it wasn't important any more. It could've been me 'n' Candy, but it ended up with just me, 'nd I couldn't have nothing like that, not without Lennie.
>
> I needed Lennie, you know. He meant a lot to me. More than you could imagine, I guess. Lennie was a part of me, he was my anchor. He kept me sane, and I was responsible for him. But I never really appreciated him, not 'till now. I could go mad with loneliness.
>
> When I left that night, I set off back to find Lennie's relatives. At first I planned to stop at places on the way, but I can't be bothered

3.2 Characters

now. I didn't think I could stop bothering, but I have. I don't care what I look like, or what I say. I understand Candy now. He was lonely, he was lonely as hell. But Candy I guess he kinda got used to it. I s'pose I will eventually. But right now it's too much. Sometimes I talk to him, even though I know he isn't there any more. I think I'm going mad, then I get kinda scared. I worry about that, the talkin' to myself.

I blame Curley. It's stupid blaming people, but I gotta do it. It makes me feel better somehow. And maybe it was Curley's fault too. From the moment he saw Lennie I knew there was gonna be trouble. I could tell he was against Lennie. But when I got talking to the man, I realised that it was just insecurity. Mind you, I wouldn't trust that wife of his. I start to think maybe it was her that was to blame, tryin' to seduce Lennie. I wonder why she did it, what she was lookin' for, or if maybe she was just tryin' to get at Curley. But you could tell that Lennie liked her the minute he saw her. But Lennie didn't like women because they were women, he treated them like mice or rats.

Sometimes I get to wishin' that I had killed myself while I was at it, but I can't see the point anymore. Whether I'm alive or dead don't make no difference, all that matters is that Lennie isn't any more. I'm lonely, an' I killed him. But I've already said that.

It was funny how Lennie could get on with some people. He got on with Crooks okay. Nobody else would have bothered about Crooks, but really I guess he jus' didn't wanna get hurt. Lennie he managed to penetrate that barrier. Even though Crooks was hostile at first, Lennie jus' didn't care. He was good like that, Lennie, not caring 'bout what you should do. Don't s'pose he realised that he gave Crooks hope for a while, but I guess that it was good of him all the same.

But it was Lennie's strange way of carin' about people that killed him wasn't it? Sometimes I think maybe I'll get myself another friend, somebody like Lennie but then I know that only time will make me better eventually.

It's grief that's my trouble. But this ain't no ordinary grief, not like when my pop died. No, 'cos I didn't kill my pop, did I? Candy 'n' Crooks got good friends. They got a-talking after I'd killed Lennie. Funny combination that. Candy's as lonely as anything, but then I s'pose Crooks was too. Both of 'em had got something up with them physically an' all. Crooks got a bad back, 'n' Candy, he only had one arm. S'pose I'm lucky really, I'm still in one piece. Lennie was like a limb to me I guess. But Candy, he recovered from using an arm so I s'pose I'll get over it soon. I know one thing though, it'll take a long time, probably more time than I got. So I guess I'll spend the rest of my life missing Lennie 'n' regretting decisions. But life's lonely as hell without someone...

Examiner's tip

- Know the characters in the novel you are studying by listing their actions and drawing conclusions.
- When you write an examination answer avoid just repeating the story of the novel; you must be able to draw conclusions.

How should we respond to this? In order to assess this work you should look at the following points.
- Is there factual accuracy?
- Have the events in the novel been used well and appropriately?
- What is being said about George's attitude and feelings towards Lennie?
- Are these expressed in a way that is appropriate for George?

In fact this is a very successful way of tackling this task. There is a fine use of the novel itself: this is just the sort of thing we might expect George to say; and what gives it real quality is that this is just how George might have said it.

3.3 Themes

Themes are the main ideas that run through a novel. If you ask the question 'What is such and such a novel about?' the answer might come back, 'love and hatred', or 'greed and avarice' or 'the struggle for power'. All of these ideas describe the way readers see something behind the story. It is not just a matter of what happens, or even of what interesting people take part in these events, but what else can be identified as important.

This, then, is the third important way in which a novel may be studied. Three basic questions can be asked:
- What theme can I recognise here?
- What is the author's way of presenting it?
- Do I agree with what he/she seems to be saying?

GCSE examination questions often take up these ideas and ask a candidate to discuss themes from a novel and draw conclusions about the writing.

Exploring a novel's themes: examples

The most straightforward way of exploring a novel's themes is to ask: 'What issues does it deal with? What themes are to be found?' If we apply these questions to the three texts we have looked at so far in this chapter we might come up with the following answers.

- *Of Mice and Men* is about friendship and loyalty; it is about dreams, hopes and also about loneliness.

- *Great Expectations* is about money, class distinctions, love and loyalty.

- *The Mayor of Casterbridge* is about a fatal mistake, the attempt to recover from it but the disastrous effects of a serious weakness of character; it is about suffering, both deserved and undeserved.

Examination questions will, of course, suggest to you what a theme is: they may ask you to look at the evidence in a novel for such a conclusion and then produce the evidence to support the idea or to refute it.

We might wonder which came first for the novelist: the theme, or the story or the characters. This would not be easy to answer and it might not even be possible for the novelist to tell you. But novels come from real people who have certain experiences. These experiences affect the way they think and what they write about. Take John Steinbeck, for example. *Of Mice and Men* was published in 1937. It is a very American book and deals with issues which came up with the Depression and about which Steinbeck had both experience and strong feelings.

Look elsewhere and you will find that George Orwell wrote *Animal Farm* during the Second World War; it was published in 1945. It deals specifically with the Russian Revolution of 1917 and the years after, but it deals too with power and corruption. George Orwell had strong feelings about totalitarianism and wrote his book accordingly.

When Harper Lee published *To Kill a Mockingbird* she had a story to tell set some thirty years earlier in the southern USA. She herself is an American and was living at the time in New York. It is a funny and a tragic book; it deals with racial prejudice and its effect on individuals and a community. We cannot doubt that she had strong feelings about racism in the USA.

We do not know exactly what made these novelists write; we cannot even say with certainty how important their themes were. What we can observe is that no one can read their novels and enjoy them without looking at these issues.

Examiner's tip

- Be ready to spot a theme that is being explored, but do not be too hasty in making up your mind about it.
- Be cautious in attributing views to a writer.

3.4 Setting

It helps to know something about the 'setting' when you are reading and studying a novel. Very simply this means being aware of the time and place in which the novel is set. You understand more of what is happening if you have some background knowledge of the customs and beliefs of the time. Many of these issues are dealt with in Chapter 2 on 'historical, social and cultural' aspects, but it is worth repeating them here.

Read the following extract from Mildred Taylor's novel, *Roll of Thunder, Hear My Cry*.

> We stood patiently waiting behind the people in front of us and when our turn came, T.J. handed his list to the man. 'Mr Barnett, sir,' he said, 'I got me this here list of things my mamma want.'
>
> The storekeeper studied the list and without looking up asked, 'You one of Mr Granger's people?'
>
> 'Yessir,' answered T.J.
>
> Mr Barnett walked to another counter and began filling the order, but before he finished a white woman called, 'Mr Barnett, you waiting on anybody just now?'
>
> Mr Barnett turned around. 'Just them,' he said, indicating us with a wave of his hand. 'What can I do for you, Miz Emmaline?' The woman handed him a list twice as long as T.J.'s and the storekeeper, without a word of apology to us, proceeded to fill it.
>
> 'What's he doing?' I objected.
>
> 'Hush, Cassie,' said Stacey, looking very embarrassed and uncomfortable. T.J.'s face was totally bland, as if nothing at all had happened.
>
> When the woman's order was finally filled, Mr Barnett again picked up T.J.'s list, but before he had gotten the next item his wife called, 'Jim Lee, these folks needing help over here and I got my hands full.' And as if we were not even there, he walked away.
>
> 'Where's he going?' I cried.
>
> 'He'll be back,' said T.J., wandering away.
>
> After waiting several minutes for his return, Stacey said 'Come on, Cassie, let's get out of here.' He started toward the door and I followed. But as we passed one of the counters, I spied Mr Barnett wrapping an order of pork chops for a white girl. Adults were one thing; I could almost understand that. They ruled things and there was nothing that could be done about them. But some kid who was no bigger than me was something else again. Certainly Mr Barnett had simply forgotten about T.J.'s order. I decided to remind him and, without saying anything to Stacey, I turned around and marched over to Mr Barnett.
>
> 'Uh ... 'scuse me, Mr Barnett,' I said as politely as I could, waiting a moment for him to look up from his wrapping. 'I think you forgot, but you was waiting on us 'fore you was waiting on this girl here, and we been waiting a good while now for you to get back.'
>
> The girl gazed at me strangely, but Mr Barnett did not look up. I assumed that he had not heard me. I was near the end of the counter so I merely went to the other side of it and tugged on his shirt sleeve to get his attention.
>
> He recoiled as if I had struck him.
>
> 'Y-you was helping us,' I said, backing to the front of the counter again.
>
> 'Well, you just get your little black self back over there and wait some more,' he said in a low, tight voice.
>
> I was hot. I had been as nice as I could be to him and here he was talking like this. 'We been waiting on you for near an hour,' I hissed, 'while you 'round here waiting on everybody else. And it ain't fair. You got no right—'

Chapter 3 Responding to prose: novels

> 'Whose little nigger is this!', bellowed Mr Barnett.
>
> Everybody in the store turned and stared at me. 'I ain't nobody's little nigger!' I screamed, angry and humiliated. 'And you ought not be waiting on everybody 'fore you wait on us.'
>
> 'Hush up, child, hush up,' someone whispered behind me. I looked around. A woman who had occupied the wagon next to ours at the market looked down upon me. Mr Barnett, his face red and eyes bulging, immediately pounced on her.
>
> 'This gal yourn, Hazel?'
>
> 'No, suh,' answered the woman meekly, stepping hastily away to show she had nothing to do with me. As I watched her turn her back on me, Stacey emerged and took my hand.
>
> 'Come on, Cassie, let's get out of here.'
>
> 'Stacey!' I exclaimed, relieved to see him by my side. 'Tell him! You know he ain't fair making us wait—'
>
> 'She your sister, boy?' Mr Barnett spat across the counter.
>
> Stacey bit his lower lip and gazed into Mr Barnett's eyes. 'Yessir.'
>
> 'Then you get her out of here,' he said with hateful force. 'And make sure she don't come back till yo' mammy teach her what she is.'
>
> 'I already know what I am!' I retaliated. 'But I betcha you don't know what you are! And I could sure tell you, too, you ole—'
>
> Stacey jerked me forward, crushing my hand in the effort, and whispered angrily, 'Shut up, Cassie!' His dark eyes flashed malevolently as he pushed me in front of him through the crowd.
>
> As soon as we were outside, I whipped my hand from his. 'What's the matter with you? You know he was wrong!'

The story is told by Cassie and it is impossible to read what she writes without feeling angry. There is so much injustice here. The racism in the story is overt. You can feel Cassie's anger. What adds to all of this is a fuller awareness of the situation from which the story comes. The setting for the novel is Mississipi, one of the southern states of the USA. The time is the 1930s. The 'racism' is a part of life, we could almost say an accepted part of life. Mr Barnett, the store-owner, would not feel that he was behaving badly by making black children wait. He would not regard himself as insulting Cassie by calling her a 'nigger'. Perhaps even more surprisingly the adults in Cassie's family also accept that this is the way white people treat black people. They may not like it but they accept it and expect Cassie to fit in and accept the situation just as they do. It is these facts that makes the whole passage so shocking.

3.5 Style, form and structure

At the highest grades in GCSE candidates are expected to discuss the way in which novelists write. When you are studying a novel this is an important issue. Here are some of the things that need to be thought about in looking a the way a novelist writes.

1. The ordering of events in the telling of the story. Do the events occur in strict chronological order or is there use of flashback and foreshadowing?

2. The narration of the story. Most novels are written by an omniscient third-person narrator, but some, such as *Great Expectations* and *To Kill a Mockingbird* are first-person narrations.

3.5 Style, form and structure

3 The use made of description: of characters, times of the year, weather. How do these things create feelings and moods in a particular part of the novel?

4 The use made of dialogue. When characters speak is it convincing? Are the grammar and vocabulary they use an important part of their characterisation?

5 To what extent things are explained by the writer. Does he/she leave the reader to come to his/her own conclusions?

6 The way that events are chosen in the development of the novel. Are they natural or contrived?

Putting this into practice

Here is an examination question based on an extract from *To Kill a Mockingbird* by Harper Lee.

■ **In what ways is this extract effective in emphasising the prejudice and injustice that exists in Maycomb?**

MEG (specimen)

> It was Jem's turn to cry. His face was streaked with angry tears as we made our way through the cheerful crowd. 'It ain't right,' he muttered, all the way to the corner of the square where we found Atticus waiting. Atticus was standing under the street light looking as though nothing had happened; his vest was buttoned, his collar and tie were neatly in place, his watch-chain glistened, he was his impassive self again.
>
> 'It ain't right Atticus,' said Jem.
>
> 'No son, it's not right.'
>
> We walked home.
>
> Aunt Alexandra was waiting up. She was in her dressing gown, and I could have sworn she had on her corset underneath it. 'I'm sorry, brother,' she murmured. Having never heard her call Atticus 'brother' before, I stole a glance at Jem, but he was not listening. He would look up at Atticus, then down at the floor, and I wondered if he thought Atticus somehow responsible for Tom Robinson's conviction.
>
> 'Is he all right?' Aunty asked, indicating Jem.
>
> 'He'll be so presently,' said Atticus. 'It was a little too strong for him.' Our father sighed. 'I'm going to bed,' he said. 'If I don't wake up in the morning, don't call me.'
>
> 'I didn't think it wise in the first place to let them –'
>
> 'This is their home, sister,' said Atticus. 'We've made it this way for them, they might as well learn to cope with it.'
>
> 'But they don't have to go to the court-house and wallow in it –'
>
> 'It's just as much Maycomb County as missionary teas.'
>
> 'Atticus –' Aunt Alexandra's eyes were anxious. 'You are the last person I thought would turn bitter over this.'
>
> 'I'm not bitter, just tired. I'm going to bed.'
>
> 'Atticus –' said Jem bleakly.
>
> He turned in the doorway. 'What, son?'
>
> 'How could they do it, how could they?'
>
> 'I don't know, but they did it. They've done it before and they did it tonight and they'll do it again and when they do it – seems only children weep. Good night.'
>
> But things are always better in the morning. Atticus rose at his usual ungodly hour and was in the living-room behind the *Mobile Register* when we stumbled in. Jem's morning face posed the question his sleepy lips struggled to ask.

> 'It's not time to worry yet,' Atticus reassured him, as we went to the dining-room. 'We're not through yet. There'll be an appeal, you can count on that. Gracious alive, Cal, what's all this?' He was staring at his breakfast plate.
>
> Calpurnia said, 'Tom Robinson's daddy sent you along this chicken this morning. I fixed it.'
>
> 'You tell him I'm proud to get it – bet they don't have chicken for breakfast at the White House. What are these?'
>
> 'Rolls,' said Calpurnia. 'Estelle down at the hotel sent 'em.'
>
> Atticus looked up at her, puzzled, and she said, 'You'd better step out here and see what's in the kitchen, Mr Finch.'
>
> We followed him. The kitchen table was loaded with enough food to buy the family: hunks of salt pork, tomatoes, beans, even scuppernongs. Atticus grinned when he found a jar of pickled pigs' knuckles. 'Reckon Aunty'll let me eat these in the dining-room?'
>
> Calpurnia said, 'This was all 'round the back steps when I got here this morning. They – they 'preciate what you did, Mr Finch. They – they aren't oversteppin' themselves, are they?'
>
> Atticus's eyes filled with tears. He did not speak for a moment. 'Tell them I'm very grateful,' he said. 'Tell them – tell them they must never do this again. Times are too hard…'

Anyone answering this question has a great deal to choose from. You could begin by observing that the setting is the evening after Tom's trial (with its verdict of guilty) and the following morning. The mood in the two sections is quite different. As Atticus and the children set off for home, Jem is in tears, tears which are described as 'angry'. Jem's 'muttering' indicates his own state of confusion and anger. By contrast, Atticus looks collected and as much in control of himself as ever. His neat appearance shows him to be in charge of his feelings, 'his impassive self again'. But Atticus does not try to hide or cover up the truth: indeed he wants his children to face it. This becomes apparent in his conversation with his sister, who had come to Maycomb while the trial was on, and the tension was high. Aunt Alexandra is ready to criticise her brother for allowing the children to be at Tom's trial, but Atticus is quietly assertive, pointing out that what the children saw was a real part of Maycomb life. He expresses this in a way that leads his sister to accuse him of being bitter, but instead of the argument that we might expect, Atticus refers only to his tiredness and his readiness to sleep in on the following morning – something that would be very unusual for him. But before Atticus finally goes, Jem asks the question that the reader too wants to find the answer to: 'How could they do it?' Atticus replies with feeling, and perhaps with resignation, that this has happened before and will happen again, and (most poignantly) that 'only children weep'.

Scout is the narrator of the story. Here she notices her brother – his anger, his bitterness, the way he asks his question 'bleakly'. She has never seen Jem like this and it makes a great impression on her. Because she is the narrator it makes an impression on us too. But the next morning the mood is different, although no one has forgotten the trial and Jem is keen to know what comes next. His father, always presented in the novel as a sensitive man, aims to reassure his son: there will be an appeal against the verdict.

The fourth person with the family this morning is Calpurnia (Cal), not Aunt Alexandra. The atmosphere between them is relaxed and there is gentle humour here. The chicken breakfast is a thank you and a tribute from Tom's 'daddy' and we don't have to be told that he can't afford such luxury. But matters go further, for the kitchen is full of food, all the grateful gifts from Tom's friends and family. These gifts were left for Atticus outside his back door. Once again there are tears. Previously, Jem's tears were bitter and angry, but Atticus cries because he is moved and overcome at what has been done out of gratitude and appreciation. He is so full of emotion that he cannot speak. When he does it is gently to say that 'they' must never do this again, for times are hard.

The scene here is full of feeling. It starts with anger and confusion, and ends with a sort of sad pleasure at what happens even in difficult times. We see all of this through Scout's eyes. We sense her admiration for her father, her close observation of Jem – but about herself she says nothing. And, of course, we cannot miss the point: Tom was found guilty because he was black. To the whites he is an inferior being and the word of a white girl (Mayella Ewell) cannot be challenged. But in what does this superiority consist? In this passage the irony is clear. The 'superior' whites lie and deceive themselves, they condemn an innocent. The blacks retaliate, not with angry word or violent demonstration, but with appreciation and kindness: they give abundantly from the little that they have. Throughout the passage our feelings are engaged too: we share Jem's anger and Atticus' overwhelming gratitude; but we have little hope for a successful appeal.

We could, if we wished, be a little critical of Harper Lee too. Is this too sentimental? The characterisation of Atticus is open to the criticism that he is too good to be true, too much the ideal father. Perhaps the gratitude here is overdone; after all, Tom is about to be sentenced for a crime he did not commit.

> **Examiner's tip**
> - Look closely at the passage and the question. There will always be plenty to say without going outside the passage, unless you are told to do so.
> - Use your knowledge of the whole book only when there is a real opportunity to do so. Don't bring things in to impress if they don't really fit. You won't succeed!

3.6 Response

'Response' is a word which signals that what you think and feel while reading a novel is very important; it is important to you and it is important to those who read what you write. Education is not just about acquiring knowledge, but about having the knowledge on which to base sensible opinions and real feelings. So the word 'I' is very important in what you have to say about literature.

But there are warnings here too! The fact that you are asked for an opinion does not mean that any opinions will do, or that one opinion is necessarily as acceptable as another. If you offer your thoughts to others for them to judge (as you do when you enter an examination) then you must play by the rules. That means you must:
- base your opinions on a sound working knowledge of the text;
- be sensitive to the way a book is written, its suggestions and the way they are expressed;
- take into account what other people have said or written about the novel;
- be ready to re-read, to think and to change your mind;
- be prepared to be tentative in expressing opinions – 'maybe', 'might be', 'I think', are all important phrases.

Some examples of response

Here are four responses to some of the texts that have been referred to in this chapter.

> When Tom Robinson was found guilty after the trial in 'To Kill a Mockingbird' I felt both sad and angry. I was sad because I knew he was innocent. In fact everyone in the court room at Maycomb knew that he was innocent. I was angry because Atticus Finch was the only person prepared to do anything for Tom. Everyone else connived in a lie. How could people behave like this, I wondered.

> I had very mixed feelings when I learned that Pip had gained such a large fortune. Because he came from a poor background I was glad to see him have a chance of doing something with his life. Getting all that money was perhaps a bit like winning the Lottery nowadays. But somehow I sensed that it wouldn't do Pip any good. I had already heard him tell Biddy about his ambitions, and I knew he was ashamed of his brother-in-law and his home. I was upset as I read on to find how right I was.

Chapter 3 Responding to prose: novels

> *Everybody has dreams and hopes for the future. Poor Lennie so wanted that special place where he could 'tend the rabbits' and George wanted it too. When I was reading 'Of Mice and Men' I tried very hard to believe there would be a happy ending. In my heart of hearts I knew that it wouldn't happen. Despite all George's efforts to control Lennie I just knew that history would repeat itself; that what had happened in Weed would happen again. And it did! What would I have done if I had been George I don't know. I would like to think that I would have had the courage, and the love, to do what he did. I really believe that the only way for George to show his love for Lennie was to kill him.*

> *Napoleon is a vile and calculating animal. Snowball had worked hard for the revolution; he had shown more personal bravery, at the Battle of the Cowshed, than Napoleon. After the animals' success he had wanted to go the next step and improve everyone's life by the building of the windmill. But Napoleon was jealous. He was also power-crazy. Sadly for Snowball and all the animals, except the pigs, he was ruthless too. He drove Snowball out, he lied to the others and exploited their simplicity and good will. I never hated Napoleon more than when he sold Boxer. He was totally despicable in my eyes then.*

Examiner's tip
- Do not hesitate to express your views.
- Make sure that your views are considered and supported.

It is impossible to read these reactions without seeing that the writers have put a lot of themselves in what they say. They show evidence of 'real engagement' with the text. They know what they are talking about, they provide evidence to back up their opinions. But they also write about their feelings – and literature is about feelings.

3.7 Using a reading log

Reading and studying any novel can be demanding. Long novels, with many characters and twists of plot, may pose special problems. One way to cope is to keep a **reading log** covering the points made in this chapter. Below is a reading log to help you study any GCSE set book or coursework text.

READING LOG

Plot
- What are the main points in the story? It is particularly important to notice where significant changes occur.
- When are new characters or new developments introduced?
- How many different stories are there? How are they connected?
- As you read you will be working out what is going to happen next. Where were you right? Where was there something surprising?

Characters
- Who are the main characters? What are your first impressions of each of them? How do your ideas change as your read?
- Which characters are not 'main' characters, but are very important to the story? What are your views about them?

- Which characters do you like and which do you dislike? Can you work out how the writer wants you to feel about the characters? Does he or she write in any particular way to encourage you or put you off?

Themes

- What are the important themes (broad ideas or types of experience) running through the novel? They may be ones that are often written about – love, hatred, conflict, relationships – or they may be specific to this book.
- How do the themes develop?
- Do you think the writer is trying to make a point or teach you something?

Setting

- At what historical time (approximately) is the novel set? Note the things which fit to this period as well as any unusual customs or ideas which surprise you.
- The novel may be set in particular places. What are the important places in the novel? How does the writer help you to imagine these?

Style form and structure

This can be the most difficult part of your work – but it does not need to be. Once you know what happens, the characters and the setting, you are in a position to think about the way the story is put together.

- Look at the story-telling. Who tells the story? From what point of view? Does this add interest to what is said?
- Look at any particularly interesting ways of saying or describing things. Note them down.
- Dialogue (conversation) is important in the telling of a story. How is it used? Is it effective. Are there ways individual characters speak which you think are memorable?

Your response

- A good book will give you many experiences – anger, fear, excitement, annoyance, anxiety, pleasure. What are your feelings – about characters, events, the way things turn out, the whole story?
- Have you been made to think about the themes or ideas in the book? Do you agree or disagree with things that are said?

Chapter 4
Responding to prose: short stories

Getting started

To the casual observer the most notable thing about short stories is their length! Some are very short indeed while others seem almost like novels. But there are many short stories in English literature that are well worth reading. If you are interested in the writing of other cultures the short story was a form of writing that flourished in America in the nineteenth century.

There is an increased awareness of short stories in English literature courses, probably because of the emphasis on writing from the period before 1900. If this is the case then it is to be greatly welcomed for there is a rich diet of stories ready for the hungry reader. And if you find difficulty sustaining interest in one of the long novels that were so popular in Victorian England, then the short story is for you.

Making generalised statements about any aspects of literature is neither easy nor advisable. But what you can probably say with some safety about short stories is:
- they deal with one event;
- they have a small or limited number of characters;
- they deal with background knowledge and description in a very economical way.

We should remember that many short stories were first published in magazines. In this sense they are similar to longer novels, many of which, in the last century, came out in serial form. There was as much interest in the serial or short story among the reading public in the nineteenth century, as perhaps there is today in a 'soap' among television viewers. Arthur Conan Doyle, for example, reached a wide audience eager to read about the exploits of Sherlock Holmes in the *Strand* magazine. When Holmes was 'killed' by Moriarty there was a great national outcry – and Doyle had to do something about it!

In this section we are going to consider four stories; two published before 1900 and two in the twentieth century.

1. *Barbara of the House of Grebe*, by Thomas Hardy, was published in a magazine called *The Graphic* in 1890.
2. *The Adventure of the Speckled Band*, by Arthur Conan Doyle, was also published in the 1890s.
3. *Tickets, Please*, by D. H. Lawrence, is set during the First World War, and has a background of changing times caused by the absence of so many men in the army.
4. *Life Drawing* is by Bernard MacLaverty and was published in 1982.

The aim here will be to identify the main characteristics of these stories and look at how we might study them and other types of short story.

4.1 A pre-1900 short story: *Barbara of the House of Grebe*

Barbara of the House of Grebe by Thomas Hardy is a strange story – and a long one! Indeed when it was first published it was criticised for being both 'unnatural' and 'disgusting'. In studying the story you should consider:
- the three main characters – Barbara, Edmond Willowes and Lord Uplandtowers – and their characteristics;
- the main episodes of the story, together with the use of time;
- the role of the narrator and the way atmosphere is created;
- the conditions in which characters are living;
- the theme or main idea of the story.

One way of looking at the story is to consider that, in different ways, all the main characters are victims. You can then explore in what ways they may be victims – either of each other, of the actions of other people, of the society in which they live or the beliefs and habits of the time.

Below is a coursework task on the story.

- How much can you learn about life in the last century from reading this story? How far are Barbara and Lord Uplandtowers victims of the society in which they live and how far are they victims of their own personalities?

When writing your answer you might like to consider:
- social class and attitudes;
- homes, lifestyles and occupations of the rich;
- travel and methods of travel;
- communications;
- how far social attitudes influence the decisions taken by Lord Uplandtowers and Barbara;
- how far their own personalities lead to, or influence, the decisions and choices they make.

This coursework task is very full and gives detailed guidance to the student. It is, of course, the teacher's choice how much detail is provided in a task such as this. Clearly, the focus of work in the classroom was on the story and its characters; but the teacher must also have realised the need to emphasise social, cultural and historical details. She clearly wished her pupils to take these factors into account when writing about the story.

The main task falls into two sections. Here is what one student wrote in reply to the second part.

> Owing to the conventions of the day, the way in which people behaved and the decisions they made in life were greatly influenced by social attitudes. Through the story we see how both Barbara and Lord Uplandtowers were victims of society in the last century. Lord Uplandtowers had great expectations placed upon him from a very early age, '... his succession to the Earldom and its accompanying local honours in childhood... He had only reached his twelfth year when his father, the fourth Earl, died.' These demands placed on such a young boy would have changed his personality and the way in which he behaved for the rest of his life. Having inherited the Earldom from such a young age, Lord Uplandtowers was determined to pass it all down to an heir of his own, keeping it all in his immediate family, 'the heir-presumptive to the title was a remote relative, whom Lord Uplandtowers did not exclude from the dislike he entertained towards many persons.' His extreme determination over having an heir and preventing his distant relation from inheriting the Earldom caused Lord Uplandtowers to feel great

resentment and bitterness towards Barbara as she couldn't bear children for him. His attitude towards Barbara and her difficulty to conceive make Lord Uplandtowers seem selfish and it seems that he only married Barbara in order for her to produce an heir for him. It is not only Lord Uplandtowers' desire for an heir that influences him, but succumbing to social attitudes. It was the 'done' thing, that everything should be passed on to the next male in your family, usually your son. Lord Uplandtowers' relentless determination gave him a lot of extra work in life. His pride wouldn't let him give in to anything. After telling a friend of his love for Barbara, he is told, '"You'll never get her — sure; you'll never get her!"', but, all the more determined, he said impassively, '"We'll see"', not giving away the fact that he wanted to 'win' her love even more. When Barbara and Lord Uplandtowers are married, he is determined to get her to love him instead of being infatuated with the statue of Edmond Willowes. '"Ha, ha!... This is where we evaporate — this is where my hopes of a successor in the title dissolve — ha! ha!! This must be seen to, verily."', 'Lord Uplandtowers was a subtle man once he had set himself to strategy...' Lord Uplandtowers was easily angered when things didn't work the way he wanted them to; this is seen when he discovers that Barbara has eloped with Edmond Willowes. '"Damn her!" said Lord Uplandtowers, as he drove homeward that night, "Damn her for a fool!"' — which shows the kind of love he bore her.'

It could be said that Lord Uplandtowers' personality caused him the most difficulty in life. All he wanted was to win Barbara's love, but his cruel-hearted attitude and superciliousness drove her further away, back to the memories of her first husband whom she loved. We see many examples of Lord Uplandtowers' cruelty towards Barbara throughout the story. '...whisper of stern reproach: "It need not have been thus if you had listened to me."', '... chuckled like a caustic fogey... when he heard of Barbara's terror and flight at her husband's return', '...and he conducted himself towards her with resentfulness', 'and he asked her "what she was good for?"'

Lord Uplandtowers needed to feel important. His power and control over people made him feel superior. 'Firm in enforcing his ferocious correctives ... till the nerves of the poor lady were ... in agony.' By treating Barbara in such a cruel manner, Lord Uplandtowers felt a sense of power and control. It could be said that his need for such powers comes from damaged pride. Lord Uplandtowers knows that he is Barbara's second choice for a husband and that 'Barbara did not love him.' This caused him bitterness, which resulted in him treating her cruelly, in an attempt to feel powerful and in control. 'Before their marriage her husband had seemed to care little about her inability to love him passionately ... But now her lack of warmth seemed to irritate him and he conducted himself towards her with a resentfulness which led to her passing many hours with him in painful silence.'

If it wasn't for social pressures to marry someone of equal match, Lord Uplandtowers would have cared about Barbara in a different way, not because she was a good match but because he loved her. Lord Uplandtowers may not have intended to treat Barbara cruelly but may have not been able or known how to express the deep felt love which he had for her.

4.1 A pre-1900 short story: Barbara of the House of Grebe

In contrast to Lord Uplandtowers, Barbara rebels by going against social convention and elopes with a man way beneath her in class. She does this to escape from doing the acceptable thing of marrying a man who is of equal match yet whom she doesn't love. 'She had taken this extreme step ... because she had seen closing around her the doom of marriage to Lord Uplandtowers.' This shows quite a strong personality in Barbara, by being able to go against everything that was expected of her and do what she thought would make her happy. Barbara thought she loved Edmond Willowes but because she was such a shallow person, she didn't get to know him, but just married him for his good looks. ' ...shallow lady ... there is no doubt that an infatuation ... of young Willowes was the chief feeling that induced her to marry him ... in that his beauty was the least of his recommendations ... he must have been a man of steadfast nature, bright intelligence and promising life.' Barbara married Willowes for his good looks and to escape from marrying Lord Uplandtowers; this shows that she is looking after herself, to make herself happy. After Willowes died, Barbara eventually married back into her own class for acceptance and to escape from the loneliness. 'Barbara did not love him', but she married Lord Uplandtowers as he ' ... was a more desirable husband, socially considered.' Barbara did not really want to marry Lord Uplandtowers, but he was the only option; she married him not because she loved him but because she had to marry someone.

Through the two marriages, we see contrasts in Barbara's behaviour. She marries Willowes because of infatuation and to go against society yet when she marries Lord Uplandtowers it's because she has accepted convention and that it's the right thing to do.

Throughout this story we see several examples of Barbara being influenced by her personality, feelings and emotions. When Barbara learns of Edmond's death, her reaction and way of coping is to do good works for the poor and vagabonds. 'She determined at least to be charitable ... soon had the satisfaction of finding her porch thronged every morning by the raggedest, idlest, most drunken ... worthless tramps in Christendom.'

As a way of coping with her loneliness after being away from Edmond so long, without thinking she pours her heart out to Lord Uplandtowers '"You here — and alone, my dear Mrs Willowes?" ... she was surprised to find herself talking earnestly and warmly to him; her impulsiveness was in truth but the natural consequence of her late existence — a somewhat desolate one ...' Barbara's loneliness stems from her insecurity and her not wanting to be alone. '"We can put up with the loneliness" said Barbara with less zest' when discussing the house her father is giving them '... "some friends will come no doubt."'

Barbara's emotional insecurity almost wrecks her marriage. She makes her own life more difficult because she can't let go of Edmond and is obsessed with the statue of him. '... standing with her arms clasped tightly round the neck of her Edmond, and her mouth on his ... appearance of a second statue embracing the first ... "My only love — how could I be so cruel to you, my perfect one — so good and true — I am ever faithful to you, ... O Edmond, I am always yours!"' Barbara loved the statue to try and keep

> *Edmond real and near to her. She was unstable and needed something to cling on to.*
>
> *Barbara had a change of personality forced upon her by Lord Uplandtowers in an attempt to rid her of all obsession with Edmond Willowes and the statue. She was forced to look at the statue of Edmond – disfigured. "'O, take it away" ... "All in good time; namely when you love me best."'*
>
> *In the last century everything anyone did was influenced by social conventions. People were judged by their actions and what was and wasn't acceptable in everyone's eyes.*
>
> *Throughout this story we see that on one hand Barbara and Lord Uplandtowers are shaped and moulded by the society in which they live but on the other had they have their lives determined by their own personalities.*

4.2 A pre-1900 short story: *The Adventure of the Speckled Band*

The Adventure of the Speckled Band, by Arthur Conan Doyle, is a detective story featuring Sherlock Holmes and his assistant Dr Watson. Like the Hardy story it comes from the 1890s. The Sherlock Holmes stories have remained popular throughout the twentieth century, but as detective fiction they have been followed by many others in the same genre. Both as novels and as television or radio adaptations, there have been other detectives who have captured the imagination. Amongst them are Lord Peter Wimsey (Dorothy L. Sayers), Hercule Poirot and Miss Marple (Agatha Christie), Morse (Colin Dexter), George Wexford (Ruth Rendell), Commander Dalgleish (P. D. James) and Brother Cadfael (Ellis Peters). If you read the Conan Doyle mystery you may be able to identify key elements in detective fiction which were later taken up by some of the writers mentioned above. These include:

- discovery of a crime (usually murder);
- baffling nature of the circumstances;
- calling in of the 'great detective';
- detective accompanied by less astute assistant;
- examining clues and discarding 'red herrings';
- working out both motive and opportunity;
- finding the solution and announcing the conclusion, often to the surprise of everyone else.

Conan Doyle includes all these features in his short story. Dr Watson tells the story from the point of view of someone who admires Holmes and is baffled by the crime and the clues. Holmes takes specific notice of minute details, putting together both a method of committing the crime and the motive for it. He visits the scene of the crime and puts himself in personal danger in order to find a solution. Justice is achieved in the end.

Points worth thinking about here are:
- the characters of the detective and his assistant;
- the way the story is told;
- how the reader becomes involved;
- how soon the reader knows who committed the crime and the method employed;
- what makes the story a good read.

4.3 A twentieth-century short story: *Tickets, Please*

Tickets, Please is the story of a tram line running from a Midland town into the countryside. D. H. Lawrence tells us:

> To ride on these cars is always an adventure.
>
> …the drivers are men unfit for active service (in the war) … so they have the spirit of the devil in them.
>
> This, the most dangerous tram-service in England … is entirely conducted by girls.

The story is about John Thomas, an inspector on the tramway, and the women who act as conductors. John Thomas plays fast and loose with their affections, playing one girl off against another. So the story is one of revenge. Lawrence's story lasts only sixteen pages in the 1989 Heinemann edition of *Selected Tales*, and yet here we have all the elements of a full narrative:

- the background – both the tram service and the war years;
- the role of the men;
- the involvement of the women;
- the romantic interest;
- John Thomas' treatment of the women;
- their revenge.

The interest here, then, is how Lawrence creates character, mood and setting so successfully in such a short space of time. Most important among the women is Annie. Here is what one GCSE student wrote for his coursework on the question:

■ Is Annie justified or not in her wishes and feelings about John Thomas?

> The women in this story have carefully planned their attack on John Thomas. They have realised that he has been taking advantage of them for a long time. Of course, they find him attractive: he would be a 'good catch' for anyone of them. All he has seemed interested in, however, is flirting with any one of them as opportunity arose. A good example of this is his meeting with Annie at the Statutes fair: they had a wonderful time together and Annie was excited by his presence. After their time together Annie's hopes were high or at least she had very positive feelings towards him. He, however, was not interested in a serious relationship. He merely wished to remain 'a nocturnal presence'.
>
> So the women plan their assault. The man so confident and full of himself is to be humiliated. The first stage is an intense physical attack. Lawrence describes them as 'strange, wild creatures' delighted now 'to have their own back'. The attack is described in detail and we are made to feel the sheer animal pleasure of the women. The sign of their triumph is when he was knocked down and they were kneeling upon his prostrate body. Foremost among them was Annie who acts as a kind of leader throughout the episode. It's as if her need for revenge is more powerful than that of the others. In her voice – for it is she who speaks first – there is, Lawrence tells us, a 'terrifying, cold triumph'.
>
> It is at this point in the narrative that a new turn is taken. Annie wishes to use his physical humiliation to advantage: Polly, Emma and Muriel perhaps think it's time to call a halt. At least that's what their giggling suggests to me. But Annie will have none of it.

> The ferocity of her words matches the violence of all their actions. He ought to be 'killed' she insists.
>
> The women insist on taking the episode into another round. Now, they demand, he must choose. After all it is his indiscriminate attention paid to them that has given offence. So they need to know which one he really wants. The word 'choose' is repeated time and again and to reinforce it Annie slaps John Thomas across the face. He is bemused, perplexed and fearful but finally he chooses and his choice is Annie.
>
> This is a new development. Annie we know is attracted to him, had wanted him. It was his refusal to take her seriously that started this off. Now he has chosen her. Will she accept him so that his defeat can be turned to triumph? Or will her pride, her refusal to be taken up at his whim, give her the courage to say no?
>
> I believe that Lawrence is saying two things. First, that she genuinely loves him, wants him. Secondly, that her wanting is too profound just to be satisfied by his choice now. Her powerful emotions lead her to reject him and thus complete his humiliation. He cannot have what he has chosen, even in defeat. Annie's assertion 'I don't want him' changes the mood again: this is not the ending they had envisaged, if they'd envisaged one at all.
>
> In silence he gathers up his things. The women back off, themselves stunned. The door is opened — by Annie — and he's set free. But what are the women feeling? I think Nora's cry of 'Coddy' suggests she would accept him even now if only he would choose her. And Annie knows this for she, who really loves him, is 'in torture'. Who has won? Who has lost? The story's powerful ending leaves us wondering. Certainly the relationship between this man and these women will never be the same again.

4.4 A twentieth-century short story: *Life Drawing*

Life Drawing, by Bernard MacLaverty, was published in 1982. It is a story which deals with time in two dimensions: the present, where a father is dying; and the past, where father and son had a difficult relationship. It is also a story which uses setting and description to great effect.

The main character in the story is Liam Diamond and he is travelling 'home' where his father is dying. It is worth looking at the construction of the plot, the histories of the two main characters and the use of description.

Plot

- Liam is travelling home by train.
- He reaches the house where he used to live and where his father is now dying.
- When the neighbours have gone he is left alone with his father.
- As he sits with his father he remembers the past.
- He thinks particularly about his wish to be an artist and how his father made fun of him.
- He draws a picture of his father.
- While he is drawing his father dies.

These are the main events in the story as it happens. What is interesting, of course, is how what is happening in the present makes Liam think of the past, so that much of the story is about his childhood.

Characters

What happens is seen through Liam Diamond's eyes: what he does and thinks is shared with the reader. Whatever we think about Liam's father only comes to us from Liam himself. Their rows and disagreements and the physical violence that was part of their relationship are very clear. But we learn of all these things with one dominating picture in our minds: a man lying in bed, unable to speak, dying. It is truly sad.

The use of description and background.

It is as if this story is itself a drawing, but using words. Everything about setting and description fits the mood and feeling here. Look at how the story starts:

> After darkness fell and he could no longer watch the landscape from the train window, Liam Diamond began to read his book.

So the mood is set – 'darkness', the landscape that can be seen no more. What is it, the reader wonders, that lies ahead of Liam? It is bleak and uncertain.

In the second paragraph there is a repetition of the same idea:

> Occasionally he would look up to see if he knew where he was but saw only the darkness and himself reflected in it.

Then Liam makes his way through the darkness to the house where his father lives: at first, he is even uncertain about finding this house. Inside nothing really has changed since his childhood:

> In twenty years he [his father] hadn't changed the wallpaper, yellow roses looping on an umber trellis.

Once Liam is alone with his father he recalls the rows that they used to have about eating habits. On one occasion, when Liam went to grab a sausage that was being served, his father made a lunge at him with his fork, jabbing it into the back of his hand. As this is recalled, we learn:

> The bedroom was cold and when he [Liam] got round to drinking his tea it was tepid.

Finally, there is the recollection of his father's anger because Liam wanted to be an artist. The father poured scorn on his son's ambition: he made fun of him. Liam tells the story of the night he sat up painting on the glass from a picture frame. When his father discovered him at three-thirty in the morning there was a violent row, Liam was struck and his painting destroyed. Now all of this comes back to him as he undertakes a charcoal drawing of his father. This time there is nothing his father can say or do. Indeed while Liam is attending to the drawing, his father dies.

> He knelt beside the bed and tried to think of something good from the time he had spent with his father. Anger and sneers and nagging was all that he could picture.

4.5 Studying short stories: a summary

Examiner's tip

- Short stories are not an easy alternative to the long novel. Readers may prefer several short stories because they provide variety.
- Be able to identify what a writer is doing in the story and how this has been achieved.

The four stories in this section illustrate how very different short stories can be, not only in plot and characterisation but in approach and technique. Good short stories need a great deal of skill to write; it is often more difficult to write less than to write more. You should, therefore, ask yourself:

1. How has the short story format helped the writer?
2. What aspects of the short story has this writer taken advantage of?
3. What is the mood of the story and how has it been achieved?
4. How do stories by the same writer differ?

Section 4 Drama

Chapter 5
Responding to drama: twentieth-century plays

Getting started

A play is rather different from other types of literature because the initial concept is not words on a page but a visual image in the mind of a reader. When we study a play for English, in one sense we are probably only doing half the job. We read the play and we consider plot, character, themes and so on; we might go to see the play if we have a chance, but we leave the detailed work on the visual interpretation to theatre studies and drama. However, it is important that we are also aware of plays as theatre.

We are deliberately using three twentieth-century plays in this section because the vast majority of syllabuses are constructed in such a way that you will study a play by Shakespeare as pre-1900 drama and will then study a twentieth-century play. If you are studying a pre-1900 play other than by Shakespeare, or, for that matter, you are studying several one-act plays, you will find that you need to apply the same techniques because they are all relevant. (See pp.85–92 and Chapters 6 and 7.)

We are going to use three plays to find our way around. The first, *An Inspector Calls* by J.B. Priestley is on the lists of several of the GCSE Boards. The play concerns the Birling family, all of whom, in some way or another have been connected with a young woman called Eva Smith. Eva has committed suicide and it could be argued that the different members of the family have all helped her along the road to suicide. This interests Inspector Goole who calls on the family to discuss what has happened.

The second play is *A Taste of Honey* by Shelagh Delaney. This play was written when Shelagh Delaney was only nineteen and it was seen to have a spontaneity and life that was very relevant to life in the 1960s. It concerns a girl called Jo and, most especially, her relationship with her irresponsible mother. Jo looks for happiness outside and becomes involved with a black sailor who leaves her pregnant, and a homosexual art student who tries to help her.

The third play is *Educating Rita* by Willy Russell. This is about a young woman in Liverpool who wants to be educated and who decides that the way to do it is through the Open University. She meets her tutor, Frank, and the play explores their relationship and how it changes as time goes on.

It is sometimes quite difficult to categorise types of play. However, we can say that *An Inspector Calls* is middle-class and in some ways is a mystery thriller, although it is also a psychological drama, putting attitudes and relationships under a microscope. *A Taste of*

Honey belongs to the era of 'kitchen sink drama' which was very consciously working-class and which looked at social issues and problems. Many people would say that this sort of drama started with a play called *Look Back in Anger* by John Osborne. *Educating Rita* is the most modern of the plays. It is a 'two-hander': in other words there are only two characters in the cast, and, unlike the other two plays which would be categorised as 'serious', this is a comedy. Class is irrelevant. Here we have two characters who are simply and gloriously different.

5.1 The importance of openings

Given that a play needs to make an impact on its audience, it is important that the opening has a clear purpose, and dialogue which catches the attention. Let's look at the openings of our three plays.

An Inspector Calls

ACT ONE

The dining-room of a fairly large suburban house, belonging to a prosperous manufacturer. It has good solid furniture of the period. The general effect is substantial and heavily comfortable, but not cosy and homelike. (If a realistic set is used, then it should be swung back, as it was in the Old Vic production at the New Theatre. By doing this, you can have the dining-table centre downstage during Act One, when it is needed there, and then, swinging back, can reveal the fireplace for Act Two, and then for Act Three can show a small table with telephone on it, downstage of fireplace; and by this time the dining-table and its chairs have moved well upstage. Producers who wish to avoid this tricky business, which involves two re-settings of the scene and some very accurate adjustments of the extra flats necessary, would be well advised to dispense with an ordinary realistic set, if only because the dining-table becomes a nuisance. The lighting should be pink and intimate until the INSPECTOR *arrives, and then it should be brighter and harder.)*

At the rise of curtain, the four BIRLINGS *and* GERALD *are seated at the table, with* ARTHUR BIRLING *at one end, his wife at the other,* ERIC *downstage, and* SHEILA *and* GERALD *seated upstage.* EDNA, *the parlour-maid, is just clearing the table, which has no cloth, of dessert plates and champagne glasses, etc., and then replacing them with decanter of port, cigar box and cigarettes. Port glasses are already on the table. All five are in evening dress of the period, the men in tails and white ties, not dinner-jackets.* ARTHUR BIRLING *is a heavy-looking, rather portentous man in his middle fifties with fairly easy manners but rather provincial in his speech. His wife is about fifty, a rather cold woman and her husband's social superior.* SHEILA *is a pretty girl in her early twenties, very pleased with life and rather excited.* GERALD CROFT *is an attractive chap about thirty, rather too manly to be a dandy but very much the easy well-bred young man-about-town.* ERIC *is in his early twenties, not quite at ease, half shy, half assertive. At the moment they have all had a good dinner, are celebrating a special occasion, and are pleased with themselves.*

BIRLING: Giving us the port, Edna? That's right. [*He pushes it towards* ERIC.] You ought to like this port, Gerald. As a matter of fact, Finchley told me it's exactly the same port your father gets from him.

GERALD: Then it'll be all right. The governor prides himself on being a good judge of port. I don't pretend to know much about it.

SHEILA [*gaily, possessively*]: I should jolly well think not, Gerald. I'd hate you to know all about port – like one of these purple-faced old men.

BIRLING: Here, I'm not a purple-faced old man.

SHEILA: No, not yet. But then you don't know all about port – do you?

BIRLING [*noticing that his wife has not taken any*]: Now then, Sybil, you must take a little tonight. Special occasion, y'know, eh?

SHEILA: Yes, go on Mummy. You must drink our health.

MRS BIRLING [*smiling*]: Very well, then. Just a little, thank you. [*To* EDNA, *who is about to go, with tray*] All right, Edna. I'll ring from the drawing-room when we want coffee. Probably in about half an hour.

EDNA [*going*]: Yes, ma'am.

[EDNA *goes out. They now have all the glasses filled.* BIRLING *beams at them and clearly relaxes.*]

BIRLING: Well, well – this is very nice. Very nice. Good dinner too, Sybil. Tell cook from me.

GERALD [*politely*]: Absolutely first-class.

MRS BIRLING [*reproachfully*]: Arthur, you're not supposed to say such things –

BIRLING: Oh – come, come – I'm treating Gerald like one of the family. And I'm sure he won't object.

SHEILA [*with mock aggressiveness*]: Go on, Gerald – just you object!

GERALD [*smiling*]: Wouldn't dream of it. In fact, I insist upon being one of the family now. I've been trying long enough, haven't I? [*As she does not reply, with more insistence.*] Haven't I? You know I have.

MRS BIRLING [*smiling*]: Of course she does.

SHEILA [*half serious, half playful*]: Yes – except for all last summer, when you never came near me, and I wondered what had happened to you.

GERALD: And I've told you – I was awfully busy at the works all that time.

SHEILA [*same tone as before*]: Yes, that's what *you* say.

MRS BIRLING: Now, Sheila, don't tease him. When you're married you'll realize that men with important work to do sometimes have to spend nearly all their time and energy on their business. You'll have to get used to that, just as I had.

SHEILA: I don't believe I will. [*Half playful, half serious, to Gerald.*] So you be careful.

GERALD: Oh – I will, I will.[ERIC *suddenly guffaws. His parents look at him.*]

SHEILA [*severely*]: Now – what's the joke?

ERIC: I don't know – really. Suddenly I felt I just had to laugh.

SHEILA: You're squiffy.

ERIC: I'm not.

MRS BIRLING: What an expression, Sheila! Really, the things you girls pick up these days!

ERIC: If you think that's the best she can do –

SHEILA: Don't be an ass, Eric.

MRS BIRLING: Now stop it, you two. Arthur, what about this famous toast of yours?

5.1 The importance of openings

> BIRLING: Yes, of course. [*Clears his throat.*] Well, Gerald, I know you agreed that we should only have this quiet little family party. It's a pity Sir George and – er – Lady Croft can't be with us, but they're abroad and so it can't be helped. As I told you, they sent me a very nice cable – couldn't be nicer. I'm not sorry that we're celebrating quietly like this –
>
> MRS BIRLING: Much nicer really.
>
> GERALD: I agree.
>
> BIRLING: So do I, but it makes speech-making more difficult –
>
> ERIC [*not too rudely*]: Well, don't do any. We'll drink their health and have done with it.
>
> BIRLING: No, we won't. It's one of the happiest nights of my life. And one day, I hope, Eric, when you've a daughter of your own, you'll understand why. Gerald, I'm going to tell you frankly, without any pretences, that your engagement to Sheila means a tremendous lot to me. She'll make you happy, and I'm sure you'll make her happy. You're just the kind of son-in-law I always wanted. Your father and I have been friendly rivals in business for some time now – though Crofts Limited are both older and bigger than Birling and Company – and now you've brought us together, and perhaps we may look forward to the time when Crofts and Birlings are no longer competing but are working together – for lower costs and higher prices.
>
> GERALD: Hear, hear! And I think my father would agree to that.
>
> MRS BIRLING: Now, Arthur, I don't think you ought to talk business on an occasion like this.
>
> SHEILA: Neither do I. All wrong.
>
> BIRLING: Quite so, I agree with you. I only mentioned it in passing. What I did want to say was – that Sheila's a lucky girl – and I think you're a pretty fortunate young man too, Gerald.
>
> GERALD: I know I am – this once anyhow.
>
> BIRLING [*raising his glass*]: So here's wishing the pair of you – the very best that life can bring. Gerald and Sheila.

You will see that the stage directions at the beginning of the play are very long and contain a great deal of detail. Playwrights have different attitudes to stage directions. In Shakespeare's plays you will find very few other than directions for characters to come in and go out. Others have fairly cursory and general directions. Others have what we have here. It tells us exactly what is going on and where the play is situated, and makes a few introductory comments about the characters.

The type of family that we are introduced to is established not only by the description of what they are wearing but by the very first words, 'Giving us the port, Edna?', which establishes that they are having a rather formal dinner. The dialogue is jovial and you might say a little stilted. It becomes obvious that Mr Birling is very anxious that everything should be right because Gerald is important to him in business terms as well as in terms of becoming a member of the family. Birling has bought the port because it is the same brand as Gerald's father buys. Gerald's parents have titles. Gerald's father has a rather larger business than Mr Birling.

There are two instances of behaviour or tone which do not quite fit the general mood. The first occurs in an exchange between Sheila and Gerald:

> SHEILA [*half serious, half playful*]: Yes – except for all last summer, when you never came near me, and I wondered what had happened to you.
>
> GERALD: And I've told you – I was awfully busy at the works all that time.
>
> SHEILA: [*same tone as before*]: Yes, that's what *you* say.

The lines are light-hearted in a way but they link up with later events and it will eventually be established that Gerald was not telling the truth.

The second is when Eric suddenly laughs loudly for no apparent reason after a long silence and shows clearly that he has had too much to drink.

What is happening at the beginning of the play is a convenient format to enable all members of the family to be introduced. This means that the entrance of the Inspector, which comes later, can be clearly significant. So we have characters introduced, the setting established and perhaps just a hint of everything not being quite so perfect as might appear at first sight.

A Taste of Honey
ACT ONE
Scene One

The stage represents a comfortless flat in Manchester and the street outside. Jazz music. Enter HELEN, *a semi-whore, and her daughter,* JO. *They are loaded with baggage.*

HELEN: Well! This is the place.

JO: And I don't like it.

HELEN: When I find somewhere to live I have to consider something far more important than your feelings ... the rent. It's all I can afford.

JO: You can afford something better than this old ruin.

HELEN: When you start earning you can start moaning.

JO: Can't be soon enough for me. I'm cold and my shoes let water ... what a place ... and we're supposed to be living off her immoral earnings.

HELEN: I'm careful. Anyway, what's wrong with this place? Everything in it's falling apart, it's true, and we've no heating – but there's a lovely view of the gasworks, we share a bathroom with the community and this wallpaper's contemporary. What more do you want? Anyway it'll do for us. Pass me a glass, Jo.

JO: Where are they?

HELEN: I don't know.

JO: You packed 'em. She'd lose her head if it was loose.

HELEN: Here they are. I put 'em in my bag for safety. Pass me that bottle – it's in the carrier.

JO: Why should I run round after you? [*Takes whisky bottle from bag.*]

HELEN: Children owe their parents these little attentions.

JO: I don't owe you a thing.

HELEN: Except respect, and I don't seem to get any of that.

JO: Drink, drink, drink, that's all you're fit for. You make me sick.

HELEN: Others may pray for their daily bread, I pray for ...

JO: Is that the bedroom?

HELEN: It is. Your health, Jo.

JO: We're sharing a bed again, I see.

HELEN: Of course, you know I can't bear to be parted from you.

JO: What I wouldn't give for a room of my own! God! It's freezing! Isn't there any sort of fire anywhere, Helen?

HELEN: Yes, there's a gas-propelled thing somewhere.

JO: Where?

HELEN: Where? What were you given eyes for? Do you want me to carry you about? Don't stand there shivering; have some of this if you're so cold.

JO: You know I don't like it.

HELEN: Have you tried it?

JO: No.

5.1 The importance of openings

> HELEN: Then get it down you! [*She wanders around the room searching for fire.*] 'Where!' she says. She can never see anything till she falls over it. Now. where's it got to? I know I saw it here somewhere … one of those shilling in the slot affairs; the landlady pointed it out to me as part of the furniture and fittings. I don't know. Oh! It'll turn up. What's up with you now?
>
> JO: I don't like the smell of it.
>
> HELEN: You don't smell it, you drink it! It consoles you.
>
> JO: What do you need consoling about?
>
> HELEN: Life! Come on, give it to me if you've done with it. I'll soon put it in a safe place. [*Drinks.*]
>
> JO: You're knocking it back worse than ever.
>
> HELEN: Oh! Well, it's one way of passing time while I'm waiting for something to turn up. And it usually does if I drink hard enough. Oh my God! I've caught a shocking cold from somebody. Have you got a clean hanky, Jo? Mine's wringing wet from dabbing at my nose all day.
>
> JO: Have this, it's nearly clean. Isn't that light awful? I do hate to see an unshaded electric light bulb dangling from the ceiling like that.
>
> HELEN: Well, don't look at it then.
>
> JO: Can I have that chair, Helen? I'll put my scarf round it. [Jo *takes chair from* HELEN, *stands on it and wraps her scarf round light bulb – burning herself in the process.*]
>
> HELEN: Wouldn't she get on your nerves? Just when I was going to take the weight off my feet for five minutes. Oh! my poor old nose.
>
> JO: Christ! It's hot.
>
> HELEN: Why can't you leave things alone? Oh! she gets me down. I'll buy a proper shade tomorrow. It's running like a tap. This is the third hanky today.
>
> JO: Tomorrow? What makes you think we're going to live that long? The roof's leaking!
>
> HELEN: Is it? No, it's not, it's just condensation.
>
> JO: Was it raining when you took the place?
>
> HELEN: It is a bit of a mess, isn't it.
>
> JO: You always have to rush off into things. You never think.
>
> HELEN: Oh well, we can always find something else.
>
> JO: But what are you looking for? Every place we find is the same.
>
> HELEN: Oh! Every time I turn my head my eyeballs hurt. Can't we have a bit of peace for five minutes?

Here we have very little in the way of stage direction, perhaps just enough to establish an atmosphere. What is established very quickly is the relationship between Helen and Jo. In one sense they are dependent on each other and in another they are very antagonistic towards each other.

> HELEN: Well! This is the place.
>
> JO: And I don't like it.

The fact that Helen has a cold and is perpetually blowing her nose, at one point on Jo's 'nearly clean' hanky emphasises that not only is the flat grotty but so is Helen. It is a simple uncomplicated opening establishing the place and the two central characters.

Educating Rita

ACT ONE

Scene One

A room on the first floor of a Victorian-built university in the north of England.

There is a large bay window with a desk placed in front of it and another desk covered with various papers and books. The walls are lined with books and on one wall hangs a good print of a nude religious scene.

FRANK, *who is in his early fifties, is standing holding an empty mug. He goes to the bookcases and starts taking books from the shelves, hurriedly replacing them before moving on to another section.*

FRANK [*looking along the shelves*]: Where the hell ...? Eliot? [*He pulls out some books, and looks into the bookshelf.*] No. [*He replaces the books.*] 'E' [*He thinks for a moment.*] 'E', 'e', 'e' ... [*Suddenly he remembers.*] Dickens. [*Jubilantly he moves to the Dickens section and pulls out a pile of books to reveal a bottle of whisky. He takes the bottle from the shelf and goes to the small table by the door and pours himself a large slug into the mug in his hand.*]

[*The telephone rings and startles him slightly. He manages a gulp at the whisky before he picks up the receiver and although his speech is not slurred, we should recognise the voice of a man who shifts a lot of booze.*]

Yes? ... Of course I'm still here ... Because I've got this Open University woman coming, haven't I? ... Tch ... Of course I told you ... But darling, you shouldn't have prepared dinner should you? Because I said, I distinctly remember saying that I would be late ... Yes. Yes, I probably shall go to the pub afterwards, I shall need to go to the pub afterwards, I shall need to wash away the memory of some silly woman's attempts to get into the mind of Henry James or whoever it is we're supposed to study on this course ... Oh God, why did I take this on? ... Yes ... Yes I suppose I did take it on to pay for the drink ... Oh, for God's sake, what is it? ... Yes, well – erm – leave it in the oven ... Look if you're trying to induce some feeling of guilt in me over the prospect of a burnt dinner you should have prepared something other than lamb and ratatouille ... Because, darling, I like my lamb done to the point of abuse and even I know that ratatouille cannot be burned ... Darling, you could incinerate ratatouille and still it wouldn't burn ... What do you mean am I determined to go to the pub? I don't need determination to get me into a pub ...

[*There is a knock at the door.*]

Look, I'll have to go ... There's someone at the door ... Yes, yes I promise ... Just a couple of pints ... Four ...

[*There is another knock at the door.*]

[*Calling in the direction of the door.*] Come in! [*He continues on the telephone.*] Yes ... All right ... yes ... Bye, bye ... [*He replaces the receiver.*] Yes, that's it, you just pop off and put your head in the oven. [*Shouting.*] Come in! Come in!

[*The door swings open revealing* RITA.]

RITA [*from the doorway*]: I'm comin' in, aren't I? It's that stupid bleedin' handle on the door. You wanna get it fixed! [*She comes into the room.*]

FRANK [*staring, slightly confused*]: Erm – yes, I suppose I always mean to ...

RITA [*going to the chair by the desk and dumping her bag*]: Well that's no good always meanin' to, is it? Y' should get on with it; one of these days you'll be shoutin' 'Come in' an' it'll go on forever because the poor sod on the other side won't be able to get in. An' you won't be able to get out.

5.1 The importance of openings

[FRANK *stares at* RITA *who stands by the desk.*]

FRANK: You are?

RITA: What am I?

FRANK: Pardon?

RITA: What?

FRANK [*looking for the admission papers*]: Now you are?

RITA: I'm a what?

[FRANK *looks up and then returns to the papers as* RITA *goes to hang her coat on the door hooks.*]

RITA [*noticing the picture*]: That's a nice picture, isn't it? [*She goes up to it.*]

FRANK: Erm – yes, I suppose it is – nice …

RITA [*studying the picture*]: It's very erotic.

FRANK [*looking up*]: Actually I don't think I've looked at it for about ten years, but yes, I suppose it is.

RITA: There's no suppose about it. Look at those tits.

[*He coughs and goes back to looking for the admission paper.*]

Is it supposed to be erotic? I mean when he painted it do y' think he wanted to turn people on?

FRANK: Erm – probably.

RITA: I'll bet he did y'know. Y' don't paint pictures like that just so that people can admire the brush strokes, do y'?

FRANK [*giving a short laugh*]: No – no – you're probably right.

RITA: This was the pornography of its day, wasn't it? It's sort of like *Men Only*, isn't it? But in those days they had to pretend it wasn't erotic so they made it religious, didn't they? Do *you* think it's erotic?

FRANK [*taking a look*]: I think it's very beautiful.

RITA: I didn't ask y' if it was beautiful.

FRANK: But the term 'beautiful' covers the many feelings I have about that picture, including the feeling that, yes, it is erotic.

RITA [*coming back to the desk*]: D'y' get a lot like me?

FRANK: Pardon?

RITA: Do you get a lot of students like me?

FRANK: Not exactly, no …

RITA: I was dead surprised when they took me. I don't suppose they would have done if it'd been a proper university. The Open University's different though, isn't it?

FRANK: I've – erm – not had much more experience of it than you. This is the first O.U. work I've done.

RITA: D'y' need the money?

FRANK: I do as a matter of fact.

RITA: It's terrible these days, the money, isn't it? With the inflation an' that. You work for the ordinary university, don't y'? With the real students. The Open University's different, isn't it?

FRANK: It's supposed to embrace a more comprehensive studentship, yes.

RITA [*inspecting a bookcase*]: Degrees for dishwashers.

FRANK: Would you – erm – would you like to sit down?

RITA: No! Can I smoke? [*She goes to her bag and rummages in it.*]

FRANK: Tobacco?

RITA: Yeh. [*She half-laughs.*] Was that a joke? [*She takes out a packet of cigarettes and a lighter.*] Here – d'y' want one? [*She takes out two cigarettes and dumps the packet on the desk.*]

FRANK [*after a pause*]: Ah – I'd love one.

RITA: Well, have one.

Chapter 5 Responding to drama: twentieth-century plays

If we look at the beginning of *Educating Rita* we find again a slightly different technique. The scene and the atmosphere are established by a not over-long stage direction, and Frank is introduced very clearly. The opening speech is partly soliloquy and partly one end of a telephone conversation. The speech is jerky and disjointed, and humour is very quickly established because we are led to believe that Frank is looking for a book when in fact he is looking for a bottle of whisky which is hidden behind the book. Frank's partner never appears in the play but we certainly know something about their relationship by the end of that first speech where he says:

> Yes, that's it, you just pop off and put your head in the oven.

This is the cue for the entrance of Rita and, whatever we, or Frank, are expecting, it is probably not her opening line:

> I'm comin' in, aren't I? It's that stupid bleedin' handle on the door.
> You wanna get it fixed!

The intention is to establish her as startlingly different from Frank – open, honest and certainly not someone who would hide anything behind a book. After her opening line, she goes on to talk about a picture in a way which is very different from the way Frank would expect his students to talk.

During the scene their conversation goes on to establish their relationship.

> **Examiner's tip**
>
> Have a look at the opening of the play which you are studying and decide what the writer is doing in the first couple of pages. Is the writer concentrating on characters? Or is it necessary to fill in story details so that you understand the characters more fully. Is there immediate speed and action or is it a 'slow burn'? How effective do you think your opening is?

5.2 The importance of endings

The ending of a play, similarly, needs to make an impact so that we are left with a positive memory. If we look at the comedies and tragedies of Shakespeare then we can be pretty certain how they are going to end: with either a death or a marriage. With more modern plays where playwrights sometimes deliberately end plays in unexpected ways, things are rather less predictable. Let us look at our three plays again.

An Inspector Calls

BIRLING [*looking at them all, triumphantly*]: Now answer that one. Let's look at it from this fellow's point of view. We're having a little celebration here and feeling rather pleased with ourselves. Now he has to work a trick on us. Well, the first thing he has to do is to give us such a shock that after that he can bluff us all the time. So he starts right off. A girl has just died in the Infirmary. She drank some strong disinfectant. Died in agony –

ERIC: All right, don't pile it on.

BIRLING [*triumphantly*]: There you are, you see. Just repeating it shakes you a bit. And that's what he had to do. Shake us at once – and then start questioning us – until we didn't know where we were. Oh – let's admit that. He had the laugh of us all right.

ERIC: He could laugh his head off – if I knew it really was all a hoax.

BIRLING: I'm convinced it is. No police inquiry. No one girl that all this happens to. No scandal –

SHEILA: And no suicide?

GERALD [*decisively*]: We can settle that at once.

SHEILA: How?

GERALD: By ringing up the Infirmary. Either there's a dead girl there or there isn't.

BIRLING [*uneasily*]: It will look a bit queer, won't it – ringing up at this time of night –

GERALD: I don't mind doing it.

MRS BIRLING [*emphatically*]: And if there isn't –

5.2 The importance of endings

GERALD: Anyway we'll see. [*He goes to telephone and looks up number. The others watch tensely.*] Brumley eight nine eight six. ... Is that the Infirmary? This is Mr Gerald Croft – of Crofts Limited ... Yes ... We're rather worried about one of our employees. Have you had a girl brought in this afternoon who committed suicide by drinking disinfectant – or any like suicide? Yes, I'll wait.

[*As he waits, the others show their nervous tension.* BIRLING *wipes his brow,* SHEILA *shivers,* ERIC *clasps and unclasps his hands, etc.*]

Yes? ... You're certain of that. ... I see. Well, thank you very much. ... Good night. [*He puts down telephone and looks at them.*] No girl has died in there today. Nobody's been brought in after drinking disinfectant. They haven't had a suicide for months.

BIRLING [*triumphantly*]: There you are! Proof positive. The whole story's just a lot of moonshine. Nothing but an elaborate sell! [*He produces a huge sigh of relief.*] Nobody likes to be sold as badly as that – but for all that – [*He smiles at them all.*] Gerald, have a drink.

GERALD [*smiling*]: Thanks, I think I could just do with one now.

BIRLING [*going to sideboard*]: So could I.

MRS BIRLING [*smiling*]: And I must say, Gerald, you've argued this very cleverly, and I'm most grateful.

Gerald [*going for his drink*]: Well, you see, while I was out of the house I'd time to cool off and think things out a little.

BIRLING [*giving him a drink*]: Yes, he didn't keep you on the run as he did the rest of us. I'll admit he gave me a bit of a scare at the time. But I'd a special reason for not wanting any public scandal just now. [*Has his drink now, and raises his glass.*] Well, here's to us. Come on, Sheila, don't look like that. All over now.

SHEILA: The worst part is. But you're forgetting one thing I still can't forget. If it didn't end tragically, then that's lucky for us. But it might have done.

BIRLING [*jovially*]: But the whole thing's different now. Come, come, you can see that, can't you? [*Imitating Inspector in his final speech*] You all helped to kill her. [*Pointing at* SHEILA *and* ERIC, *and laughing.*] And I wish you could have seen the look on your faces when he said that. [SHEILA *moves towards door.*] Going to bed, young woman?

SHEILA [*tensely*]: I want to get out of this. It frightens me the way you talk.

BIRLING [*heartily*]: Nonsense! You'll have a good laugh over it yet. Look, you'd better ask Gerald for that ring you gave back to him, hadn't you? Then you'll feel better.

SHEILA [*passionately*]: You're pretending everything's just as it was before.

ERIC: I'm not!

SHEILA: No, but these others are.

BIRLING: Well, isn't it? We've been had, that's all.

SHEILA: So nothing really happened. So there's nothing to be sorry for, nothing to learn. We can all go on behaving just as we did.

MRS BIRLING: Well, why shouldn't we?

SHEILA: I tell you – whoever that Inspector was, it was anything but a joke. You knew it then. You began to learn something. And now you've stopped. You're ready to go on in the same old way.

BIRLING [*amused*]: And you're not, eh?

SHEILA: No, because I remember what he said, how he looked, and what he made me feel. Fire and blood and anguish. And it frightens me the way you talk, and I can't listen to any more of it.

Chapter 5 Responding to drama: twentieth-century plays

> ERIC: And I agree with Sheila. It frightens me too.
>
> BIRLING: Well, go to bed then, and don't stand there being hysterical.
>
> MRS BIRLING: They're over-tired. In the morning they'll be as amused as we are.
>
> GERALD: Everything's all right now, Sheila. [*Holds up the ring.*] What about this ring?
>
> SHEILA: No, not yet. It's too soon. I must think.
>
> BIRLING [*pointing to* ERIC *and* SHEILA]: Now look at the pair of them – the famous younger generation who know it all. And they can't even take a joke –
>
> [*The telephone rings sharply. There is a moment's complete silence.* BIRLING *goes to answer it.*] Yes? … Mr Birling speaking. … What? – Here –
>
> [*But obviously the other person has rung off. He puts the telephone down slowly and looks in a panic-stricken fashion at the others.*]
>
> BIRLING: That was the police. A girl has just died – on her way to the Infirmary – after swallowing some disinfectant. And a police inspector is on his way here – to ask some – questions –
>
> [*As they stare guiltily and dumbfounded, the curtain falls.*]
>
> **END OF PLAY**

Over the course of the play the inspector has affected the characters in very different ways. Some members of the family are able to pretend that nothing has happened whereas others, notably the two youngest, are very much affected. It then transpires that the Inspector is probably a fraud, as there is no record of him at the police station. This discovery reinforces the lack of concern shown by some members of the family; interestingly it does not change the attitude of the younger family members. Perhaps most significantly, the engagement which was being celebrated at the beginning of the play and which had been broken off during the course of events is still off.

The play then has a twist in the tail. The phone rings and it turns out that … a girl has swallowed some disinfectant and has died. A police inspector is on his way round to talk about the incident and to ask some questions … the cycle has begun again.

> ### A Taste of Honey
>
> HELEN: It's all right, love, I'm here and everything's all right. Are you awake now?
>
> JO: Hello. Yes … What's it like?
>
> HELEN: What?
>
> JO: Is there much pain?
>
> HELEN: No! It's not so much pain as hard work, love. I was putting my Christmas pudding up on a shelf when you started on me. There I was standing on a chair singing away merry as the day is long …
>
> JO: Did you yell?
>
> HELEN: No, I ran.
>
> JO: Do you know, I had such a funny dream just now.
>
> HELEN: Oh Jo, you're always dreaming, aren't you. Well, don't let's talk about your dreams or we'll get morbid.
>
> JO: Where would you like those flowers putting?
>
> HELEN: Over … over there … Come on, you come and do it, love.
>
> JO: Hasn't Geof come back yet?
>
> HELEN: No, he hasn't.
>
> JO: Well, where are you going to sleep, Helen?
>
> HELEN: It's all right, love. Don't fall over now.

5.2 The importance of endings

JO: You know, I've got so used to old Geof lying there on that couch like – like an old watchdog. You aren't …

HELEN: It's all right, love, don't you worry about me, I'll find somewhere.

JO: I wonder where he is … Oh!

HELEN: Oh Jo, careful … Hold on, love, hold on! It'll be all right. The first one doesn't last long. Oh my God, I could do with a drink now. Hold on.

[JO *kneels on bed,* HELEN *strokes her hair.*]

JO: That's better.

HELEN: Are you all right now? There we are. [*Children sing outside.*] Can you hear those children singing over there on the croft, Jo?

JO: Yes, you can always hear them on still days.

HELEN: You know when I was young we used to play all day long at this time of the year; in the summer we had singing games and in the spring we played with tops and hoops, and then in the autumn there was the Fifth of November, then we used to have bonfires in the street, and gingerbread and all that. Have I ever told you about the time when we went to a place called Shining Clough? Oh, I must have done. I used to climb up there every day and sit on the top of the hill, and you could see the mills in the distance, but the clough itself was covered in moss. Isn't it funny how you remember these things? Do you know, I'd sit there all day long and nobody ever knew where I was. Shall I go and make us a cup of tea?

[HELEN *enters kitchen and fiddles with stove.*]

Oh Jo, I've forgotten how we used to light this thing.

JO: Turn on all the knobs. Mind you don't gas yourself.

HELEN: I still can't do it.

JO: Geof'll fix it.

HELEN: No, it's all right.

JO: Helen.

HELEN: Yes.

JO: My baby may be black.

HELEN: You what, love.

JO: My baby will be black.

HELEN: Oh, don't be silly, Jo. You'll be giving yourself nightmares.

JO: But it's true. He was black.

HELEN: Who?

JO: Jimmie.

HELEN: You mean to say that … that sailor was a black man? … Oh my God! Nothing else can happen to me now. Can you see me wheeling a pram with a … Oh my God. I'll have to have a drink.

JO: What are you going to do?

HELEN: I don't know. Drown it. Who knows about it?

JO: Geoffrey.

HELEN: And what about the nurse? She's going to get a bit of a shock, isn't she?

JO: Well, she's black too.

HELEN: Good, perhaps she'll adopt it. Dear God in heaven!

JO: If you don't like it you can get out. I didn't ask you to come here.

HELEN: Where's my hat?

JO: On your head.

HELEN: Oh yes … I don't know what's to be done with you, I don't really. [*To the audience.*] I ask you, what would you do?

> JO: Are you going?
>
> HELEN: Yes.
>
> JO: Are you just going for a drink?
>
> HELEN: Yes.
>
> JO: Are you coming back?
>
> HELEN: Yes.
>
> JO: Well, what are you going to do?
>
> HELEN: Put it on the stage and call it Blackbird. [*She rushes out.*]
>
> [JO *watches her go, leaning against the doorpost. Then she looks round the room, smiling a little to herself – she remembers* GEOF.]
>
> JO: As I was going up Pippin Hill,
>   Pippin Hill was dirty.
>   And there I met a pretty miss,
>   And she dropped me a curtsy.
>   Little miss, pretty miss,
>   Blessings light upon you.
>   If I had half a crown a day,
>   I'd gladly spend it on you.
>
> **CURTAIN**

The ending of *A Taste of Honey* takes us full circle in a slightly different way. All the characters who have entered the lives of Jo and Helen have gone and the two of them are back by themselves, still, of course, not able to cope with each other. There is just one moment when Helen tries to act like a mother and talks about what they used to do together when they were young, but the moment passes when Jo starts talking about her baby: Helen can't cope.

The message of this play seems to be that, for people like Jo and Helen, nothing ever changes.

> ### Educating Rita
>
> RITA *enters and shuts the door. She is wrapped in a large winter coat. She lights a cigarette and moves across to the filing cabinet and places a Christmas card with the others already there. She throws the envelope in the waste-bin and opens the door revealing* FRANK *with a couple of tea-chests either side of him. He is taken aback at seeing her and then he gathers himself and, picking up one of the chests, enters the room.* RITA *goes out into the corridor and brings in the other chest.*
>
> FRANK *gets the chair from the end of his desk and places it by the bookcase. He stands on it and begins taking down the books from the shelves and putting them into the chests.* RITA *watches him but he continues as if she is not there.*
>
> RITA: Merry Christmas, Frank. Have they sacked y'?
>
> FRANK: Not quite.
>
> RITA: well, why y' – packing your books away?
>
> FRANK: Australia. [*After a pause.*] Some weeks ago – made rather a night of it.
>
> RITA: Did y' bugger the bursar?
>
> FRANK: Metaphorically. And as it was metaphorical the sentence was reduced from the sack to two years in Australia. Hardly a reduction in sentence really – but …
>
> RITA: What y' gonna do?
>
> FRANK: *Bon voyage.*
>
> RITA: She's not going with y'?

[FRANK *shakes his head.* RITA *begins helping him take down the books from the shelves and putting them in the chests.*]

RITA: What y' gonna do?

FRANK: What do you think I'll do? Aussie? It's a paradise for the likes of me.

RITA: Tch. Come on, Frank …

FRANK: It is. Don't you know the Australians named their favourite drink after a literary figure. Forster's Lager they call it. Of course they get the spelling wrong – rather like you once did!

RITA: Be serious.

FRANK: For God's sake, why did you come back here?

RITA: I came to tell you you're a good teacher. [*After a pause.*] Thanks for enterin' me for the exam.

FRANK: That's all right. I know how much it had come to mean to you.

[RITA *perches on the small table while* FRANK *continues to take books from the upper shelves.*]

RITA: You didn't want me to take it, did y'? Eh? You woulda loved it if I'd written, 'Frank knows all the answers', across me paper, wouldn't y'? I nearly did an' all. When the invigilator said, 'Begin', I turned over me paper with the rest of them, and while they were all scribbling away against the clock, I just sat there, lookin' at the first question. Y' know what it was, Frank? 'Suggest ways in which one might cope with some of the staging difficulties in a production of *Peer Gynt*.'

[FRANK *gets down, sits on the chair and continues to pack the books.*]

FRANK: Well, you should have had no trouble with that.

RITA: I did though. I just sat lookin' at the paper an' thinkin' about what you'd said. I tried to ignore it, to pretend that you were wrong. You think you gave me nothing; did nothing for me. You think I just ended up with a load of quotes and empty phrases; an' I did. But that wasn't your doin'. I was so hungry. I wanted it all so much that I didn't want it to be questioned. I told y' I was stupid. It's like Trish, y' know me flatmate, I thought she was so cool an' together – I came home the other night an' she'd tried to top herself. Magic, isn't it? She spends half her life eatin' wholefoods an' health foods to make her live longer, an' the other half tryin' to kill herself. [*After a pause.*] I sat lookin' at the question, an' thinkin' about it all. Then I picked up me pen an' started.

FRANK: And you wrote, 'Do it on the radio'?

RITA: I could have done. An' you would have been proud of me if I'd done that an' rushed back to tell you – wouldn't ye? But I chose not to. I had a choice. I did the exam.

FRANK: I know. A good pass as well.

RITA: Yeh. An' it might be worthless in the end. But I had a choice. I chose, me. Because of what you'd given me I had a choice. I wanted to come back an' tell y' that. That y' a good teacher.

FRANK: [*stopping working and looking at her*]: You know – erm – I hear very good things about Australia. Things are just beginning there. The thing is, why don't you – come as well? It'd be good for us to leave a place that's just finishing for one that's just beginning.

RITA: Isn't that called jumpin' a sinking ship?

FRANK: So what? Do you really think there's any chance of keeping it afloat?

[*She looks at him and then at the shelves.*]

RITA [*seeing the empty whisky bottles*]: 'Ey, Frank, if there was threepence back on each of those bottles you could buy Australia.

Chapter 5 Responding to drama: twentieth-century plays

> FRANK [*smiling*] You're being evasive.
>
> RITA [*going and sitting on a tea-chest*]: I know. Tiger's asked me to go down to France with his mob.
>
> FRANK: Will you?
>
> RITA: I dunno. He's a bit of a wanker really. But I've never been abroad. An' me mother's invited me to hers for Christmas.
>
> FRANK: What are you going to do?
>
> RITA: I dunno. I might go to France. I might go to me mother's. I might even have a baby. I dunno. I'll make a decision, I'll choose. I dunno.
>
> [FRANK *has found a package hidden behind some of the books. He takes it down.*]
>
> FRANK: Whatever you do, you might as well take this ...
>
> RITA: What?
>
> FRANK [*handing it to her*]: It's erm – well, it's er – it's a dress really. I bought it some time ago – for erm – for an educated woman friend – of mine ...
>
> [RITA *takes the dress from the bag.*]
>
> FRANK: I erm – don't – know if it fits, I was rather pissed when I bought it ...
>
> RITA: An educated woman, Frank? An' is this what you call a scholarly neckline?
>
> FRANK: When choosing it I put rather more emphasis on the word woman than the word educated.
>
> RITA: All I've ever done is take from you. I've never given anything.
>
> FRANK: That's not true you've ...
>
> RITA: It is true. I never thought there was anythin' I could give you. But there is. Come here, Frank ...
>
> FRANK: What?
>
> RITA: Come here... [*She pulls out a chair.*] Sit on that ...
>
> [FRANK *is bewildered.*]
>
> RITA: Sit...
>
> [FRANK *sits and* RITA, *eventually finding a pair of scissors on the desk, waves them in the air.*]
>
> RITA: I'm gonna take ten years off you ...
>
> [*She goes across to him and begins to cut his hair.*]
>
> **BLACKOUT**

Examiner's tip

Have a look at the way in which the play you are studying ends. Decide why it ends how it does and where it leaves the audience. Ask yourself whether it is an effective ending.

The last scene of *Educating Rita* is designed to leave us with a question mark. You might argue that, in a sense, we, as well as Rita, have been educated and it is right that we should be able to judge how both Frank and Rita have gained from the experience of meeting each other. Clearly in terms of knowing much more about literature Rita has been educated, but where does she go now? Will her life really change or will she carry on with the sort of life she has always led? We can wonder what Frank has learnt. It is ironic that, at the end of the play, Rita not Frank has the role of providing what is necessary – she gives him a haircut.

Sometimes then a play leaves you with questions rather than answers.

5.3 Climaxes

Plays often come to a series of climaxes as an integral part of their structure. We will look at one of our plays to see how this is the case.

5.3 Climaxes

An Inspector Calls is written in three acts and each act reaches its own climax. We have already discussed the climax at the end of the last act when the telephone rings and the 'genuine' police are on the line. This is an unexpected climax and certainly affects the central characters. It also comes as a surprise to the audience who are left buzzing.

In the first act we could say that the arrival of the inspector is a sort of climax, but the key is to look at the end of the act where the real climax occurs. This is the confrontation between Sheila, the daughter of the family, and Gerald, her fiancé, when Sheila comes to realise that there is a connection between Gerald and Eva Smith. When we were looking at the beginning of the play we pointed out lines where Sheila refers to the summer Gerald ignored her, and it is significant that the act ends with a return to this. The pieces of the jigsaw begin, inevitably, to fit together.

> GERALD [*trying to smile*]: Well what, Sheila?
>
> SHEILA: How did you come to know this girl – Eva Smith?
>
> GERALD: I didn't.
>
> SHEILA: Daisy Renton then – it's the same thing.
>
> GERALD: Why should I have known her?
>
> SHEILA: Oh don't be stupid. We haven't much time. You gave yourself away as soon as he mentioned her other name.
>
> GERALD: All right. I knew her. Let's leave it at that.
>
> SHEILA: We can't leave it at that.
>
> GERALD [*approaching her*]: Now listen, darling –
>
> SHEILA: No, that's no use. You not only knew her but you knew her very well. Otherwise, you wouldn't look so guilty about it. When did you first get to know her? [*He does not reply.*] Was it after she left Milwards? When she changed her name, as he said, and began to lead a different sort of life? Were you seeing her last spring and summer, during that time when you hardly came near me and said you were so busy? Were you? [*He does not reply but looks at her.*] Yes, of course you were.
>
> GERALD: I'm sorry, Sheila. But it was all over and done with, last summer. I hadn't set eyes on the girl for at least six months. I don't come into this suicide business.
>
> SHEILA: I thought I didn't, half an hour ago.
>
> GERALD: You don't. Neither of us does. So – for God's sake – don't say anything to the Inspector.
>
> SHEILA: About you and this girl?
>
> GERALD: Yes. We can keep it from him.
>
> SHEILA [*laughs rather hysterically*]: Why – you fool – *he knows*. Of course he knows. And I hate to think how much he knows that we don't know yet. You'll see. You'll see. [*She looks at him almost in triumph.*]
>
> [*He looks crushed. The door slowly opens and the* INSPECTOR *appears, looking steadily and searchingly at them.*]
>
> INSPECTOR: Well?
>
> **END OF ACT ONE**

The end of the second act reaches a similar climax, and again there is an inevitability about what will be revealed. The audience is allowed to see, just before Mrs Birling, the mother of the family, what is happening. We are helped in this by Sheila who is first to realise and who tries to stop her mother speaking. The climax is intensified by the entrance of Eric, the son, but the curtain falls before he is able to say anything.

Chapter 5 Responding to drama: twentieth-century plays

MRS BIRLING: I'm sorry she should have come to such a horrible end. But I accept no blame for it at all.

INSPECTOR: Who is to blame then?

MRS BIRLING: First, the girl herself.

SHEILA [*bitterly*]: For letting Father and me have her chucked out of her jobs!

MRS BIRLING: Secondly I blame the young man who was the father of the child she was going to have. If, as she said, he didn't belong to her class, and was some drunken young idler, then that's all the more reason why he shouldn't escape. He should be made an example of. If the girl's death is due to anybody, then it's due to him.

INSPECTOR: And if her story is true – that he was stealing money –

MRS BIRLING [*rather agitated now*]: There's no point in assuming that –

INSPECTOR: But suppose we do, what then?

MRS BIRLING: Then he'd be entirely responsible – because the girl wouldn't have come to us, and have been refused assistance, if it hadn't been for him –

INSPECTOR: So he's the chief culprit anyhow.

MRS BIRLING: Certainly. And he ought to be dealt with very severely –

SHEILA [*with sudden alarm*]: Mother – stop – stop!

BIRLING: Be quiet, Sheila!

SHEILA: But don't you see –

MRS BIRLING [*severely*]: You're behaving like an hysterical child tonight. [SHEILA *begins crying quietly.* MRS BIRLING *turns to* INSPECTOR.] And if you'd take some steps to find this young man and then make sure that he's compelled to confess in public his responsibility – instead of staying here asking quite unnecessary questions – then you really would be doing your duty.

INSPECTOR [*grimly*]: Don't worry, Mrs Birling. I shall do my duty. [*He looks at his watch.*]

MRS BIRLING [*triumphantly*]: I'm glad to hear it.

INSPECTOR: No hushing up, eh? Make an example of the young man, eh? Public confession of responsibility – um?

MRS BIRLING: Certainly. I consider it your duty. And now no doubt you'd like to say good night.

INSPECTOR: Not yet. I'm waiting.

MRS BIRLING: Waiting for what?

INSPECTOR: To do my duty.

SHEILA [*distressed*]: Now, Mother – don't you see?

MRS BIRLING [*understanding now*]: But surely ... I mean ... it's ridiculous ... [*She stops, and exchanges a frightened glance with her husband.*]

BIRLING [*terrified now*]: Look, Inspector, you're not trying to tell us that – that my boy – is mixed up in this –?

INSPECTOR [*sternly*]: If he is, then we know what to do, don't we? Mrs Birling has just told us.

BIRLING [*thunderstruck*]: My God! But – look here –

MRS BIRLING [*agitated*]: I don't believe it. I *won't* believe it...

SHEILA: Mother – I begged you and begged you to stop –

[INSPECTOR *holds up a hand. We hear the front door. They wait, looking towards door.* ERIC *enters, looking extremely pale and distressed. He meets their inquiring stares.*
Curtain falls quickly.]

END OF ACT TWO

> **Examiner's tip**
>
> The play you are studying may not be divided into acts in the same way as *An Inspector Calls* but it will undoubtedly have one or more climaxes which you can identify. These are very significant moments in the play. What are the climaxes in the play you are studying and where do they occur? What would you say about them?

Notice that another detail from the very beginning of the play – that Eric drinks too much – is picked up here and becomes significant.

5.4 Characters and the interaction between them

Shakespearean plays operate with a huge panoply of characters covering a whole range of social types. Our twentieth-century plays, on the other hand, tend to operate with far fewer characters and, although we might find characters of very different types, they are frequently a very tight-knit group. In *Educating Rita* a key to the relationship of the two characters is that they are so very different. They have different social backgrounds, different academic backgrounds, different aspirations and so on.

In looking at characters we are going to concentrate on *A Taste of Honey*. There are five characters in the play, and each one could be described as a stereotype. Jo's relationship with each character produces predictable complications.

First there is Jo herself. She is a teenage girl from a single-parent family who wants to leave school as soon as she can. She has problems in her relationship with her mother and, as a consequence of the sort of life she has led, tends to latch on to misfits like Geof. She is a perfectly pleasant girl but is not mature enough to control her own life and, almost inevitably, things go wrong.

Helen, Jo's mother, is described in the opening stage directions as a 'semi-whore', which is best translated as meaning she is involved with a whole string of men. Like Billy in *Kes*, Jo has probably had very many 'uncles' during her childhood. In the play Helen is involved with Peter, a drunkard who has enough money to keep her happy, at least for a while. She also drinks, and her complete irresponsibility is shown when she tries to persuade Jo to drink whisky, even though Jo doesn't want to. You could argue that she is the eternal romantic, willing to marry Peter and probably believing that it will all be perfect. At the end of the play we find that she is prejudiced in various ways. She has difficulty coping with the fact that Geof is homosexual and that Jo's boyfriend is black.

There is little to add to what has already been said about Peter. He is a drunkard; he claims to be a war hero and wears an eyepatch; he seems to be able to lay his hands on a lot of money when he needs it; he is selfish and certainly is not concerned about Jo. What is perhaps surprising is that he doesn't leave Helen immediately as it is quite clear that she has been deceiving him about her age; we can tell this from a comment he makes when he meets Jo.

Boy doesn't play a particularly large part in the action. There is nothing malicious about him and he doesn't really pretend or make promises to Jo. He is a sailor and he will disappear back to his boat and Jo knows that; the statement that he will come back is just an automatic response that neither he nor Jo believes. He likes Jo, she likes him and they simply have some irresponsible enjoyment together. We might make a moral judgement about him in the light of what happens, but that would probably be harsh.

Geof is the most responsible character in the play. He is the one hope that Jo has, it would seem, of being able to cope with her pregnancy. He is sensitive, he is caring, he is undemanding. The fact that he is homosexual gives Jo the hope of a safe relationship and she appreciates this. He prepares for the birth of the baby. Had Helen not come back, he would have undoubtedly stayed and he would have made sure that the baby was cared for, probably doing the caring himself while Jo ignored them both. Helen does, however, come back and his gentle personality is such that there is no way in which he can compete with her. We, as the audience, almost certainly feel on his departure that the one hope which the baby really had goes with him.

Stereotypes they may be but the interaction between them makes us feel that Shelagh Delaney has observed life and is showing us a glimpse of reality.

> **Examiner's tip**
>
> It is unlikely that the characters in the play you are studying are so clearly stereotypical. Take the central characters of your play and write a brief analysis of each of them in the same way as we have written about the characters above. Then examine their relationships and the way in which the play is constructed around them and summarise briefly how the play works.

5.5 Plot and sub-plot

> **Examiner's tip**
>
> Take the play which you are studying and, in one or two short paragraphs, summarise the plot. You may well find that the story is straightforward and controlled and you may be able to summarise it very briefly. You may, by contrast, find that there is more than one story line and you might want to summarise each story line in its own short paragraph. Remember all you are doing is telling the story of what happens. There is no need for any comment or analysis.

The plot is what happens in the play, the story line. *An Inspector Calls* has a clear plot in that the Inspector visits, and involves each member of the family in the situation one at a time. The story of what happened to Eva Smith is thus told. There is nothing outside this central story line.

The plot of *A Taste of Honey* is a simple story. Helen and Jo move. Helen links up with Peter and goes off for a time. Jo meets Boy and becomes pregnant before he leaves. Geof moves in to help. Helen comes back and Geof moves out.

If we try to tease out the plot of *Educating Rita*, in a sense it is even simpler. Frank and Rita meet each other and affect each other's lives. Here, character is more important than plot.

5.6 Themes

> **Examiner's tip**
>
> Consider the themes which are explored in the play you are studying. You might find that there are several themes which you think are of equal importance; there might be one clearly predominant theme. Write brief paragraphs explaining how each theme is explored during the play.

Themes are different from the plot. They are the underlying ideas which the play explores. Below is a list of themes which apply to the three plays we have been using. Which themes fit with which play?

- snobbery
- irresponsibility
- love
- guilt
- prejudice
- family values

You will find that the themes suggested above do not neatly belong to just one of our plays; in fact several of them might be themes which belong to all three plays.

5.7 Language

In a number of places in this book we have considered the language of literature in different ways. Always be prepared to ask yourself why writers have used particular words. Below you will find three pages selected quite arbitrarily from the plays we have been using. You will see we have deleted the names of the characters. Your task is to:

1. Decide which page belongs to which play – quite easy because you should know enough about what happens in the plays to be able to decide from what is being said.

2. Look at the language of the dialogue in each play and decide what sort of person is speaking. You should look at the way sentences are put together and the vocabulary which is used. You might be able to tell from the vocabulary which is the oldest play and which is the most modern. You might be able, both from the general language and from what they say, to put a name to each speaker.

3. Take a page at random from the play you are studying and analyse the language in the same way.

5.7 Language

Play 1

—— *is sitting at his desk typing poetry. He pauses, stubs out a cigarette, takes a sip from the mug at his side, looks at his watch and then continues typing.*

—— *bursts through the door. She is dressed in new, second-hand clothes.*

—— ——! [*She twirls on the spot to show off her new clothes.*]

—— [*smiling*]: And what is this vision, returning from the city? [*He gets up and moves towards* ——.] Welcome back.

—— ——, it was fantastic.
[*She takes off her shawl and gives it to* —— *who hangs it on the hook by the door.* —— *goes to the desk.*]
[*Putting down her bag on the desk.*] Honest, it was – ogh!

—— What are you talking about, London or summer school?

—— Both. A crowd of us stuck together all week. We had a great time: dead late every night, we stayed up talkin', we went all round London, got drunk, went to the theatres, bought all sorts of second-hand gear in the markets ... Ogh, it was ...

—— So you won't have had time to do any actual work there?

—— Work? We never stopped. Lashin' us with it they were; another essay, lash, do it again, lash.

[—— *moves towards the desk.*]

—— Another lecture, smack. It was dead good though. [*She goes and perches on the bookcase.*]

[—— *sits in the swivel chair, facing her.*]

—— Y'know at first I was dead scared. I didn't know anyone. I was gonna come home. But the first afternoon I was standin' in this library, y'know lookin' at the books, pretendin' I was dead clever. Anyway, this tutor come up to me, he looked at the book in me hand an' he said, 'Ah, are you fond of Ferlinghetti?' It was right on the top of me tongue to say, 'Only when it's served with Parmesan cheese', but, —— I didn't. I held it back an' I heard meself sayin', 'Actually I'm not too familiar with the American poets.' —— you woulda been dead proud of me. He started talkin' to me about the American poets – we sat around for ages – an' he wasn't even...

Play 2

[*He goes to open the door while* —— *takes her mother out. Then he closes it and comes in.*]

—— When did you meet her again?

—— About a fortnight afterwards.

—— By appointment?

—— No. And I couldn't remember her name or where she lived. It was all very vague. But I happened to see her again in the Palace bar.

—— More drinks?

—— Yes, though that time I wasn't so bad.

—— But you took her home again?

—— Yes. And this time we talked a bit. She told me something about herself and I talked too. Told her my name and what I did.

—— And you made love again?

—— Yes. I wasn't in love with her or anything – but I liked her – she was pretty and a good sport –

—— [*harshly*]: So you had to go to bed with her?

83

Chapter 5 Responding to drama: twentieth-century plays

—— Well, I'm old enough to be married, aren't I, and I'm not married, and I hate these fat old tarts round the town – the ones I see some of your respectable friends with –

—— [*angrily*]: I don't want any of that talk from you –

—— [*very sharply*]: I don't want any of it from either of you. Settle it afterwards. [*To* ——] Did you arrange to see each other after that?

—— Yes, and the next time – or the time after that – she told me she thought she was going to have a baby. She wasn't quite sure. And then she was.

—— And of course she was very worried about it?

—— Yes, and so was I. I was in a hell of a state about it.

—— Did she suggest that you ought to marry her?

—— No, she didn't want me to marry her. Said I didn't love her – and all that. In a way, she treated me – as if I were a kid. Though I was nearly as old as she was.

—— So what did you propose to do?

—— Well, she hadn't a job – and didn't feel like trying again for one – and she'd no money left – so I insisted on giving her enough money to keep her going – until she refused to take any more –

—— How much did you give her altogether?

Play 3

—— Anybody at home? Well, I'm back. You see, I couldn't stay away, could I. There's some flowers for you, ——. The barrows are smothered in them. Oh! How I carried that lot from the bus stop I'll never know. The old place looks a bit more cheerful, doesn't it? I say, there's a nice homely smell. Have you been doing a bit of baking? I'll tell you one thing, it's a lovely day for flitting.

—— Would you like a cup of tea, ——?

—— Have you got anything stronger? Oh no, of course you haven't! Go on, I'll have a cup with you. Let's have a look at you, love. I arrived just in time, by the look of things, didn't I? How are you, love? Everything straightforward? Been having your regular check-up and doing all them exercises and all the things they go in for nowadays? That's a good girl. Have you got everything packed?

—— Packed?

—— Yes.

—— But I'm not going into hospital.

—— You're not having it here, are you?

—— Yes, she didn't want to go away.

—— Oh my God, is he still here? I thought he would be.

—— Do you want a piece of cake ——?

—— Yes, please.

—— You can't have a baby in this dump. Why don't you use a bit of sense for once and go into hospital? They've got everything to hand there. I mean, sometimes the first one can be a bit tricky.

—— There's going to be nothing tricky about it; it's going to be perfectly all right, isn't it, ——?

—— Who do you think you are, the Flying Doctor?

—— Look, I've made up my mind I want to have it here. I don't like hospitals.

—— Have you ever been in a hospital?

—— No.

Examiner's tip

Always take any opportunity to see the play you are studying on stage. If you cannot do that try to find a video. If all else fails at least remember that the intention of the writer was that it should be seen.

Putting this into practice

Below are a few questions which could very easily appear on examination papers. Before you practise writing answers, check the following:

- Are you being asked to consider the play in its historical context?
- Are you being asked to think of the play as a piece of theatre with the audience watching?
- Are you being asked to consider the play in its social setting?
- Is the cultural background relevant?
- Is plot relevant? Or theme? Or character? Or all three?

Remember that an essay needs planning. You will seldom write a successful essay 'off the top of your head'. Here are the questions:

- In *An Inspector Calls* is Eva Smith the victim of class prejudice?
- *A Taste of Honey* seeks to examine a whole range of social problems. Identify the problems raised and explain what the play has to say about each of them.
- Explain how Willy Russell makes *Educating Rita*, a play which has only two characters and which is quite static, work as a piece of theatre for an audience.
- Write a detailed character study of the central character in a play which you are studying. Make sure that you analyse the character's importance in the plot and his or her relationship with other characters.
- A production of a play which you have been studying is coming to your local town. Write a letter to a friend, telling them about the play, and explaining in detail why you would encourage them to go and see it.

When you have finished writing the essay go back over the checklist and ask yourself the question: *Have I dealt with all the different points which I should have put into this essay?*

5.8 One-act plays

A one-act play, in many ways, has similar features to a short story. A full-length play has time to develop a variety of characters and to involve them in a complicated plot which may have several sub-plots as well. A full-length play can also use a variety of settings in which its characters can be placed.

A one-act play, on the other hand, cannot indulge in these luxuries. If a play is only going to last for a comparatively short time then it is highly likely that there will be a single setting, only a few characters and that the plot will have a single thread. It may indeed be a monologue, the single character maintaining the play alone.

The Zoo Story: an example of a one-act play

This play, by Edward Albee, is set in a park. The scene is very simple. The initial stage direction reads as follows:

> *It is Central Park; a Sunday afternoon in summer; the present. There are two park benches, one toward either side of the stage; they both face the audience. Behind them: foliage, trees, sky. At the beginning, Peter is seated on one of the benches.*

There are only two characters in the play. Peter is in his early forties and is described as wearing tweeds, smoking a pipe and carrying horn-rimmed glasses. Jerry is described as being in his late thirties, not poorly dressed, but carelessly; he seems weary and rather older than Peter. They don't know each other and the play is about how Jerry forces himself into Peter's world by insistently talking to him. Below is an extract from the beginning of the play.

Chapter 5 Responding to drama: twentieth-century plays

JERRY: I've been to the zoo. [PETER *doesn't notice.*] I said, I've been to the zoo. MISTER, I'VE BEEN TO THE ZOO!

PETER: Hm? ... What? ... I'm sorry, were you talking to me?

JERRY: I went to the zoo, and then I walked until I came here. Have I been walking north?

PETER [*puzzled*]: North? Why ... I ... I think so. Let me see.

JERRY [*pointing past the audience*]: Is that Fifth Avenue?

PETER: Why yes; yes, it is.

JERRY: And what is that cross street there; that one, to the right?

PETER: That? Oh, that's Seventy-fourth Street.

JERRY: And the zoo is around Sixty-fifth Street; so, I've been walking north.

PETER [*anxious to get back to his reading*]: Yes; it would seem so.

JERRY: Good old north.

PETER [*lightly, by reflex*]: Ha, ha.

JERRY [*after a slight pause*]: But not due north.

PETER: I ... well, no, not due north; but, we ... call it north. It's northerly.

JERRY [*watches as* PETER, *anxious to dismiss him, prepares his pipe*]: Well, boy, you're not going to get lung cancer, are you?

PETER [*looks up, a little annoyed, then smiles*]: No, sir. Not from this.

JERRY: No, sir. What you'll probably get is cancer of the mouth, and then you'll have to wear one of those things Freud wore after they took one whole side of his jaw away. What do they call those things?

PETER [*uncomfortable*]: A prosthesis?

JERRY: The very thing! A prosthesis. You're an educated man, aren't you? Are you a doctor?

PETER: Oh, no; no. I read about it somewhere; *Time* magazine, I think. [*He turns to his book.*]

JERRY: Well, *Time* magazine isn't for blockheads.

PETER: No, I suppose not.

JERRY [*after a pause*]: Boy, I'm glad that's Fifth Avenue there.

PETER [*vaguely*]: Yes.

JERRY: I don't like the west side of the park much.

PETER: Oh? [*Then, slightly wary, but interested.*] Why?

JERRY [*offhand*]: I don't know.

PETER: Oh. [*He returns to his book.*]

JERRY [*he stands for a few seconds, looking at* PETER, *who finally looks up again, puzzled*]: Do you mind if we talk?

PETER [*obviously minding*]: Why ... no, no.

JERRY: Yes you do; you do.

PETER [*puts his book down, his pipe out and away, smiling*]: No, really; I don't mind.

JERRY: Yes, you do.

PETER [*finally decided*]: No; I don't mind at all, really.

JERRY: It's ... it's a nice day.

PETER: [*stares unnecessarily at the sky*]: Yes. Yes, it is; lovely.

JERRY: I've been to the zoo.

PETER: Yes, I think you said so ... didn't you?

JERRY [*out of the blue*]: Do you have TV and everything?

PETER: Why yes, we have two; one for the children.

JERRY: You're married!

> PETER [*with pleased emphasis*]: Why, certainly.
> JERRY: It isn't a law, for God's sake.
> PETER: No ... no, of course not.
> JERRY: And you have a wife.
> PETER [*bewildered by the seeming lack of communication*]: Yes!
> JERRY: And you have children.
> PETER: Yes; two.
> JERRY: Boys?
> PETER: No, girls ... both girls.
> JERRY: But you wanted boys.
> PETER: Well ... naturally, every man wants a son but ...
> JERRY [*lightly mocking*]: But that's the way the cookie crumbles?
> PETER [*annoyed*]: I wasn't going to say that.

Whether Peter is getting annoyed or not is irrelevant as Jerry persists in pursuing the conversation, during which each tells something of his life story. Peter lives what could be called a perfectly ordinary life, with his wife, two daughters and their pets; Jerry, on the other hand, lives a rather more eccentric life, with a number of rather odd neighbours. Peter has possessions while Jerry has very few possessions, and so on. At one point in the play Jerry makes a long and quite extraordinary speech which you can read below. It begins with the following stage direction:

> *The following long speech, it seems to me, should be done with a great deal of action, to achieve a hypnotic effect on Peter and on the audience too. Some specific actions have been suggested, but the director and actor playing Jerry might best work it out for themselves.*

Read the speech, imagining you are the director. Don't forget that plays are written to be seen and not to be read on the page. As director, how would you advise the actor who has to deliver this long and perhaps difficult speech? You might choose to turn this into a practice answer if you wish.

> JERRY: ALL RIGHT. [*As if reading from a huge billboard.*] THE STORY OF JERRY AND THE DOG! [*Natural again.*] What I am going to tell you has something to do with how sometimes it's necessary to go a long distance out of the way in order to come back a short distance correctly; or, maybe I only think that it has something to do with that. But, it's why I went to the zoo today, and why I walked north ... northerly, rather ... until I came here. All right. The dog, I think I told you, is a black monster of a beast: an oversized head, tiny, tiny ears, and eyes ... bloodshot, infected, maybe; and a body you can see the ribs through the skin. The dog is black, all black; all black except for the bloodshot eyes, and ... yes ... and an open sore on its ... *right* forepaw; that is red, too. And, oh yes; the poor monster, and I do believe it's an old dog ... it's certainly a misused one ... almost always has an erection ... of sorts. That's red, too. And ... what else? ... oh, yes; there's a gray-yellow-white color, too, when he bares his fangs. Like this: Grrrrrrr! Which is what he did when he saw me for the first time ... the day I moved in. I worried about that animal the very first minute I met him. Now, animals don't take to me like Saint Francis had birds hanging off him all the time. What I mean is: animals are indifferent to me ... like people [*He smiles slightly.*] ... most of the time. But this dog wasn't indifferent. From the very beginning he'd snarl and then go for me, to get one of my legs. Not like he was rabid, you know; he was sort of a stumbly dog, but he wasn't half-assed, either. It was a good, stumbly run; but I always got away. He got a piece of my trouser leg, look, you can see right here, where it's mended;

he got that the second day I lived there; but, I kicked free and got upstairs fast, so that was that. [*Puzzles.*] I still don't know to this day how the other roomers manage it, but you know what I *think*: I think it had to do only with me. Cozy. So. Anyway, this went on for over a week, whenever I came in; but never when I went out. That's funny. Or, it *was* funny. I could pack up and live in the street for all the dog cared. Well, I thought about it up in my room one day, one of the times after I'd bolted upstairs, and I made up my mind. I decided: First, I'll kill the dog with kindness, and if that doesn't work ... I'll just kill him. [PETER *winces.*] Don't react, Peter; just listen. So, the next day I went out and bought a bag of hamburgers, medium rare, no catsup, no onion; and on the way home I threw away all the rolls and kept just the meat. [*Action for the following, perhaps.*] When I got back to the roominghouse the dog was waiting for me. I half opened the door that led to the entrance hall, and there he was; waiting for me. It figured. I went in, very cautiously, and I had the hamburgers, you remember; I opened the bag, and I set the meat down about twelve feet from where the dog was snarling at me. Like so! He snarled; stopped snarling; sniffed; moved slowly; then faster; then faster toward the meat. Well, when he got to it he stopped, and he looked at me. I smiled; but tentatively, you understand. He turned his face back to the hamburgers, smelled, sniffed some more, and then ... RRRAAAAGGGGGHHHH, like that ... he tore into them. It was as if he had never eaten anything in his life before, except like garbage. Which might very well have been the truth. I don't think the landlady ever eats anything but garbage. But. He ate all the hamburgers, almost all at once, making sounds in his throat like a woman. *Then*, when he'd finished the meat, the hamburger, and tried to eat the paper, too, he sat down and smiled. I think he smiled; I know cats do. It was a very gratifying few moments. Then, BAM, he snarled and made for me again. He didn't get me this time, either. So, I got upstairs, and I lay down on my bed and started to think about the dog again. To be truthful, I was offended, and I was damn mad, too. It was six perfectly good hamburgers with not enough pork in them to make it disgusting. I was offended. But, after a while, I decided to try it for a few more days. If you think about it, this dog had what amounted to an antipathy toward me; really. And, I wondered if I mightn't overcome this antipathy. So, I tried it for five more days, but it was always the same: snarl, sniff; move; faster; stare; gobble; RAAGGGHHH; smile; snarl; BAM. Well, now; by this time Columbus Avenue was strewn with hamburger rolls and I was less offended than disgusted. So, I decided to kill the dog.

[PETER *raises a hand in protest.*]

Oh, don't be so alarmed, Peter; I didn't succeed. The day I tried to kill the dog I bought only one hamburger and what I thought was a murderous portion of rat poison. When I bought the hamburger I asked the man not to bother with the roll, all I wanted was the meat. I expected some reaction from him, like: we don't sell no hamburgers without rolls; or, wha'd'ya wanna do, eat it out'a ya han's? But no; he smiled benignly, wrapped up the hamburger in waxed paper, and said: A bite for ya pussy-cat? I wanted to say: No, not really; it's part of a plan to poison a dog I know. But, you can't say 'a dog I know' without sounding funny; so I said, a little too loud, I'm afraid, and too formally: YES, A BITE FOR MY PUSSY-CAT. People looked up. It always happens when I try to simplify things; people look up. But that's neither hither nor thither. So. On my way back to the roominghouse, I kneaded the hamburger and the rat poison together between my hands, at that point feeling as much sadness as disgust. I opened the door to the entrance hall, and there the monster was, waiting to take the offering and then jump me. Poor bastard; he never learned that the moment he took to smile before he went for me gave me time enough to get out of range. BUT, there he was; malevolence with an erection, waiting. I put the poison patty down, moved toward the stairs and watched. The poor animal gobbled the food down as usual, smiled, which made me almost sick, and then, BAM. But, I sprinted up the stairs, as usual, and the dog didn't get me, as usual. AND IT CAME TO PASS THAT THE BEAST WAS DEATHLY ILL. I knew this because he no longer attended me, and because the landlady sobered up. She stopped me in the hall the same evening of the attempted murder and confided the information that God had struck her puppy-dog a surely fatal blow. She had forgotten her bewildered lust, and her eyes were wide open for the first time. They looked like the dog's eyes. She sniveled and implored me to pray for the animal. I wanted to say to her: Madam, I have myself to pray for, the colored queen, the Puerto Rican family, the person in the front room whom I've never seen, the woman who cries deliberately behind her closed door, and the rest of the people in all roominghouses, everywhere; besides, Madam, I don't understand how to pray. But ... to simplify things ... I told her I would pray. She looked up. She said that I was a liar, and that I probably wanted the dog to die. I told her, and there was so much truth here, that I didn't want the dog to die. I didn't, and not just because I'd poisoned him. I'm afraid that I must tell you I wanted the dog to live so that I could see what our new relationship might come to.

[PETER *indicates his increasing displeasure and slowly growing antagonism*.]

Please understand, Peter; that sort of thing is important. You must believe me; it *is* important. We have to know the effect of our actions. [*Another deep sigh.*] Well, anyway; the dog recovered. I have no idea why, unless he was a descendant of the puppy that guarded the gates of hell or some such resort. I'm not up on my mythology. [*He pronounces the word myth-o-logy.*] Are you?

[PETER *sets to thinking, but* JERRY *goes on.*]

At any rate, and you've missed the eight-thousand-dollar question, Peter; at any rate, the dog recovered his health and the landlady recovered her thirst, in no way altered by the bow-wow's deliverance. When I came home from a movie that was playing on Forty-second Street, a movie I'd seen, or one that was very much like one or several I'd seen, after the landlady told me puppykins was better, I was so hoping for the dog to be waiting for me. I was ... well, how would you put it ... enticed? ... fascinated? ... no, I don't think so ... heart-shatteringly anxious, that's it; I was heart-shatteringly anxious to confront my friend again.

[PETER *reacts scoffingly.*]

Yes, Peter; friend. That's the only word for it. I was heart-shatteringly et cetera to confront my doggy friend again. I came in the door and advanced, unafraid, to the center of the entrance hall. The beast was there ... looking at me. And, you know, he looked better for his scrape with the nevermind. I stopped; I looked at him; he looked at me. I think ... I think we stayed a long time that way ... still, stone-statue ... just looking at one another. I looked more into his face than he looked into mine. I mean, I can concentrate longer at looking into a dog's face than a dog can concentrate at looking into mine, or into anybody else's face, for that matter. But during that twenty seconds or two hours that we looked into each other's face, we made contact. Now, here is what I had wanted to happen: I loved the dog now, and I wanted him to love me. I had tried to love, and I had tried to kill, and both had been unsuccessful by themselves. I hoped ... and I don't really know why I expected the dog to understand anything, much less my motivations ... I hoped that the dog would understand.

[*Peter seems to be hypnotized.*]

It's just ... it's just that ... [JERRY *is abnormally tense, now.*] ... it's just that if you can't deal with people, you have to make a start somewhere. WITH ANIMALS! [*Much faster now, and like a conspirator.*] Don't you see? A person has to have some way of dealing with SOMETHING. If not with people ... if not with people ... SOMETHING. With a bed, with a cockroach, with a mirror ... no, that's too hard, that's one of the last steps. With a cockroach, with a ... with a ... with a carpet, a roll of toilet paper ... no, not that either ... that's a mirror, too; always check bleeding. You see how hard it is to find things? With a street corner, and too many lights, all colours reflecting on the oily-wet streets ... with a wisp of smoke, a wisp ... of smoke ... with ... with pornographic playing cards, with a strongbox ... WITHOUT A LOCK ... with love, with vomiting, with crying, with fury because the pretty little ladies aren't pretty little ladies, with making money with your body which is an act of love and I could prove it, with howling because you're alive; with God. How about that? WITH GOD WHO IS A COLORED QUEEN WHO WEARS A KIMONO AND PLUCKS HIS EYEBROWS, WHO IS A WOMAN WHO CRIES WITH DETERMINATION BEHIND HER CLOSED DOOR ... with God who, I'm told, turned his back on the whole thing some time ago ... with ... some day, with people. [JERRY *sighs the next word heavily.*] People. With an idea; a concept. And where better, where ever better in this humiliating excuse for a jail, where better to communicate one single, simple-minded idea than in an entrance hall? Where? It would be A START! Where better to make a beginning ... to understand and just possibly be understood ... a beginning of an understanding, than with ...

[*Here* JERRY *seems to fall into almost grotesque fatigue.*]

... than with A DOG. Just that; a dog.

[*Here there is a silence that might be prolonged for a moment or so; then* JERRY *wearily finishes his story.*]

A dog. It seemed like a perfectly sensible idea. Man is a dog's best friend, remember. So: the dog and I looked at each other. I longer than the dog. And what I saw then has been the same ever since. Whenever the dog and I see each other we both stop where we are. We regard each other with a mixture of sadness and suspicion, and then we feign indifference. We walk past each other safely; we have an understanding. It's very sad, but you'll have to admit that it is an understanding. We had made many attempts at contact, and we had failed. The dog has returned to garbage, and I to solitary but free passage. I have not returned. I mean to say, I have *gained* solitary free passage, if that much further loss can be said to be gain. I have learned that neither kindness nor cruelty by themselves, independent of each other, creates any effect beyond themselves; and I have learned that the two combined, together, at the same time, are the teaching emotion. And what is gained is loss. And what has been the result: the dog and I have attained a compromise; more of a bargain, really. We neither love nor hurt because we do not try to reach each other. And, *was* trying to feed the dog an act of love? And, perhaps, was the dog's attempt to bite me *not* an act of love? If we can so misunderstand, well then, why have we invented the word love in the first place?

> [*There is silence.* JERRY *moves to* PETER's *bench and sits down beside him. This is the first time* JERRY *has sat down during the play.*]
>
> The Story of Jerry and the Dog: the end.
>
> [PETER *is silent.*]
>
> Well, Peter? [JERRY *is suddenly cheerful.*] Well, Peter? Do you think I could sell that story to the *Reader's Digest* and make a couple of hundred bucks for The Most Unforgettable Character I've Ever Met? Huh?

After this speech things become progressively more violent, with Jerry trying to take possession of the bench on which they are sitting and Peter threatening to call the police. Jerry eventually produces a knife and is stabbed and killed. As you will see from the very end of the play below, Peter has no intention of killing Jerry. You could argue that Jerry committed suicide by running onto the knife.

> JERRY: There you go. Pick it up. You have the knife and we'll be more evenly matched.
>
> PETER [*horrified*]: No!
>
> JERRY [*rushes over to* PETER, *grabs him by the collar*; PETER *rises; their faces almost touch*]: Now you pick up that knife and you fight with me. You fight for your self-respect; you fight for that goddamned bench.
>
> PETER [*struggling*]: No! Let ... let go of me! He ... Help!
>
> JERRY [*slaps* PETER *on each 'fight'*]: You fight, you miserable bastard; fight for that bench; fight for your parakeets; fight for your cats; fight for your two daughters; fight for your wife; fight for your manhood, you pathetic little vegetable. [*Spits in* PETER's *face.*] You couldn't even get your wife with a male child.
>
> PETER [*breaks away, enraged*]: It's a matter of genetics, not manhood, you ... you monster.
>
> [*He darts down, picks up the knife and backs off a little; he is breathing heavily.*]
>
> I'll give you one last chance; get out of here and leave me alone!
>
> [*He holds the knife with a firm arm, but far in front of him, not to attack, but to defend.*]
>
> JERRY [*sighs heavily*]: So be it!
>
> [*With a rush he charges* PETER *and impales himself on the knife. Tableau: For just a moment, complete silence,* JERRY *impaled on the knife at the end of* PETER's *still firm arm. Then* PETER *screams, pulls away, leaving the knife in* JERRY. JERRY *is motionless, on point. Then he, too, screams, and it must be the sound of an infuriated and fatally wounded animal. With the knife in him, he stumbles back to the bench that* PETER *had vacated. He crumbles there, sitting, facing* PETER, *his eyes wide in agony, his mouth open.*]
>
> PETER [*whispering*]: Oh my God, oh my God, oh my God ...
>
> [*He repeats these words many times, very rapidly.*]
>
> JERRY [JERRY *is dying; but now his expression seems to change. His features relax, and while his voice varies, sometimes wrenched with pain, for the most part he seems removed from his dying. He smiles*]: Thank you, Peter. I mean that, now; thank you very much.
>
> [PETER's *mouth drops open. He cannot move; he is transfixed.*]
>
> Oh, Peter, I was so afraid I'd drive you away. [*He laughs as best he can.*] You don't know how afraid I was you'd go away and

Chapter 5 Responding to drama: twentieth-century plays

> leave me. Peter ... Peter? ... Peter ... thank you. I came unto you [*He laughs, so faintly.*] and you have comforted me. Dear Peter.
>
> PETER [*almost fainting*]: Oh my God!
>
> JERRY: You'd better go now. Somebody might come by, and you don't want to be here when anyone comes.
>
> PETER [*does not move, but begins to weep*]: Oh my God, oh my God.
>
> JERRY [*most faintly, now; he is very near death*]: You won't be coming back here any more, Peter; you've been dispossessed. You've lost your bench, but you've defended your honor. And Peter, I'll tell you something now; you're not really a vegetable; it's all right, you're an animal. You're an animal, too. But you'd better hurry now, Peter. Hurry, you'd better go ... see?
>
> [JERRY *takes a handkerchief and with great effort and pain wipes the knife and handle clean of fingerprints.*]
>
> Hurry away, Peter.
>
> [PETER *begins to stagger away.*]
>
> Wait ... wait, Peter. Take your book ... book. Right here ... beside me ... on your bench ... my bench, rather. Come ... take your book.
>
> [PETER *starts for the book but retreats.*]
>
> Hurry ... Peter.
>
> [PETER *rushes to the bench, grabs the book, retreats.*]
>
> Very good, Peter ... very good. Now ... hurry away.
>
> [PETER *hesitates for a moment, then flees, stage-left.*]
>
> Hurry away ... [*His eyes are closed now.*] Hurry away, your parakeets are making the dinner ... the cats ... are setting the table ...
>
> PETER [*off stage: a pitiful howl*]: OH MY GOD!
>
> JERRY [*his eyes still closed, he shakes his head and speaks; a combination of scornful mimicry and supplication*]: Oh ... my ... God.
>
> [*He is dead.*]
>
> **CURTAIN**

That is the play. As a piece of writing of your own you might like to invent two characters and put them in a similar situation. Write a few pages of the dialogue. Remember that, in a short play, you have to establish characters quickly if they are to come alive. As in a full-length play, though, you must also think beyond plot to theme. From even the comparatively brief extracts you have read from *The Zoo Story* and from the brief account of the plot, you should know enough to be able to see themes such as 'family life', 'friendship', 'security', 'the importance of ownership' and even 'the value of life'.

If you study a one-act play for GCSE look for speed of development and tight control of form.

Chapter 6
Responding to drama: pre-1900 plays

Getting started

A number of you will meet the requirement to study drama written before 1900 by studying Shakespeare. In this guide there is a separate chapter on Shakespeare. Some of you will, however, be studying plays written by other authors.

In this chapter we are going to take three plays, all written before 1900, and look at some of their features. The plays are *Doctor Faustus* by Christopher Marlowe, *The School for Scandal* by Richard Brinsley Sheridan and *The Importance of Being Earnest* by Oscar Wilde.

These three plays were written over a period of more than three hundred years and are very different from each other. They show a number of distinct features. We are going to take them in chronological order and explore their different features.

6.1 *Dr Faustus*

Dr Faustus or, to give it its full title, *The Tragical History of Dr Faustus* cannot be dated exactly but was first performed in the last decade of the sixteenth century. Its writer, Christopher Marlowe, led a colourful career; he went to Cambridge University and it is probable that while he was there he became a spy. It is also probable that it was his shady background which led to his murder in a public house during an argument over who should pay the bill for a day's drinking. The play wasn't performed until after his death and this accounts for parts of it probably having been changed or written by others.

The plot

The play tells the story of the German Faust, or Doctor Faustus, who sells his soul to the devil in return for twenty-four years of having anything he wants. The devil is represented in the play by a character called Mephastophilis who looks so horrible when he first appears that Dr Faustus asks him to come back dressed as a monk. This is a play about Good and Evil and it uses a number of the conventions of ancient morality plays.

The theme of Good and Evil

Good and Evil are represented in the play in a number of ways. We have the Good Angel and the Evil Angel who appear as characters and who fight for the soul of Dr Faustus. Somehow, though, the Evil Angel always seems to have the better arguments:

> GOOD ANGEL: Sweet Faustus, think of heaven and heavenly things.
>
> EVIL ANGEL: No Faustus, think of honour and of wealth.

Good is further represented towards the end of the play by an old man who speaks to Faustus and dissuades him from suicide, although he realises that he cannot actually save Faustus.

> OLD MAN: Ah Doctor Faustus, that I might prevail
> To guide thy steps unto the way of life,
> By which sweet path thou may'st attain the goal
> That shall conduct thee to celestial rest.
> Break heart, drop blood, and mingle it with tears,
> Tears falling from repentant heaviness …
>
> … Ah stay, good Faustus, stay thy desperate steps!
> I see an angel hovers o'er thy head,
> And with a vial full of precious grace
> Offers to pour the same into thy soul!
> Then call for mercy and avoid despair …
>
> … I go, sweet Faustus, but with heavy cheer,
> Fearing the ruin of thy hopeless soul.

Evil is represented very much more strongly because, from the outset, Faustus has decided that he is going to side with the devil. At times Evil is represented as entertainment for him, to take his mind off the horrors which are to come. For instance, a tableau of the seven deadly sins appears in this way.

> ENVY: I am envy, begotten of a chimney-sweeper, and an oyster-wife. I cannot read, and therefore wish all books were burnt; I am lean with seeing others eat – O that there would come a famine through all the world that all might die, and I live alone; then thou should'st see how fat I would be! But must thou sit and I stand? Come down, with a vengeance.
>
> GLUTTONY: Who, I sir? I am Gluttony. My parents are all dead, and the devil a penny they have left me, but a bare pension, and that is thirty meals a day and ten bevers – a small trifle to suffice nature. O, I come of a royal parentage: my grandfather was a gammon of bacon, my grandmother a hogshead of claret wine; my godfathers were these: Peter Pickled-Herring, and Martin Martlemas-beef. O, but my godmother! She was a jolly gentlewoman, and well-beloved in every good town and city; her name was Mistress Margery March-Beer. Now, Faustus, thou hast heard all my progeny; wilt thou bid me to supper?

These types of representation of Good and Evil were very common in morality plays.

Characters

The characters in the play are very much paste-board characters, representing types with little character development. Characters we have already mentioned clearly come into that type; so do characters such as the group of students who work with Dr Faustus, and other characters who are conjured up by Mephastophilis for Faustus' entertainment – characters like the Pope, the Emperor Charles V and Helen of Troy.

The two characters who are full and rounded are Dr Faustus himself and Mephastophilis. Interestingly, Mephastophilis comes across as a very sympathetic character at times.

> FAUSTUS: And what are you that live with Lucifer?
>
> MEPHASTOPHILIS: Unhappy spirits that fell with Lucifer,
> Conspired against our God with Lucifer,
> And are forever damned with Lucifer.

> **Examiner's tip**
>
> You might take a history of the English theatre out of the library and scan the development of theatre through the centuries. This will help you not only to put the plays we are looking at in context, but will also help you to put Shakespeare in his historical place in theatrical development.

FAUSTUS: Where are you damned?

MEPHASTOPHILIS: In hell.

FAUSTUS: How comes it then that thou art out of hell?

MEPHASTOPHILIS: Why this is hell, nor am I out of it.
    Think'st thou that I, who sawe the face of God,
    And tasted the eternal joys of heaven,
    Am not tormented with ten thousand hells
    In being deprived of everlasting bliss!
    O Faustus, leave these frivolous demands,
    Which strike a terror to my fainting soul.

Faustus himself, as a character, ranges from bravado, through analytical sense to profound fear. This will be clear when we explore the language of Christopher Marlowe, using examples from what he writes.

As is common in Shakespeare, Marlowe also uses comic minor characters alongside the main characters. Here we have Wagner and Robin and Rafe who conjur up devils and who have similar, if lesser, aspirations than Faustus himself.

ROBIN: True Rafe! And more, Rafe, if thou hast any mind to Nan Spit, our kitchen maid, then turn her and wind her to thy own use, as often as thou wilt, and at midnight.

RAFE: O brave Robin! Shall I have Nan Spit, and to mine own use? On that condition I'll feed thy devil with horsebread as long as he lives, of free cost.

ROBIN: No more, sweet Rafe; let's go and make clean our boots which lie foul upon our hands, and then to our conjuring in the devil's name.

The language and poetry of the play

As was common with plays at this period, *Dr Faustus* is written in a mixture of prose and poetry. Christopher Marlowe's poetry is often referred to as 'the mighty line' and below follow two speeches from the play, showing the power of Marlowe's poetry.

In the first speech Mephastophilis has brought Helen of Troy to Faustus so that he can see the woman who, in mythology, was considered to be the most beautiful in the world. Faustus is overcome with her beauty, and the lines which he speaks convey this in their softness and control. They are written in iambic pentameters (see pp.128–9 for an explanation of the iambic pentameter), and they refer to the events of Helen's legendary life.

FAUSTUS: Was this the face that launched a thousand ships,
    And burnt the topless towers of Ilium?
    Sweet Helen, make me immortal with a kiss:
    Her lips suck forth my soul, see where it flies!
    Come Helen, come, give me my soul again.
    Here will I dwell, for heaven be in these lips,
    And all is dross that is not Helena!

[*Enter* OLD MAN.]

I will be Paris, and for love of thee,
Instead of Troy shall Wittenberg be sacked;
And I will combat with weak Menelaus,
And wear thy colours on my plumed crest:
Yea, I will wound Achilles in the heel,
And then return to Helen for a kiss.
O thou art fairer than the evening air,
Clad in the beauty of a thousand stars,
Brighter art thou than flaming Jupiter
When he appeared to hapless Semele;
More lovely than the monarch of the sky
In wanton Arethusa's azured arms;
And none but thou shalt be my paramour.

The second speech is the very last speech of Faustus before he is dragged off to hell. Again it is written in iambic pentameters. It begins with the works, 'Ah Faustus, Now thou hast but one bare hour to live' and is remarkable for the way in which it tracks the passing of time through the final hour, culminating in the desperate offer to burn his books, the symbol of everything he has lived for.

[*The clock strikes eleven.*]
FAUSTUS: Ah Faustus,
  Now hast thou but one bare hour to live,
  And then thou must be damned perpetually.
  Stand still, you ever-moving spheres of heaven,
  That time may cease, and midnight never come.
  Fair Nature's eye, rise, rise again, and make
  Perpetual day, or let this hour be but
  A year, a month, a week, a natural day,
  That Faustus may repent and save his soul.
  O lente, lente currite noctis equi!
  The stars move still, time runs, the clock will strike,
  The devil will come, and Faustus must be damned.
  O I'll leap up to my God! Who pulls me down?
  See, see where Christ's blood streams in the firmament!
  One drop would save my soul, half a drop: ah my Christ -
  Ah, rend not my heart for naming of my Christ;
  Yet will I call on him – O spare me, Lucifer!
  Where is it now? 'Tis gone: and see where God
  Stretcheth out his arm and bends his ireful brows!
  Mountains and hills, come, come and fall on me,
  And hide me from the heavy wrath of God.
  No, no?
  Then will I headlong run into the earth:
  Earth, gape! O no, it will not harbour me.
  You stars that reigned at my nativity,
  Whose influence hath allotted death and hell,
  Now draw up Faustus like a foggy mist
  Into the entrails of yon labouring cloud,
  That when you vomit forth into the air
  My limbs may issue from your smoky mouths,
  So that my soul may but ascend to heaven.
[*The watch strikes.*]
  Ah, half the hour is past: 'twill all be past anon.
  O God, if thou wilt not have mercy on my soul,
  Yet for Christ's sake, whose blood hath ransomed me,
  Impose some end to my incessant pain:
  Let Faustus live in hell a thousand years,
  A hundred thousand, and at last be saved.
  O, no end is limited to damned souls!
  Why wert thou not a creature wanting soul?
  Or why is this immortal that thou hast?
  Ah, Pythagoras' *metempsychosis* – were that true,
  This soul should fly from me, and I be changed
  Unto some brutish beast:
  All beasts are happy, for when they die,
  Their souls are soon dissolved in elements;
  But mine must live still to be plagued in hell.
  Cursed be the parents that engendered me:
  No Faustus, curse thy self, curse Lucifer,
  That hath deprived thee of the joys of heaven!
[*The clock striketh twelve.*]
  O it strikes, it strikes! Now body, turn to air,
  Or Lucifer will bear thee quick to hell.
[*Thunder and lightning.*]

> O soul, be changed into little water drops,
> And fall into the ocean, ne'er be found.
> My God, my God, look not so fierce on me!
>
> [*Enter* DEVILS.]
>
> Adders and serpents, let me breathe awhile!
> Ugly hell gape not! Come not, Lucifer!
> I'll burn my books – ah, Mephastophilis!

> **Examiner's tip**
>
> Take a few lines of the last speech of *Dr Faustus* and refer to p.129 in Chapter 7 to enable you to mark the stressed and unstressed syllables demonstrating that they are iambic pentameters.

We can sum up by saying that *Dr Faustus* looks back both to the morality plays of earlier centuries and to the dramas of the sixteenth century, where it belongs alongside Shakespeare.

Characters are very much the same mixture of rounded and paste-board as used by Shakespeare. Language reaches the supreme heights of poetry. Perhaps we ought also to remember that it was written for the same type of theatre as were Shakespeare's plays, and we have the mix of spectacular set-piece scenes and intimate scenes which would have been performed on the inner stage as opposed to the full apron stage.

Mention of the type of stage and theatre leads us on to our second play.

6.2 *The School for Scandal*

The School for Scandal was first performed in 1777, some two hundred years after *Dr Faustus* and a great deal had happened to the theatre in the meantime; it had even been suppressed for a while under the puritan regime of Oliver Cromwell. Most especially, theatre had become more intimate. The open air stages had gone and been replaced by stages behind a proscenium arch with curtains which could be drawn across to allow changes of scenery to signify different places.

The plot

The play tells the story of two brothers, Charles and Joseph Surface, and reflects the view which their uncle, Sir Oliver, holds of them. Charles is rather rash and happy-go-lucky but he is very honest, open and generous in the way in which he leads his life. Joseph, by contrast, is sly and unpleasant, although he cunningly tries to appear the opposite. Sir Oliver appears in two disguises while he finds out the truth about the brothers. There is also Maria, the honest heroine, who must end up with Charles if there is to be any justice in the world. The other fully rounded characters in the plot are Sir Peter and Lady Teazle. Sir Peter is an honest and upright older man whose life has been in the city. He has married a rather naïve young woman who lived her early life in the country. Her naïvety means that she can be influenced by Joseph Surface and his circle of friends, although she eventually escapes from their influence. The circle of friends form the background against which much of the play takes place. They are 'the school for scandal' whose names indicate precisely their characters: Lady Sneerwell, Mrs Candour, Sir Benjamin Backbite, Snake, and so on. They do not care who they hurt by spreading gossip of the most malicious kind.

Characters

The characters who make up this school are essentially very unpleasant. Maria sums up Sir Benjamin Backbite with the words 'his conversation is a perpetual libel on all his acquaintance'. Their unpleasantness is shown in the two extracts which follow.

LADY SNEERWELL: Nay, but we should make allowance. Sir Benjamin is a wit and a poet.

MARIA: For my part, I confess, madam, wit loses its respect with me when I see it in company with malice. What do you think, Mr Surface?

JOSEPH: Certainly, madam. To smile at the jest which plants a thorn in another's breast is to become a principal in the mischief.

LADY SNEERWELL: Pshaw, there's no possibility of being witty without a little ill nature. The malice of a good thing is the barb that makes it stick. What's your opinion, Mr Surface?

JOSEPH: To be sure, madam, that conversation where the spirit of raillery is suppressed will ever appear tedious and insipid.

MARIA: Well, I'll not debate how far scandal may be allowable; but in a man, I am sure, it is always contemptible. We have pride, envy, rivalship, and a thousand motives to depreciate each other; but the male slanderer must have the cowardice of a woman before he can traduce one.

[*Enter* SERVANT.]

SERVANT: Madam, Mrs Candour is below, and if your ladyship's at leisure, will leave her carriage.

LADY SNEERWELL: Beg her to walk in.

[*Exit* SERVANT.]

Now, Maria, here is a character to your taste, for though Mrs Candour is a little talkative, everybody allows her to be the best-natured and best sort of woman.

MARIA: Yes, with a very gross affectation of good nature and benevolence, she does more mischief than the direct malice of old Crabtree.

JOSEPH: I'faith that's true, Lady Sneerwell. Whenever I hear the current running against the characters of my friends, I never think them in such danger as when Candour undertakes their defence.

LADY SNEERWELL: Hush! Here she is.

[*Enter* MRS CANDOUR.]

MRS CANDOUR: My dear Lady Sneerwell, how have you been this century? Mr Surface, what news do you hear? Though indeed it is no matter, for I think one hears nothing else but scandal.

JOSEPH: Just so, indeed, ma'am.

MRS CANDOUR: Ah, Maria, child! What, is the whole affair off between you and Charles? His extravagance, I presume? The town talks of nothing else.

MARIA: Indeed! I am very sorry, ma'am, the town is not better employed.

MRS CANDOUR: True, true, child; but there's no stopping people's tongues. I own I was hurt to hear it, as indeed I was to learn from the same quarter that your guardian, Sir Peter, and Lady Teazle have not agreed lately as well as could be wished.

MARIA: 'Tis strangely impertinent for people to busy themselves so.

MRS CANDOUR: Very true, child, but what's to be done? People will talk; there's no preventing it. Why, it was but yesterday I was told that Miss Gadabout had eloped with Sir Filigree Flirt. But, Lord, there's no minding what one hears; though to be sure, I had this from very good authority.

MARIA: Such reports are highly scandalous.

MRS CANDOUR: So they are, child – shameful, shameful! But the world is so censorious, no character escapes. Lord, now who would have suspected your friend, Miss Prim, of an indiscretion? Yet such is the ill nature of people that they say her uncle stopped her last week, just as she was stepping into the York diligence with her dancing-master.

MARIA: I'll answer for't there are no grounds for that report.

MRS CANDOUR: Oh, no foundation in the world, I dare swear. No more, probably, than for the story circulated last month of Mrs Festino's affair with Colonel Cassino – though, to be sure, that matter was never rightly cleared up.

JOSEPH: The licence of invention some people take is monstrous indeed.

LADY TEAZLE: What's the matter, Mrs Candour?

MRS CANDOUR: They'll not allow our friend Miss Vermilion to be handsome.

LADY SNEERWELL: Oh, surely she is a pretty woman.

CRABTREE: I am very glad you think so, ma'am.

MRS CANDOUR: She has a charming fresh colour.

LADY TEAZLE: Yes, when it is fresh put on.

MRS CANDOUR: Oh, fie! I'll swear her colour is natural: I have seen it come and go.

LADY TEAZLE: I daresay you have, ma'am: it goes off at night and comes again in the morning.

SIR BENJAMIN: True, ma'am, it not only comes and goes, but, what's more, egad – her maid can fetch and carry it.

MRS CANDOUR: Ha, ha, ha! How I hate to hear you talk so! But surely now, her sister is – or *was* – very handsome.

CRABTREE: Who – Mrs Evergreen? Oh, Lord, she's six and fifty if she's an hour.

MRS CANDOUR: Now positively you wrong her. Fifty-two or fifty-three is the utmost – and I don't think she looks more.

SIR BENJAMIN: Ah, there is no judging by her looks unless one could see her face.

LADY SNEERWELL: Well, well, if Mrs Evergreen does take some pains to repair the ravages of time, you must allow she effects it with great ingenuity; and surely that's better than the careless manner in which the widow Ochre chalks her wrinkles.

SIR BENJAMIN: Nay, now, Lady Sneerwell, you are severe upon the widow. Come, come, 'tis not that she paints so ill – but when she has finished her face, she joins it on so badly to her neck that she looks like a mended statue, in which the connoisseur sees at once that the head's modern, though the trunk's antique.

CRABTREE: Ha, ha, ha! Well said, nephew!

MRS CANDOUR: Ha, ha, ha! Well, you make me laugh, but I vow I hate you for it. What do you think of Miss Simper?

SIR BENJAMIN: Why, she has very pretty teeth.

LADY TEAZLE: Yes, and on that account, when she is neither speaking nor laughing (which very seldom happens), she never absolutely shuts her mouth, but leaves it always on a jar, as it were, thus.

[*Shows her teeth.*]

MRS CANDOUR: How can you be so ill-natured?

LADY TEAZLE: Nay, I allow even that's better than the pains Mrs Prim takes to conceal her losses in front. She draws her mouth till it positively resembles the aperture of a poor's-box and all her words appear to slide out edgewise, as it were thus, *How do you do, madam? – Yes, madam.*

LADY SNEERWELL: Very well, Lady Teazle; I see you can be a little severe.

LADY TEAZLE: In defence of a friend it is but justice. But here comes Sir Peter to spoil our pleasantry.

[Enter SIR PETER TEAZLE.]

SIR PETER: Ladies, your most obedient. [*Aside.*] Mercy on me, here is the whole set! A character dead at every word, I suppose.

MRS CANDOUR: I am rejoiced you are come, Sir Peter. They have been so censorious and Lady Teazle as bad as anyone.

SIR PETER: It must be very distressing to you, Mrs Candour, I dare swear.

MRS CANDOUR: Oh, they will allow good qualities to nobody – not even good nature to our friend Mrs Pursy.

LADY TEAZLE: What, the fat dowager who was at Mrs Quadrille's last night?

MRS CANDOUR: Nay, her bulk is her misfortune; and when she takes such pains to get rid of it, you ought not to reflect on her.

LADY SNEERWELL: That's very true, indeed.

LADY TEAZLE: Yes, I know she almost lives on acids and small whey; laces herself by pulleys; and often in the hottest noon in summer, you may see her on a little squat pony, with her hair plaited up behind like a drummer's, and puffing round the Ring on a full trot.

MRS CANDOUR: I thank you, Lady Teazle, for defending her.

SIR PETER: Yes, a good defence truly!

MRS CANDOUR: Truly, Lady Teazle is as censorious as Miss Sallow.

CRABTREE: Yes, and she is a curious being to pretend to be censorious – an awkward gawky, without any one good point under heaven!

MRS CANDOUR: Positively you shall not be so very severe. Miss Sallow is a near relation of mine by marriage, and as for her person, great allowance is to be made; for, let me tell you, a woman labours under many disadvantages who tries to pass for a girl at six and thirty.

LADY SNEERWELL: Though surely she is handsome still – and for the weakness in her eyes, considering how much she reads by candle-light, it is not to be wondered at.

MRS CANDOUR: True, and then as to her manner – upon my word I think it is particularly graceful, considering she never had the least education. For you know her mother was a Welsh milliner and her father a sugar-baker at Bristol.

SIR BENJAMIN: Ah, you are both of you too good-natured!

SIR PETER [*aside*]: Yes, damned good-natured! This their own relation! Mercy on me!

MRS CANDOUR: For my part, I own I cannot bear to hear a friend ill spoken of.

In both extracts we see how these people operate to attack anyone who they feel is vulnerable. We can also see how they have brought Lady Teazle into their circle. We have to remember, though, that this is a comedy and, however cruel they are, there is always the possibility of humour in the background as we know that they will eventually be caught out.

The comedy

One of the most amusingly inventive scenes in the play is what is often known as the 'screen scene'. Joseph begins by entertaining Lady Teazle and, when Sir Peter Teazle arrives, he has to improvise quickly by hiding Lady Teazle behind a screen. Joseph pretends to be the exhausted student with his book. When Joseph's brother Charles is about to arrive, Sir Peter wants to hide and Joseph has to invent, very quickly, a 'little French milliner' who is hidden there. Eventually everything is revealed when Charles pulls down the screen, but Joseph never gives up trying to defend himself.

Below is the scene, Act Four Scene Three.

[JOSEPH SURFACE *and* SERVANT *in the library in* JOSEPH's *house.*]

JOSEPH: No letter from Lady Teazle?

SERVANT: No, sir.

JOSEPH [*aside*]: I am surprised she has not sent, if she is prevented from coming. Sir Peter certainly does not suspect me. Yet, I wish I may not lose the heiress, through the scrape I have drawn myself in with the wife; however, Charles's imprudence and bad character are great points in my favour.

[*Knocking heard without.*]

SERVANT: Sir, I believe that must be Lady Teazle.

JOSEPH: Hold! See whether it is or not before you go to the door; I have a particular message for you, if it should be my brother.

SERVANT: 'Tis her ladyship, sir; she always leaves her chair at the milliner's in the next street.

JOSEPH: Stay, stay; draw that screen before the window – that will do. My opposite neighbour is a maiden lady of so curious a temper.

[SERVANT *draws the screen, and exit.*]

I have a difficult hand to play in this affair. Lady Teazle has lately suspected my views on Maria; but she must by no means be let into the secret – at least, not till I have her more in my power.

[*Enter* LADY TEAZLE.]

LADY TEAZLE: What! Sentiment in soliloquy now? Have you been very impatient? O lud, don't pretend to look grave. I vow I couldn't come before.

JOSEPH: Oh, madam, punctuality is a species of constancy, a very unfashionable quality in a lady.

LADY TEAZLE: Upon my word, you ought to pity me. Do you know Sir Peter is grown so ill-tempered to me of late – and so jealous of Charles too! That's the best of the story, isn't it?

JOSEPH [*aside*]: I am glad my scandalous friends keep that up.

LADY TEAZLE: I am sure I wish he would let Maria marry him and then perhaps he would be convinced; don't you, Mr Surface?

JOSEPH [*aside*]: Indeed I do not. [*Aloud.*] Oh, certainly I do. For then my dear Lady Teazle would also be convinced how wrong her suspicions were of my having any design on the silly girl.

LADY TEAZLE: Well, well, I'm inclined to believe you. But isn't it provoking, to have the most ill-natured things said of one? And there's my friend Lady Sneerwell has circulated I don't know how many scandalous tales of me, and all without any foundation too – that's what vexes me.

JOSEPH: Aye, madam, to be sure, that is the provoking circumstance – without foundation. Yes, yes, there's the mortification, indeed; or, when a scandalous story is believed against one, there certainly is no comfort like the consciousness of having deserved it.

LADY TEAZLE: No, to be sure, then I'd forgive their malice. But to attack me, who am really so innocent and who never say an ill-natured thing of anybody – that is, of any friend; and then Sir Peter, too, to have him so peevish and so suspicious, when I know the integrity of my own heart – indeed, 'tis monstrous!

JOSEPH: But, my dear Lady Teazle, 'tis your own fault if you suffer it. When a husband entertains a groundless suspicion of his wife and withdraws his confidence from her, the original compact is broken, and she owes it to the honour of her sex to endeavour to outwit him.

LADY TEAZLE: Indeed! So that if he suspects me without cause, it follows that the best way of curing his jealousy is to give him reason for it?

JOSEPH: Undoubtedly – for your husband should never be deceived in you; and in that case it becomes you to be frail in compliment to his discernment.

LADY TEAZLE: To be sure, what you say is very reasonable, and when the consciousness of my own innocence –

JOSEPH: Ah, my dear madam, there is the great mistake! 'Tis this very conscious innocence that is of the greatest prejudice to you. What is it makes you negligent of forms, and careless of the world's opinion? Why, the consciousness of your own innocence. What makes you thoughtless in your conduct, and apt to run into a thousand little imprudences? Why, the consciousness of your own innocence. What makes you impatient of Sir Peter's temper, and outrageous at his suspicions? Why, the consciousness of your innocence.

LADY TEAZLE: 'Tis very true.

JOSEPH: Now, my dear Lady Teazle, if you would but once make a trifling *faux pas*, you can't conceive how cautious you would grow, and how ready to humour and agree with your husband.

LADY TEAZLE: Do you think so?

JOSEPH: Oh, I am sure on't; and then you would find all scandal would cease at once, for, in short, your character at present is like a person in a plethora, absolutely dying from too much health.

LADY TEAZLE: So, so; then I perceive your prescription is that I must sin in my own defence, and part with my virtue to secure my reputation?

JOSEPH: Exactly so, upon my credit, ma'am.

LADY TEAZLE: Well, certainly this is the oddest doctrine, and the newest receipt for avoiding calumny.

JOSEPH: An infallible one, believe me. Prudence, like experience, must be paid for.

LADY TEAZLE: Why, if my understanding were once convinced –

JOSEPH: Oh, certainly, madam, your understanding should be convinced. Yes, yes – heaven forbid I should persuade you to do anything you thought wrong. No, no, I have too much honour to desire it.

LADY TEAZLE: Don't you think we may as well leave honour out of the argument?

JOSEPH: Ah, the ill effects of your country education, I see, still remain with you.

LADY TEAZLE: I doubt they do indeed; and I will fairly own to you that if I could be persuaded to do wrong, it would be by Sir Peter's ill usage sooner than your honourable logic after all.

JOSEPH: Then, by this hand, which he is unworthy of – [*Taking her hand.*]

6.2 The School for Scandal

[*Enter Servant.*]

'Sdeath, you blockhead – what do you want?

SERVANT: I beg your pardon, sir, but I thought you wouldn't choose Sir Peter to come up without announcing him.

JOSEPH: Sir Peter! Oons – the devil!

LADY TEAZLE: Sir Peter! O lud, I'm ruined! I'm ruined!

SERVANT: Sir, 'twasn't I let him in.

LADY TEAZLE: Oh, I'm undone! What will become of me now, Mr Logic? Oh, mercy, he's on the stairs. I'll get behind here – and if ever I'm so imprudent again –

[*Hides behind screen.*]

JOSEPH: Give me that book.

[*Sits down.* SERVANT *pretends to adjust his hair.*]

[*Enter* SIR PETER TEAZLE.]

SIR PETER: Aye, ever improving himself! Mr Surface, Mr Surface –

JOSEPH: Oh, my dear Sir Peter, I beg your pardon. [*Gaping, and throws away the book.*] I have been dozing over a stupid book. Well, I am much obliged to you for this call. You haven't been here, I believe, since I fitted up this room. Books, you know, are the only things I am a coxcomb in.

SIR PETER: 'Tis very neat indeed. Well, well, that's proper; and you make even your screen a source of knowledge – hung, I perceive, with maps.

JOSEPH: Oh, yes, I find great use in that screen.

SIR PETER: I dare say you must. Certainly when you want to find anything in a hurry.

JOSEPH [*aside*]: Aye, or to hide anything in a hurry either.

SIR PETER: Well, I have a little private business –

JOSEPH [*to* SERVANT]: You needn't stay.

SERVANT: No, sir.

[*Exit.*]

JOSEPH: Here's a chair, Sir Peter. I beg –

SIR PETER: Well, now we are alone, there is a subject, my dear friend, on which I wish to unburden my mind to you – a point of the greatest moment to my peace; in short, my dear friend, Lady Teazle's conduct of late has made me extremely unhappy.

JOSEPH: Indeed! I am very sorry to hear it.

SIR PETER: Aye, 'tis too plain she has not the least regard for me; but, what's worse, I have pretty good authority to suppose she must have formed an attachment to another.

JOSEPH: Indeed! You astonish me!

SIR PETER: Yes; and, between ourselves, I think I've discovered the person.

JOSEPH: How! You alarm me exceedingly.

SIR PETER: Aye, my dear friend, I knew you would sympathize with me.

JOSEPH: Yes – believe me, Sir Peter, such a discovery would hurt me just as much as it would you.

SIR PETER: I am convinced of it. Ah, it is a happiness to have a friend whom one can trust even with one's family secrets. But have you no guess who I mean?

JOSEPH: I haven't the most distant idea. It can't be Sir Benjamin Backbite?

SIR PETER: Oh, no! What say you to Charles?

JOSEPH: My brother! Impossible!

SIR PETER: Ah, my dear friend, the goodness of your own heart misleads you. You judge of others by yourself.

JOSEPH: Certainly, Sir Peter, the heart that is conscious of its own integrity is ever slow to credit another's treachery.

SIR PETER: True, but your brother has no sentiment; you never hear him talk so.

JOSEPH: Yet I can't but think Lady Teazle herself has too much principle.

SIR PETER: Aye, but what is principle against the flattery of a handsome, lively young fellow?

JOSEPH: That's very true.

SIR PETER: And then, you know, the difference of our ages makes it very improbable that she should have any very great affection for me; and, if she were to be frail, and I were to make it public, why, the town would only laugh at me – the foolish old bachelor who had married a girl.

JOSEPH: That's true, to be sure – they would laugh.

SIR PETER: Laugh – aye, and make ballads and paragraphs and the devil knows what of me.

JOSEPH: No, you must never make it public.

SIR PETER: But then, again, that the nephew of my old friend, Sir Oliver, should be the person to attempt such a wrong, hurts me more nearly.

JOSEPH: Aye, there's the point. When ingratitude barbs the dart of injury, the wound has double danger in it.

SIR PETER: Aye. I that was, in a manner, left his guardian, in whose house he had been so often entertained – who never in my life denied him my advice!

JOSEPH: Oh, 'tis not to be credited! There may be a man capable of such baseness, to be sure; but for my part, till you can give me positive proofs, I cannot but doubt it. However, if it should be proved on him, he is no longer a brother of mine; I disclaim kindred with him; for the man who can break the laws of hospitality and attempt the wife of his friend, deserves to be branded as the pest of society.

SIR PETER: What a difference there is between you! What noble sentiments!

JOSEPH: Yet I cannot suspect Lady Teazle's honour.

SIR PETER: I am sure I wish to think well of her, and to remove all ground of quarrel between us. She has lately reproached me more than once with having made no settlement on her, and in our last quarrel she almost hinted that she should not break her heart if I was dead. Now, as we seem to differ in our ideas of expense, I have resolved she shall have her own way and be her own mistress in that respect for the future; and if I were to die, she will find that I have not been inattentive to her interest while living. Here, my friend, are the drafts of two deeds, which I wish to have your opinion on. By one she will enjoy eight hundred a year independent while I live; and, by the other, the bulk of my fortune at my death.

JOSEPH: This conduct, Sir Peter, is indeed truly generous. [*Aside.*] I wish it may not corrupt my pupil.

SIR PETER: Yes, I am determined she shall have no cause to complain, though I would not have her acquainted with the latter instance of my affection yet awhile.

JOSEPH [*aside*]: Nor I, if I could help it.

SIR PETER: And now, my dear friend, if you please, we will talk over the situation of your affairs with Maria.

JOSEPH [*softly*]: Oh, no, Sir Peter; another time, if you please.

SIR PETER: I am sensibly chagrined at the little progress you seem to make in her affection.

JOSEPH [*softly*]: I beg you will not mention it. What are my disappointments when your happiness is in debate! [*Aside.*] 'Sdeath, I shall be ruined every way.

SIR PETER: And though you are so averse to my acquainting Lady Teazle with your passion for Maria, I'm sure she's not your enemy in the affair.

JOSEPH: Pray, Sir Peter, now, oblige me. I am really too much affected by the subject we have been speaking of, to bestow a thought on my own concerns. The man who is entrusted with his friend's distresses can never –

[*Enter* SERVANT.]

Well, sir?

SERVANT: Your brother, sir is speaking to a gentleman in the street, and says he knows you are within.

JOSEPH: 'Sdeath, blockhead, I'm not within; I'm out for the day.

SIR PETER: Stay, hold, a thought has struck me. You shall be at home.

JOSEPH: Well, well, let him up.

[*Exit* SERVANT.]

[*Aside.*] He'll interrupt Sir Peter, however.

SIR PETER: Now, my good friend, oblige me, I entreat you. Before Charles comes, let me conceal myself somewhere; then do you tax him on the point we have been talking on, and his answers may satisfy me at once.

JOSEPH: Oh, fie, Sir Peter! Would you have me join in so mean a trick – to trepan my brother too?

SIR PETER: Nay, you tell me you are sure he is innocent; if so, you do him the greatest service by giving him an opportunity to clear himself, and you will set my heart at rest. Come, you shall not refuse me. Here, behind this screen will be – [*Goes to the screen.*] Hey! What the devil! There seems to be one listener there already. I'll swear I saw a petticoat.

JOSEPH: Ha, ha, ha! Well, this is ridiculous enough. I'll tell you, Sir Peter, though I hold a man of intrigue to be a most despicable character, yet, you know, it doesn't follow that one is to be an absolute Joseph either. Hark'ee, 'tis a little French milliner, a silly rogue that plagues me – and having some character to lose, on your coming, sir, she ran behind the screen.

SIR PETER: Ah, you rogue! But, egad, she has overheard all I have been saying of my wife.

JOSEPH: Oh, 'twill never go any farther, you may depend upon't.

SIR PETER: No? Then i'faith let her hear it out. Here's a closet will do as well.

JOSEPH: Well, go in then.

SIR PETER: Sly rogue! sly rogue!

[*Goes into the closet.*]

JOSEPH: A narrow escape, indeed, and a curious situation I'm in, to part man and wife in this manner.

LADY TEAZLE [*peeping from the screen*]: Couldn't I steal off?

JOSEPH: Keep close, my angel.

SIR PETER [*peeping*]: Joseph, tax him home.

JOSEPH: Back, my dear friend.

LADY TEAZLE [*peeping*]: Couldn't you lock Sir Peter in?

JOSEPH: Be still, my life.

SIR PETER [*peeping*]: You're sure the little milliner won't blab?

JOSEPH: In, in, my good Sir Peter, 'Fore gad, I wish I had a key to the door.

[*Enter* CHARLES SURFACE.]

CHARLES: Hullo, brother, what has been the matter? Your fellow would not let me up at first. What, have you had a Jew or a wench with you?

JOSEPH: Neither, brother, I assure you.

CHARLES: But what has made Sir Peter steal off? I thought he had been with you.

JOSEPH: He *was* brother, but hearing you were coming, he did not choose to stay.

CHARLES: What! Was the old gentleman afraid I wanted to borrow money of him?

JOSEPH: No, sir. But I am sorry to find, Charles, you have lately given that worthy man grounds for great uneasiness.

CHARLES: Yes, they tell me I do that to a great many worthy men. But how so, pray?

JOSEPH: To be plain with you, brother, he thinks you are endeavouring to gain Lady Teazle's affections from him.

CHARLES: Who, I? O lud, not I, upon my word. Ha, ha, ha! So the old fellow has found out that he has got a young wife, has he? Or, what is worse, her ladyship has found out she has an old husband?

JOSEPH: This is no subject to jest on, brother. He who can laugh —

CHARLES: True, true, as you were going to say. Then, seriously, I never had the least idea of what you charge me with, upon my honour.

JOSEPH [*aloud*]: Well, it will give Sir Peter great satisfaction to hear this.

CHARLES: To be sure, I once thought the lady seemed to have taken a fancy to me; but, upon my soul, I never gave her the least encouragement. Besides, you know my attachment to Maria.

JOSEPH: But sure, brother, even if Lady Teazle had betrayed the fondest partiality for you —

CHARLES: Why, look'ee, Joseph, I hope I shall never deliberately do a dishonourable action; but if a pretty woman was purposely to throw herself in my way — and that pretty woman married to a man old enough to be her father —

JOSEPH: Well?

CHARLES: Why, I believe I should be obliged to borrow a little of your morality, that's all. But brother, do you know now that you surprise me exceedingly by naming me with Lady Teazle; for, faith, I always understood you were her favourite.

JOSEPH: Oh, for shame, Charles! This retort is foolish.

CHARLES: Nay, I swear I have seen you exchange such significant glances —

JOSEPH: Nay, nay, sir, this is no jest —

CHARLES: Egad, I'm serious. Don't you remember, one day, when I called here —

JOSEPH: Nay, prithee, Charles —

CHARLES: And found you together —

JOSEPH: Zounds, sir, I insist —

CHARLES: And another time, when your servant —

JOSEPH: Brother, brother, a word with you. [*Aside.*] Gad, I must stop him.

CHARLES: Informed me, I say, that –

JOSEPH: Hush! I beg your pardon, but Sir Peter has overheard all we have been saying. I knew you would clear yourself, or I should not have consented.

CHARLES: How, Sir Peter! Where is he?

JOSEPH: Softly. There!

[*Points to the closet.*]

CHARLES: Oh, 'fore heaven, I'll have him out. Sir Peter, come forth!

JOSEPH: No, no –

CHARLES: I say, Sir Peter, come into court. [*Pulls in Sir Peter.*] What! My old guardian! What, turn inquisitor and take evidence incog.?

SIR PETER: Give me your hand, Charles. I believe I have suspected you wrongfully; but you mustn't be angry with Joseph. 'Twas my plan.

CHARLES: Indeed!

SIR PETER: But I acquit you. I promise you I don't think near so ill of you as I did. What I have heard has given me great satisfaction.

CHARLES: Egad then, 'twas lucky you didn't hear any more. [*Apart to* JOSEPH.] Wasn't it Joseph?

SIR PETER: Ah, you would have retorted on him.

CHARLES: Aye, aye, that was a joke.

SIR PETER: Yes, yes, I know his honour too well.

CHARLES: But you might as well have suspected him as me in this matter for all that. [*Apart to Joseph.*] Mightn't he, Joseph?

SIR PETER: Well, well, I believe you.

JOSEPH [*aside*]: Would they were both well out of the room!

[*Enter* SERVANT *and whispers* JOSEPH.]

SIR PETER: And in future, perhaps, we may not be such strangers.

[*Exit* SERVANT.]

JOSEPH: Gentlemen, I beg your pardon, I must wait on you downstairs. Here is a person come on particular business.

CHARLES: Well, you can see him in another room. Sir Peter and I have not met a long time, and I have something to say to him.

JOSEPH [*aside*]: They must not be left together. [*Aloud.*] I'll send this man away and return directly. [*Apart to Sir Peter and goes out.*] Sir Peter, not a word of the French milliner.

SIR PETER [*apart to* JOSEPH]: I? Not for the world. [*Aloud.*] Ah, Charles, if you associated more with your brother, one might indeed hope for your reformation. He is a man of sentiment. Well, there is nothing in the world so noble as a man of sentiment.

CHARLES: Pshaw, he is too moral by half – and so apprehensive of his good name, as he calls it, that I suppose he would as soon let a priest into his house as a girl.

SIR PETER: No, no! Come, come, you wrong him. No, no, Joseph is no rake, but he is no such saint either in that respect. [*Aside.*] I have a great mind to tell him; we should have a laugh.

CHARLES: Oh, hang him, he's a very anchorite, a young hermit.

SIR PETER: Hark'ee, you must not abuse him: he may chance to hear of it again, I promise you.

CHARLES: Why, you won't tell him?

SIR PETER: No. But this way. [*Aside.*] Egad, I'll tell him. [*Aloud.*] Hark'ee, have you a mind to have a good laugh at Joseph?

CHARLES: I should like it of all things.

SIR PETER: Then, i'faith, we will! [*Aside.*] I'll be quit with him for discovering me. [*Aloud.*] He had a girl with him when I called.

CHARLES: What! Joseph? You jest.

SIR PETER: Hush! A little French milliner. And the best of the jest is – she's in the room now.

CHARLES: The devil she is!

SIR PETER: Hush! I tell you.

[*Points to the screen.*]

CHARLES: Behind the screen! 'Slife, let's unveil her.

SIR PETER: No, no, he's coming – you shan't indeed.

CHARLES: Oh, egad, we'll have a peep at the little milliner.

SIR PETER: Not for the world! Joseph will never forgive me.

CHARLES: I'll stand by you.

SIR PETER: Odds, here he is!

[JOSEPH *enters just as* CHARLES *throws down the screen.*]

CHARLES: Lady Teazle – by all that's wonderful!

SIR PETER: Lady Teazle, by all that's damnable!

CHARLES: Sir Peter, this is one of the smartest French milliners I ever saw. Egad, you seem all to have been diverting yourselves here at hide and seek – and I don't see who is out of the secret. Shall I beg your ladyship to inform me? Not a word! Brother, will you be pleased to explain this matter? What, is morality dumb too? Sir Peter, though I found you in the dark, perhaps you are not so now? All mute. Well, though I can make nothing of the affair, I suppose you perfectly understand one another, so I'll leave you to yourselves. [*Going.*] Brother, I'm sorry to find you have given that worthy man cause for so much uneasiness. Sir Peter, there's nothing in the world so noble as a man of sentiment!

[*Exit* CHARLES. *They stand for some time looking at each other.*]

JOSEPH: Sir Peter, notwithstanding I confess that appearances are against me, if you will afford me your patience, I make no doubt – but I shall explain everything to your satisfaction.

SIR PETER: If you please, sir.

JOSEPH: The fact is, sir, that Lady Teazle, knowing my pretensions to your ward, Maria – I say, sir – Lady Teazle, being apprehensive of the jealousy of your temper – and knowing my friendship to the family – she, sir, I say – called here – in order that – I might explain these pretensions – but on your coming – being apprehensive – as I said – of your jealousy – she withdrew – and this, you may depend on it, is the whole truth of the matter.

SIR PETER: A very clear account, upon my word; and I dare swear the lady will vouch for every article of it.

LADY TEAZLE: For not one word of it, Sir Peter.

SIR PETER: How? Don't you even think it worth while to agree in the lie?

LADY TEAZLE: There is not one syllable of truth in what that gentleman has told you.

SIR PETER: I believe you, upon my soul, ma'am.

JOSEPH [*aside to* LADY TEAZLE]: 'Sdeath, madam, will you betray me?

LADY TEAZLE: Good Mr Hypocrite, by your leave, I'll speak for myself.

SIR PETER: Aye, let her alone, sir; you'll find she'll make out a better story than you, without prompting.

> LADY TEAZLE: Hear me, Sir Peter! I came hither on no matter relating to your ward, and even ignorant of this gentleman's pretensions to her. But I came seduced by his insidious arguments, at least to listen to his pretended passion, if not to sacrifice your honour to his baseness.
>
> SIR PETER: Now I believe the truth is coming indeed!
>
> JOSEPH: The woman's mad!
>
> LADY TEAZLE: No, sir, she has recovered her senses, and your own arts have furnished her with the means. Sir Peter, I do not expect you to credit me, but the tenderness you expressed for me, when I am sure you could not think I was a witness to it, has penetrated so to my heart, that had I left the place without the shame of this discovery, my future life should have spoken the sincerity of my gratitude. As for that smooth-tongued hypocrite, who would have seduced the wife of his too credulous friend, while he affected honourable addresses to his ward – I behold him now in a light so truly despicable that I shall never again respect myself for having listened to him.
>
> [*Exit.*]
>
> JOSEPH: Notwithstanding all this, Sir Peter, heaven knows –
>
> SIR PETER: That you are a villain! And so I leave you to your conscience.
>
> JOSEPH: You are too rash, Sir Peter; you shall hear me. The man who shuts out conviction by refusing to –
>
> [*Exeunt,* JOSEPH SURFACE *following and speaking.*]

> **Examiner's tip**
>
> Many writers use the idea of characters hiding from each other to produce humour. You have probably read other examples or have seen the technique used in plays or situation comedies on the television. Be aware of theatrical techniques of this kind when you are watching television.

It is a long scene. Use it as a basis to practise your skills of summarising plot and of making your own comments.

Read it through carefully and write your own summary under the following headings:

- The changing behaviour of Joseph Surface.
- How Sir Peter and Lady Teazle, despite everything, come together.
- The importance of the screen.

Throughout the play there are little touches of witty humour, a particularly pleasant one being an account of a supposed duel:

> CRABTREE: Sir Peter forced Charles to take one and they fired, it seems, pretty nearly together. Charles's shot took place, as I told you and Sir Peter's missed; but, what is very extraordinary, the ball struck against a little bronze Pliny that stood over the fireplace, grazed out of the window at a right angle, and wounded the postman, who was just coming to the door with a double letter from Northamptonshire.

What we have in *The School for Scandal* is a pleasant comedy of manners involving two couples who we hope will live happily together ever after: Sir Peter and Lady Teazle, and Charles and Maria. Their happiness is threatened throughout the play by the group of gossips including Joseph Surface. The nature of the comedy is such that everything is bound to turn out all right in the end.

6.3 *The Importance of Being Earnest*

Although there is none of the malice in the background of *The Importance of Being Earnest* this play, which comes about a hundred years later, could also be termed a comedy of manners. It was described by Oscar Wilde himself as 'a trivial play for serious people'.

The plot

At the beginning of the play Algernon is waiting for his aunt, Lady Bracknell, to arrive for tea. While he is waiting, his friend Ernest (Jack) Worthing arrives. He has come especially to propose to Lady Bracknell's daughter, Gwendoline. Jack is the guardian of Cecily who is a young heiress. His name is really Jack and Ernest is a supposed younger brother who he has invented simply to justify his trips to London. This intrigues Algernon as he also uses an invented character, 'Bunbury', who he pretends is ill when he wants to leave London to visit the country. Algernon takes Lady Bracknell out of the way when she arrives to enable Jack to propose to Gwendoline. Gwendoline loves him but says clearly that she also loves his name Ernest and could not tolerate any other name. Lady Bracknell decides, however, that everything is impossible because Jack can produce no parents as he was found in a handbag on Victoria Station.

The action of the play then moves to Jack's country house and Algernon arrives. He has come to see Cecily and is pretending to be Ernest. By the end of the act both girls believe that they are engaged to Ernest Worthing and when the two men walk in, the ladies are appalled and leave the room.

In the third act of the play the two young couples are reconciled but Lady Bracknell arrives and almost spoils everything by refusing her consent to the marriages. In the middle of this, Miss Prism, Cecily's governess, is revealed as having worked earlier for Lady Bracknell and it was she who had absent-mindedly left Jack in her handbag at the station. Jack is really Algernon's brother and is really named Ernest and everything ends, of course, perfectly.

The language

The plot of the play is quite trivial, but is written in a way which is light, humorous and pleasant. We could take many examples to show you how witty and clever the language is. Below, for instance, is an extract from Act One when Jack and Algernon are talking about the invented Ernest and Bunbury.

> JACK: Yes... Charming old lady she is, too. Lives at Tunbridge Wells. Just give it back to me, Algy.
>
> ALGERNON [*retreating to back of sofa*]: But why does she call herself little Cecily if she is your aunt and lives at Tunbridge Wells? [*Reading.*] 'From little Cecily with her fondest love.'
>
> JACK [*moving to sofa and kneeling upon it*]: My dear fellow, what on earth is there in that? Some aunts are tall, some aunts are not tall. That is a matter that surely an aunt may be allowed to decide for herself. You seem to think that every aunt should be exactly like your aunt! That is absurd! For Heaven's sake give me back my cigarette case. [*Follows* ALGERNON *round the room.*]
>
> ALGERNON: Yes. But why does your aunt call you her uncle? 'From little Cecily, with her fondest love to her dear uncle Jack.' There is no objection, I admit, to an aunt being a small aunt, but why an aunt, no matter what her size may be, should call her own nephew her uncle, I can't quite make out. Besides, your name isn't Jack at all; it is Ernest.
>
> JACK: It isn't Ernest; it's Jack.
>
> ALGERNON: You have always told me it was Ernest. I have introduced you to every one as Ernest. You answer to the name of Ernest. You look as if your name was Ernest. You are the most earnest-looking person I ever saw in my life. It is perfectly absurd your saying that your name isn't Ernest. It's on your cards. Here is one of them. [*Taking it from case.*] 'Mr Ernest Worthing, B.4, The Albany.' I'll keep this as a proof that your name is Ernest if ever you attempt to deny it to me, or to Gwendolen, or to any one else. [*Puts the card in his pocket.*]

JACK: Well, my name is Ernest in town and Jack in the country, and the cigarette case was given to me in the country.

ALGERNON: Yes, but that does not account for the fact that your small Aunt Cecily, who lives at Tunbridge Wells, calls you her dear uncle. Come, old boy, you had much better have the thing out at once.

JACK: My dear Algy, you talk exactly as if you were a dentist. It is very vulgar to talk like a dentist when one isn't a dentist. It produces a false impression.

ALGERNON: Well, that is exactly what dentists always do. Now, go on! Tell me the whole thing. I may mention that I have always suspected you of being a confirmed and secret Bunburyist; and I am quite sure of it now.

JACK: Bunburyist? What on earth do you mean by a Bunburyist?

ALGERNON: I'll reveal to you the meaning of that incomparable expression as soon as you are kind enough to inform me why you are Ernest in town and Jack in the country.

JACK: Well, produce my cigarette case first.

ALGERNON: Here it is. [*Hands cigarette case.*] Now produce your explanation, and pray make it improbable. [*Sits on sofa.*]

JACK: My dear fellow, there is nothing improbable about my explanation at all. In fact it's perfectly ordinary. Old Mr Thomas Cardew, who adopted me when I was a little boy, made me in his will guardian to his grand-daughter, Miss Cecily Cardew. Cecily, who addresses me as her uncle from motives of respect that you could not possibly appreciate, lives at my place in the country under the charge of her admirable governess, Miss Prism.

ALGERNON: Where is that place in the country, by the way?

JACK: That is nothing to you, dear boy. You are not going to be invited … I may tell you candidly that the place is not in Shropshire.

ALGERNON: I suspected that, my dear fellow! I have Bunburyed all over Shropshire on two separate occasions. Now, go on. Why are you Ernest in town and Jack in the country?

JACK: My dear Algy, I don't know whether you will be able to understand my real motives. You are hardly serious enough. When one is placed in the position of guardian, one has to adopt a very high moral tone on all subjects. It's one's duty to do so. And as a high moral tone can hardly be said to conduce very much to either one's health or one's happiness, in order to get up to town I have always pretended to have a younger brother of the name of Ernest, who lives in the Albany, and gets into the most dreadful scrapes. That, my dear Algy, is the whole truth pure and simple.

ALGERNON: The truth is rarely pure and never simple. Modern life would be very tedious if it were either, and modern literature a complete impossibility!

JACK: That wouldn't be at all a bad thing.

ALGERNON: Literary criticism is not your forte, my dear fellow. Don't try it. You should leave that to people who haven't been at a University. They do it so well in the daily papers. What you really are is a Bunburyist. You are one of the most advanced Bunburyists I know.

JACK: What on earth do you mean?

ALGERNON: You have invented a very useful younger brother called Ernest, in order that you may be able to come up to town as often as you like. I have invented an invaluable permanent invalid called Bunbury, in order that I may be able to go down into the country whenever I choose. Bunbury is perfectly invaluable. If it wasn't for Bunbury's extraordinary bad health, for instance, I

> wouldn't be able to dine with you at Willis's to-night, for I have been really engaged to Aunt Augusta for more than a week.
>
> JACK: I haven't asked you to dine with me anywhere to-night.
>
> ALGERNON: I know. You are absurdly careless about sending out invitations. It is very foolish of you. Nothing annoys people so much as not receiving invitations.
>
> JACK: You had much better dine with your Aunt Augusta.
>
> ALGERNON: I haven't the smallest intention of doing anything of the kind. To begin with, I dined there on Monday, and once a week is quite enough to dine with one's own relations. In the second place, whenever I do dine there I am always treated as a member of the family, and sent down with either no woman at all, or two. In the third place, I know perfectly well whom she will place me next to, to-night. She will place me next to Mary Farquhar, who always flirts with her own husband across the dinner-table. That is not very pleasant. Indeed, it is not even decent ... and that sort of thing is enormously on the increase. The amount of women in London who flirt with their own husbands is perfectly scandalous. It looks so bad. It is simply washing one's clean linen in public. Besides, now that I know you to be a confirmed Bunburyist I naturally want to talk to you about Bunburying. I want to tell you the rules.
>
> JACK: I'm not a Bunburyist at all. If Gwendolen accepts me, I am going to kill my brother, indeed I think I'll kill him in any case. Cecily is a little too much interested in him. It is rather a bore. So I am going to get rid of Ernest. And I strongly advise you to do the same with Mr ... with your invalid friend who has the absurd name.
>
> ALGERNON: Nothing will induce me to part with Bunbury, and if you ever get married, which seems to me extremely problematic, you will be very glad to know Bunbury. A man who marries without knowing Bunbury has a very tedious time of it.
>
> JACK: That is nonsense. If I marry a charming girl like Gwendolen, and she is the only girl I ever saw in my life that I would marry, I certainly won't want to know Bunbury.
>
> ALGERNON: Then your wife will. You don't seem to realise, that in married life three is company and two is none.
>
> JACK [*sententiously*]: That, my dear young friend, is the theory that the corrupt French Drama has been propounding for the last fifty years.
>
> ALGERNON: Yes; and that the happy English home has proved in half the time.

As another example of the style, below is a short extract from Act Three.

> LADY BRACKNELL: The marriage, I think, had better take place quite soon.
>
> ALGERNON: Thank you, Aunt Augusta.
>
> CECILY: Thank you, Aunt Augusta.
>
> LADY BRACKNELL: To speak frankly, I am not in favour of long engagements. They give people the opportunity of finding out each other's character before marriage, which I think is never advisable.
>
> JACK: I beg pardon for interrupting you, Lady Bracknell, but this engagement is quite out of the question. I am Miss Cardew's guardian, and she cannot marry without my consent until she comes of age. That consent I absolutely decline to give.

Lady Bracknell: Upon what grounds may I ask? Algernon is an extremely, I may almost say an ostentatiously, eligible young man. He has nothing, but he looks everything. What more can one desire?

Jack: It pains me very much to have to speak frankly to you, Lady Bracknell, about your nephew, but the fact is that I do not approve at all of his moral character. I suspect him of being untruthful. [Algernon *and* Cecily *look at him in indignant amazement.*]

Lady Bracknell: Untruthful! My nephew Algernon? Impossible! He is an Oxonian.

Jack: I fear there can be no possible doubt about the matter. This afternoon during my temporary absence in London on an important question of romance, he obtained admission to my house by means of the false pretence of being my brother. Under an assumed name he drank, I've just been informed by my butler, an entire pint bottle of my Perrier-Jouet, Brut, '89; wine I was specially reserving for myself. Continuing his disgraceful deception, he succeeded in the course of the afternoon in alienating the affections of my only ward. He subsequently stayed to tea, and devoured every single muffin. And what makes his conduct all the more heartless is, that he was perfectly well aware from the first that I have no brother, that I never had a brother, and that I don't intend to have a brother, not even of any kind. I distinctly told him so myself yesterday afternoon.

Lady Bracknell: Ahem! Mr Worthing, after careful consideration I have decided entirely to overlook my nephew's conduct to you.

Jack: That is very generous of you, Lady Bracknell. My own decision, however, is unalterable. I decline to give my consent.

Lady Bracknell [*to* Cecily]: Come here, sweet child. [Cecily *goes over.*] How old are you, dear?

Cecily: Well, I am really only eighteen, but I always admit to twenty when I go to evening parties.

Lady Bracknell: You are perfectly right in making some slight alteration. Indeed, no woman should ever be quite accurate about her age. It looks so calculating ... [*In a meditative manner.*] Eighteen, but admitting to twenty at evening parties. Well, it will not be very long before you are of age and free from the restraints of tutelage. So I don't think your guardian's consent is, after all, a matter of any importance.

Jack: Pray excuse me, Lady Bracknell, for interrupting you again, but it is only fair to tell you that according to the terms of her grandfather's will Miss Cardew does not come legally of age till she is thirty-five.

Lady Bracknell: That does not seem to me to be a grave objection. Thirty-five is a very attractive age. London society is full of women of the very highest birth who have, of their own free choice, remained thirty-five for years. Lady Dumbleton is an instance in point. To my own knowledge she has been thirty-five ever since she arrived at the age of forty, which was many years ago now. I see no reason why our dear Cecily should not be even still more attractive at the age you mention than she is at present. There will be a large accumulation of property.

Cecily: Algy, could you wait for me till I was thirty-five?

Algernon: Of course I could, Cecily. You know I could.

Cecily: Yes, I felt it instinctively, but I couldn't wait all that time. I hate waiting even five minutes for anybody. It always makes me rather cross. I am not punctual myself, I know, but I do like punctuality in others, and waiting, even to be married, is quite out of the question.

Chapter 6 Responding to drama: pre-1900 plays

> ALGERNON: Then what is to be done, Cecily?
>
> CECILY: I don't know, Mr Moncrieff.
>
> LADY BRACKNELL: My dear Mr Worthing, as Miss Cardew states positively that she cannot wait till she is thirty-five – a remark which I am bound to say seems to be to show a somewhat impatient nature – I would beg of you to re-consider your decision.
>
> JACK: But my dear Lady Bracknell, the matter is entirely in your own hands. The moment you consent to my marriage with Gwendolen, I will most gladly allow your nephew to form an alliance with my ward.
>
> LADY BRACKNELL [*rising and drawing herself up*]: You must be quite aware that what you propose is out of the question.
>
> JACK: Then a passionate celibacy is all that any of us can look forward to.
>
> LADY BRACKNELL: That is the destiny I propose for Gwendolen. Algernon, of course, can choose for himself. [*Pulls out her watch.*] Come, dear, [GWENDOLEN *rises.*] we have already missed five, if not six, trains. To miss any more might expose us to comment on the platform.

Examiner's tip

If you can, watch a video of *The Importance of Being Earnest*. This will help you to understand the style of the play. It is likely that your teacher will use videos of your texts in class. If not, it is always useful to watch a video to remember that what you will see is only one interpretation of the work and you won't necessarily agree with it.

The style of Oscar Wilde is very distinctive and the extracts you have read are two very good examples of it. One type of response to literature, mentioned elsewhere in this book (pp.45–46), is known as 're-creative literature'. It is a type of response to literature which is often included in coursework.

As an interesting exercise, invent for yourself a group of four or five characters, perhaps a group at some function like a wedding reception or a school open day, and write a few pages of their conversation in the style of Oscar Wilde. Remember that the style is witty and in no way malicious, unlike that in *The School for Scandal*.

Characters

You may find the characters in *The Importance of Being Earnest* rather superficial but remember that this is what they are meant to be. For instance, Algernon is simply a pleasant young man who has few cares in the world and who falls in love. Miss Prism is a simple caricature of a bumbling absent-minded governess. We don't have even to consider it unlikely that she would have forgotten a baby in a handbag; we can just accept the fact that she did. Similarly, Lady Bracknell is a gloriously outrageous snob who is not objectionable because she is so exaggerated.

We have now examined three plays, all of which were written before 1900. You will find them rather different from the plays of the twentieth century which we have looked at. You might like to consider those differences when you have studied both chapters.

Chapter 7
Responding to Shakespeare

Getting started

The study of Shakespeare is now a compulsory part of National Curriculum English. All GCSE English Literature courses have to include pre-twentieth century drama and it is generally agreed that the most sensible way to meet this requirement is by studying a play by Shakespeare. Shakespeare wrote mainly plays – thirty-six in all (plus two with John Fletcher) – but he also wrote poetry. The study of Shakespeare's work may include, therefore, some plays, some sonnets and, possibly, one of the longer poems.

Most examination boards expect candidates to offer writing about Shakespeare in their coursework. This is because there is a considerable amount of shared coursework between English and English Literature.

7.1 Understanding the text

Shakespeare wrote his plays between 1589 and 1613. He wrote them to be performed in the theatre. His intention was to entertain. This does not mean that he did not have serious purposes in mind when he wrote, but he had to bear in mind that he wanted to attract audiences to see the plays performed. It is very easy to forget this when studying a play for examination purposes.

It is also important to keep in mind that the words we read in a text are designed to be used by actors portraying a part. The character may be happy or distressed, angry or foolish; whatever the mood and attitude, the words have to fit the action. This should make us aware, too, that from the words we can work out the feelings, ideas and opinions of a character. Our imaginations should help us to think about what is happening.

Stage directions also help us keep in mind what is happening. In editions of Shakespeare plays these are never detailed. Basically they tell us who is on stage, who leaves, who enters. There are also indications of who hears what is being said by another character. It is important not to assume that everyone on stage hears what is going on. Other stage directions help to create atmosphere which tells us about the significance of what is happening. The weather may be important – storms, in particular, are significant in Shakespeare. Watch out, too, for directions about battles or important people: the sounding of trumpets is a good indicator that someone or something meaningful is being signalled.

Many approaches to plays in general, including those of Shakespeare, now emphasise that the student should understand and write about what happens on stage. Plays are not novels! It always helps to see plays performed in the theatre if possible; failing this there are now many excellent films, which are often available on video. These all help in the study of plays, but students should always be careful to check the text: producers have been known to cut lines, change the order of events, and omit minor characters.

Finally, it is important to remember that most speeches in Shakespeare are written in verse. When, on occasions, there is a passage in prose it is for a particular reason. As with the study of poetry it is always good to read aloud when trying to understand a speech. The rhythm and pattern of the lines, as well as the words and the sentences, help to convey meaning.

Looking at one scene in detail

In Act One Scene Three of *Macbeth*, Macbeth and his colleague Banquo are returning from battle. The battle has been important for Scotland because both the traitors (Scots fighting their own King) and the invaders have been defeated. This is the cause of great joy and Duncan the King should now feel safe on his throne. Things do not, however, turn out like that. Below is the first part of the scene where Macbeth and Banquo meet three witches. As you read it and try to imagine what is happening remember that the scene is set on a 'heath', a wild and desolate piece of countryside, and that a storm ('thunder and lightning') is raging.

Read the first part of the scene through. Imagine what is happening. Collect together all the clues you can from the text to help you. When you have done this, compare your ideas with those which follow the extract.

> [*Enter* MACBETH *and* BANQUO.]
>
> MACBETH: So foul and fair a day I have not seen.
>
> BANQUO: How far is't called to Forres? What are these,
>   So withered and so wild in their attire,
>   That look not like th'inhabitants o'th'earth,
>   And yet are on't? – Live you, or are you aught
>   That man may question? You seem to understand me,
>   By each at once her choppy finger laying
>   Upon her skinny lips; you should be women
>   And yet your beards forbid me to interpret
>   That you are so.
>
> MACBETH: Speak if you can: what are you?
>
> FIRST WITCH: All hail Macbeth, hail to thee, Thane of Glamis.
>
> SECOND WITCH: All hail Macbeth, hail to thee, Thane of Cawdor.
>
> THIRD WITCH: All hail Macbeth, that shalt be king hereafter.
>
> BANQUO: Good sir, why do you start and seem to fear
>   Things that do sound so fair? – I'th'name of truth
>   Are ye so fantastical, or that indeed
>   Which outwardly ye show? My noble partner
>   You greet with present grace and great prediction
>   Of noble having and of royal hope
>   That he seems rapt withal. To me you speak not.
>   If you can look into the seeds of time
>   And say which grain will grow and which will not,
>   Speak then to me, who neither beg nor fear
>   Your favours nor your hate.
>
> FIRST WITCH: Hail.
>
> SECOND WITCH: Hail.
>
> THIRD WITCH: Hail.
>
> FIRST WITCH: Lesser than Macbeth, and greater.
>
> SECOND WITCH: Not so happy, yet much happier.
>
> THIRD WITCH: Thou shalt get kings, though thou be none.
>   So all hail Macbeth and Banquo.
>
> FIRST WITCH: Banquo and Macbeth, all hail.

7.1 Understanding the text

> MACBETH: Stay, you imperfect speakers. Tell me more.
> By Sinel's death, I know I am Thane of Glamis,
> But how of Cawdor? The Thane of Cawdor lives
> A prosperous gentleman, and to be king
> Stands not within the prospect of belief,
> No more than to be Cawdor. Say from whence
> You owe this strange intelligence, or why
> Upon this blasted heath you stop our way
> With such prophetic greeting? Speak, I charge you.
> [*Witches vanish.*]
>
> BANQUO: The earth hath bubbles, as the water has,
> And these are of them. Whither are they vanished?
>
> MACBETH: Into the air, and what seemed corporal,
> Melted, as breath into the wind. Would they had stayed!
>
> BANQUO: Were such things here as we do speak about?
> Or have we eaten on the insane root,
> That takes the reason prisoner?
>
> MACBETH: Your children shall be kings.
>
> BANQUO: You shall be king.
>
> MACBETH: And Thane of Cawdor too: went it not so?
>
> BANQUO: To th'selfsame tune and words – who's here?

Macbeth and Banquo are returning from the battle, but they do not speak of their success. Instead, Macbeth's opening words are strange – he talks of a day both fair and foul. They are interrupted in their speech by the sight of three old women who speak directly to Macbeth. He is greeted formally as Thane of Glamis, Thane of Cawdor and as 'king hereafter'. Banquo's speech tells us that Macbeth is immediately affected by the witches' prophecies – he is 'rapt withal', in a world of his own. Noting this, Banquo asks the witches to speak to him; they say his sons will become kings, though there is no prospect of this honour for Banquo himself. None of this seems to register with Macbeth: he is thinking of what they said to him and trying to reason his way through it all. The witches will not be questioned further and they 'vanish'.

What we should notice here is the presentation of character, the setting in which these events occur and the way we are prepared for what happens next.

- We have heard a lot already of 'brave Macbeth'. Well here he is. He senses something strange about the day and the occasion – 'So foul and fair a day...'. He is the object of the witches' attention; they greet him by his present title (Glamis) and suggest two to follow – Cawdor and king. Macbeth is taken by these suggestions; he is thinking of them and of their implications. A little later he wants to know what it all means. When the witches have gone he tries to work it all out with Banquo's help. Macbeth concentrates his thoughts on the prophecies; Banquo tries to find an explanation for the women themselves.

- As we have already noted it is a barren and hostile landscape in which these things happen. Thunder and lightning signal disturbances. There is a suggestion here that unnatural things are about to happen and for Shakespeare this is an important idea: unnatural happenings have dire consequences.

- The words 'foul' and 'fair' are important here. They introduce a number of ideas in the play, such as the differences between appearance and reality and how one thing can seem different according to circumstances. In addition, we are introduced to the idea of Macbeth becoming king and it is obvious that the idea grasps his attention. Later in this extract we see that the idea of becoming king is, in Macbeth's mind, as remote a possibility as becoming Thane of Cawdor. The audience, unlike Macbeth, already knows that Cawdor is condemned to death and Macbeth is to be rewarded with his title and his lands. We should also note here that Banquo's part in the future of the Scottish monarchy is referred to: his sons will be kings.

In the second part of this scene we see Ross and Angus, messengers from the King, bringing news to Macbeth and Banquo. Look at the extract below and work out what advice should be given to actors who wish to present the scene effectively on stage.

[*Enter* Ross *and* Angus.]

Ross: The King hath happily received, Macbeth,
   The news of thy success, and when he reads
   Thy personal venture in the rebels' fight,
   His wonders and his praises do contend
   Which should be thine or his. Silenced with that,
   In viewing o'er the rest o'th'selfsame day,
   He finds thee in the stout Norwegian ranks,
   Nothing afeard of what thyself didst make,
   Strange images of death. As thick as tale
   Came post with post, and every one did bear
   Thy praises in his kingdom's great defence,
   And poured them down before him.

Angus: We are sent
   To give thee from our royal master thanks;
   Only to herald thee into his sight,
   Not pay thee.

Ross: And for an earnest of a greater honour,
   He bade me, from him, call thee Thane of Cawdor:
   In which addition, hail most worthy thane,
   For it is thine.

Banquo: What, can the devil speak true?

Macbeth: The Thane of Cawdor lives. Why do you dress me
   In borrowed robes?

Angus: Who was the thane, lives yet,
   But under heavy judgement bears that life
   Which he deserves to lose.
   Whether he was combined with those of Norway,
   Or did line the rebel with hidden help
   And vantage, or that with both he laboured
   In his country's wrack, I know not,
   But treasons capital, confessed and proved,
   Have overthrown him.

Macbeth [*aside*]:   Glamis, and Thane of Cawdor:
   The greatest is behind. – Thanks for your pains. –
   [*To Banquo.*] Do you not hope your children shall be kings,
   When those that gave the Thane of Cawdor to me
   Promised no less to them?

Banquo: That, trusted home,
   Might yet enkindle you unto the crown,
   Besides the Thane of Cawdor. But 'tis strange,
   And oftentimes, to win us to our harm,
   The instruments of darkness tell us truths;
   Win us with honest trifles, to betray's
   In deepest consequence. –
   Cousins, a word, I pray you.

Macbeth [*aside*]:   Two truths are told,
   As happy prologues to the swelling act
   Of the imperial theme. – I thank you, gentlemen. –
   This supernatural soliciting
   Cannot be ill, cannot be good. If ill,
   Why hath it given me earnest of success,
   Commencing in a truth? I am Thane of Cawdor.
   If good, why do I yield to that suggestion,
   Whose horrid image doth unfix my hair
   And make my seated heart knock at my ribs
   Against the use of nature? Present fears
   Are less than horrible imaginings.
   My thought, whose murther yet is but fantastical,
   Shakes so my single state of man
   That function is smothered in surmise,
   And nothing is, but what is not.

> BANQUO: Look how our partner's rapt.
> MACBETH: If chance will have me king, why chance may crown me
>   Without my stir.
> BANQUO: New honours come upon him
>   Like our strange garments, cleave not to their mould,
>   But with the aid of use.
> MACBETH [*aside*]:   Come what come may,
>   Time and the hour run through the roughest day.
> BANQUO: Worthy Macbeth, we stay upon your leisure.
> MACBETH: Give me your favour. My dull brain was wrought
>   With things forgotten. Kind gentlemen, your pains
>   Are registered where every day I turn
>   The leaf to read them. Let us toward the king.
>   [*To Banquo.*] Think upon what hath chanced and at more time,
>   The interim having weighed it, let us speak
>   Our free hearts each to other.
> BANQUO: Very gladly.
> MACBETH: Till then, enough. – Come friends.
>
>   [*Exeunt.*]

7.2 Getting to know the plot

By looking at a scene from *Macbeth* in detail you should now have a good idea about the way Shakespeare wrote. It is now worth trying to consider a whole play and how to approach it for the first time.

When you open a text you will notice that all the characters are listed for you at the beginning. There may be an introduction written by someone who has edited the play, but this is probably best looked at after a first reading. So turn to the play itself. It will be divided into acts and scenes. Each Shakespeare play has five acts: these are the major divisions of the play. Each act has a number of scenes and these vary in length considerably. In *Macbeth*, for example, there are seven scenes in Act One, but only three in Act Four.

Many plays have more than one story line or plot and these are interwoven. In *Twelfth Night* there is the plot concerning Count Orsino and his love for Olivia; there is also the baiting of Malvolio and the antics of Sir Toby and his friends. Commentators on Shakespeare's plays often refer to the 'main plot' and the 'sub-plot'. On any first reading of a play it is important to get a good idea of the action. It does not matter for the first read if details are unclear, but the main lines of the plot should be established.

An important part of any story is the way it develops. Stories are full of changes, surprises and the unexpected. Readers get interested in guessing what is going to happen, and working out what causes particular events. Very often in a story events build up to a disastrous climax; after that it is a question of seeing how this event changes things for the characters involved.

Examining a plot in detail

Note down the main developments in the play you are studying, perhaps using a flow diagram. Indicate the most important event or climax. Show how this changes things for the characters from then onwards.

Examiner's tip

You are probably using this guide because you are already studying a play. The following approach may be used with any play:
- Identify how many plots there are.
- Work out the main events in each plot.
- Be clear about the characters involved in them.

Here is an example, drawing upon the events in *Macbeth*.
- The play is concerned with Macbeth becoming king.
- Macbeth (with Banquo) meets the witches who suggest he will be king.
- Macbeth thinks about this and about murder.
- He becomes Thane of Cawdor so thinks that he may be king.
- He sees Malcolm named heir and realises that he must act to reach the throne.
- He tells his wife (by letter) of these events and she determines to make him king.
- When he meets his wife and Duncan comes to stay with them Lady Macbeth has already formed a plan.
- Macbeth himself keeps changing his mind and knows that murdering the king is wrong.
- *But Macbeth murders Duncan.*

The murder is the turning point of the play. Macbeth becomes king, but he never enjoys his position. He is full of worries and anxieties. He plans more murders. He grows away from his wife, who becomes less and less important in the play. He becomes desperate and goes to see the witches again. He places his trust in their answers to his questions, but their answers are full of double meanings. Deserted by so many of his followers, Macbeth fights to the last but is killed by MacDuff.

Once you have a good idea about what happens it is possible to start asking questions. Examination questions sometimes focus on why certain events occur. These are perfectly natural questions that any reader will want to ask. So, in *Macbeth*, we might consider:
- What makes Macbeth wish to be king?
- What part does Lady Macbeth play in the murder of Duncan?
- How is it that Macbeth is successful?
- Why is he not under suspicion for the murder?
- What part do the witches play in influencing Macbeth?

To answer these questions fully a good knowledge of events is required. As long as you have a fair idea of where to start, with the help of the text it is possible to work out events, stage by stage. When you do this you will be deciding on the relationship between cause and effect in the story.

7.3 Looking at characters

Plays are made up of people and what they do. We have already thought about what happens — the plot — and how to come to understand it. We must now consider the people who appear in the plays. These are referred to as 'characters'. A great deal of Shakespeare study concentrates on characters — what they do, why they do it and how the audience or reader should respond. Obviously Shakespeare's characters are not real people, no matter how much Shakespeare used ideas and experiences from those he met. What we know about them comes only from the plays themselves. Within a play we see what a character does and says and what is said about him or her. From these sources we can build up a picture of a character in our own minds.

It is common practice for examination boards to set questions on the characters in a play. One main character, or a particular aspect of his or her behaviour may be chosen. Alternatively, several minor characters may be grouped together. The idea of 'major' and 'minor' characters is a useful one. In *Macbeth* Macbeth, Lady Macbeth and MacDuff are all major characters; Donalbain, Malcolm, Ross and Angus are all minor characters. These classifications depend on the significance of a character to the whole play as well as on the amount of action or speech that he or she is involved in. In other plays, *Twelfth Night* is a good example, it is more difficult to divide the characters into 'major' or 'minor'. Orsino is vital to the plot, but he does not have a large share in the action. Is he a major or a minor character? Feste, the clown, has a very significant role to play, but is he a major or a minor character? There are other characters, too, who could be thought of in this way. Remember that it is only useful to employ the idea of major and minor characters if it helps in the study of the play.

7.3 Looking at characters

How to study a character

When you wish to study a character, here are some of the things you should do.

1. Identify the main scenes in which he or she appears.
2. Summarise for yourself what he or she does.
3. Look at what is said – which are the most important speeches telling you what the character is doing?
4. Look at what is said about the character by others, especially the most important characters.
5. Think about the reactions you have as you read. Do you like or dislike the character? Do you admire or despise him or her? Do you understand why he or she says and does particular things?
6. Remember that the whole play is the context for judging character.
7. Remember that plays are for audiences, and audiences need to be involved – so feeling angry, tense, excited, disapproving, annoyed, happy are all part of the experience of the play.

Studying a major character: Lady Macbeth

Let us look at Lady Macbeth. She is a major character although she only appears in the first three acts and the first scene of the final act. Anyone studying the play will recognise that she is an important influence on her husband and his path to the throne of Scotland. Here are some questions which might be asked about her:

- What influence does Lady Macbeth have upon Macbeth?
- Who influences Macbeth more – his wife or the witches?
- What are the important features of Lady Macbeth's character?
- What is different for Lady Macbeth after her husband has become king?
- Why does Lady Macbeth become mad?
- Why does Lady Macbeth die in the way she does?

If you are building up a full picture of Lady Macbeth, especially for examinations, you will need to cover all these points.

Let us suppose now that you have to answer this coursework or examination question:

■ Why does Lady Macbeth become mad?

An answer to this question requires a close look at Act Five Scene One, sometimes called the 'sleepwalking' scene. The scene begins with Lady Macbeth's servant talking to the Doctor who has been called in to help with a severe problem. The servant (or gentlewoman) is concerned about what she has seen Lady Macbeth do many times before, so this is no isolated incident. The servant is very worried indeed about her mistress. Lady Macbeth, she tells the Doctor, not only walks in her sleep, but performs certain actions and says certain things as well. There may be more at stake here, then, than Lady Macbeth's health.

The Doctor (and the audience) observe Lady Macbeth closely. She carries a light which is always by her side when it is dark. She rubs her hands together, imitating 'washing', the servant says. When she speaks it is to talk of a 'damned spot', of fear, of an old man and blood. Later she speaks of her hands smelling of blood and then of washing and putting on a nightgown. She also refers to the Thane of Fife (MacDuff) and to Banquo.

The audience does not need many hints to see that Lady Macbeth is constantly reliving the night of Duncan's murder. Then she was full of confidence; she mocked her husband's fear and said she would have killed Duncan herself had he not resembled her own father. On that night she had made the plans and prepared the alibi. She had even said:

> A little water clears us of this deed.
> How easy is it then!

But now it is clear that she is full of guilt; the murder is preying on her mind. When Macbeth killed Duncan he heard a voice call, 'Sleep no more' and he told us that 'the innocent sleep'. Now there is no sleep for his wife, at least no peaceful sleep that might 'knit up the sleeve of ravelled care' (Act Two Scene Two, line 37). Furthermore, Lady Macbeth had said on the night of Duncan's murder:

> These deeds must not be thought of
> After these ways; so, it will make us mad.

What she said then, has happened to her now.

It is obvious that Shakespeare wrote the 'sleepwalking' scene with the earlier scene very much in mind. What Lady Macbeth had thought easy and without difficulty has proved to be the opposite; the advice she gave to her husband to shrug off his guilt has turned against her. She has no peace, no easy mind; she is burdened with guilt. She is unbalanced, obsessed and distraught. She is of no further use to her husband and death is only a little way into the future.

This question and the example of an answer in outline, have concentrated on a particular feature of character and at a crucial point in a play. We will look next at a character in a more general way.

Studying another major character: Malvolio

Malvolio in *Twelfth Night* is a suitable character to study. An examination or coursework question might ask:

- Does Malvolio deserve the punishment he receives at the end of the play?

Such a question can only be answered by looking at his words and behaviour, particularly towards those who 'punish' him. To build up an answer you would need to look at:

- Malvolio's position in Olivia's household;
- the way he treats the other servants (including Feste, the clown);
- the way he treats Olivia's kinsman, Sir Toby Belch, and his guest, Sir Andrew Aguecheek;
- Malvolio's opinion of himself and his abilities;
- his immediate and instinctive reaction to reading the letter left in his way;
- the fact that he so easily believes it comes from his lady;
- the way he is ready to do as commanded, even though it means dressing in a ridiculous way and behaving foolishly.

From all these points it is possible to see Malvolio as self-opinionated, arrogant and lacking in any warmth or friendship for others. Once you have come to that opinion it is not difficult to see why others want to make fun of him. It is only natural to want to bring down those who give themselves airs and graces above their position or personal merits. The very fact that Malvolio believes that Olivia is in love with him, commands him to do what he does so readily ('cast thy humble slough' ... [be] surly with servants') and encourages him to do what he wants to do so often ('be opposite with a kinsman') all show an arrogant man with no idea of the way others really see him. The successful baiting of Malvolio is something that audiences delight in whenever this play is performed – probably because they can think of some 'Malvolio' of their own!

7.4 The role of minor characters and sub-plots

Quite often in Shakespeare plays you can pick out characters who seem to be a bit different, who don't fit in with the general plot, and you may well wonder what they are doing there. These are **minor characters**.

Minor characters: some examples

In Act Two Scene Three, Macbeth has just killed Duncan, Macduff is about to arrive, the murder will be discovered, Malcolm and Donalbain will run away, and Macbeth will become king. What happens? A drunken lout comes reeling about the stage, shouting and swearing.

7.4 The role of minor characters and sub-plots

He certainly is drunk as we can see from the following exchange:

> MACDUFF: Was it so late, friend, ere you went to bed,
> That you do lie so late?
>
> PORTER: Faith, Sir, we were carousing till the second cock.

He has been woken up by Macduff knocking on the great door of the castle and the knocking has been going on for some time: Macbeth and Lady Macbeth talked of it in the previous scene. The Porter eventually goes to do his job as gate keeper, and says:

> Here's a knocking indeed: If a man were Porter of Hell Gate, he should have old turning the key. [*Knocking.*] Knock, knock, knock. Who's there, i'th'name of Beelzebub? – Here's a farmer, that hang'd himself on th'expectation of plenty. – Come in, time-pleaser; have napkins enow about you, here you'll sweat for't. [*Knocking.*] Knock, knock. Who's there, i' th'other devil's name?

As you can see, he's swearing in the name of the Devil and Beelzebub; he's probably feeling hot and sweaty with his hangover and talks as if he is in charge of the gates of hell. He mentions what was possibly a well-known story of a farmer who thought the crops were going to fail and who therefore hid all his spare crop from the previous year so that he could bring it out at the right time and make a large profit. Unfortunately, there was a superb harvest and he was left with all his old crop and so hanged himself. He must have ended up going to hell. The Porter also mentions a tailor who was a thief and who also went to hell. His final words on the way to open the great door remind us that anyone, in any profession, can go the same way:

> …I had thought to have let in some of all Professions, that go the Primrose way to th'everlasting Bonfire.

When he is talking to Macduff just before he disappears, (he leaves at the moment when Macbeth reappears) it is to crack some rather crude sexual jokes concerning the effect of drink:

> …Therefore, much drink may be said to be an equivocator with lechery: it makes him, and it mars him; it sets him on, and it takes him off; it persuades him, and disheartens him; makes him stand to, and not stand to: in conclusion, equivocates him in a sleep, and giving him the lie, leaves him.

That is the Porter. He never reappears. So why does he appear?

We could look at other examples of similar characters. In *Hamlet* there are two disreputable gravediggers. They appear at a most poignant moment in the play, when Ophelia, the beautiful young heroine, has died in tragic circumstances. They are digging her grave and yet are cracking jokes and digging up bones. Like the Porter they only appear in one scene of the play.

One theory is that these characters, usually appearing in the tragedies, perform a specific function connected to the design of the Elizabethan theatre and the composition of the audience. Some members of the audience, the 'groundlings', watched the play from the centre of the theatre, in the open air, with no seats. If they were to concentrate on the very serious parts of the play perhaps they needed a few moments to fidget and let off steam. If we take our Macbeth example again, there has been a long sequence leading up to the murder of the king and the audience will soon have to concentrate on the sequence which leads up to the crowning of Macbeth as king and beyond. Visually the next bit of real excitement will be the murder of Banquo and the appearance of his ghost.

Let us suppose that, in your examination, you are tackling a question asking you to write about the minor characters in a play you have been studying. As practice, write a section of your essay, not more than a side in length, in which you analyse a character you have been examining. Your characters might be the Porter in *Macbeth* or the gravediggers in *Hamlet*; the list could go on and on.

Sometimes, especially in the comedies and the histories, these minor characters are rather more developed and, although they still cannot be termed central characters, they nevertheless have a well-developed personality of their own. If you have studied *The Merchant of Venice* you will have come across Launcelot Gobbo who, at various times, is a servant to two of the major characters in the play and Old Gobbo, his blind father. They come into this category. We are now going to look in detail at two minor characters from *Much Ado About Nothing*: Dogberry, the Constable in charge of the Watch, and Verges, the Headborough, Dogberry's partner in authority.

Examiner's tip

When you come to study one of Shakespeare's great tragedies keep an eye out for minor characters. When they appear, answer the following:
- What has happened before their appearance and what is going to happen immediately after it?
- What is their function?
- What is their relationship with the central characters of the play?
- What do they say? Analyse the type of language they use and the humour they bring with them.

The humour which these two characters generate comes in several ways. They first appear about halfway through the play in Act Three Scene Three when Dogberry takes charge of the Watchmen. It is very quickly clear that Dogberry is a pompous oaf who wants to appear very much more intelligent than he in fact is. The problem is that in trying to appear intelligent he manages to keep on muddling up words. Here are some of the things he says in Scenes Three and Five of Act Three:

> …You are thought here to be the most *senseless* and fit man for the constable of the watch; therefore bear you the lantern.
>
> …be *vigitant* I beseech you.
>
> Comparisons are *odorous*…
>
> …only get the learned writer to set down our *excommunication*, and meet me at the gaol.

He also hasn't the faintest idea how to enforce the authority which he supposedly has and so, when he is asked by the others how they should behave, his advice is preposterous:

> DOGBERRY: Well, you are to call at the ale-houses, and bid those that are drunk get them to bed.
>
> 1ST WATCHMAN: How if they will not?
>
> DOGBERRY: Why, then, let them alone till they are sober.

and

> VERGES: If you hear a child cry in the night, you must call to the nurse and bid her still it.
>
> 2ND WATCHMAN: How if the nurse be asleep and will not hear us?
>
> DOGBERRY: Why, then, depart in peace, and let the child wake her with crying; for the ewe that will not hear her lamb when it baes will never answer a calf when he bleats.

And if you think that last little saying didn't seem to make sense – it didn't!

After they have appeared in their first scene, what makes Dogberry and Verges different from characters like the Porter is that they go on and do their job. The Watch arrests two of the villains and therefore inevitably become more involved with the main characters of the play. They are required to examine these two villains and, however much Dogberry muddles his words, during the examination some very important things become clear, and they are central to the main plot of the play.

> DOGBERRY: …Masters, I charge you in the Prince's name, accuse these men.
>
> 1ST WATCHMAN: This man said, sir, that Don John, the Prince's brother, was a villain.
>
> DOGBERRY: Write down 'Prince John a villain'. Why, this is flat perjury, to call a Prince's brother villain.
>
> BORACHIO: Master Constable –
>
> DOGBERRY: Pray thee, fellow, peace. I do not like thy look, I promise thee.
>
> SEXTON: What heard you him say else?
>
> 2ND WATCHMAN: Marry, that he had received a thousand ducats of Don John for accusing the Lady Hero wrongfully.
>
> DOGBERRY: Flat burglary as ever was committed …O villain! Thou wilt be condemned into everlasting redemption for this.

Towards the end of the play the villains admit their guilt to the central characters and the jobs of Dogberry and Verges are complete. Dogberry remains incomprehensible to the end, and interestingly, perhaps to move the play towards its happy conclusion, the Prince picks up the language and speaks in similar vein.

> DON PEDRO: Officers, what offence have these men done?
>
> DOGBERRY: Marry, sir, they have committed false report; moreover they have spoken untruths; secondarily, they are slanders; sixth and lastly, they have belied a lady; thirdly, they have verified unjust things; and, to conclude, they are lying knaves.

Examiner's tip

Does the play you are studying have characters whose roles might be analysed in a similar way? If so:
- How often do they appear?
- Do they interact with the main characters of the play?
- How do they speak?
- Do they move the plot of the play forward?
- What would you judge their importance to be?

7.4 The role of minor characters and sub-plots

DON PEDRO: First, I ask thee what they have done; thirdly I ask thee what's their offence; sixth and lastly, why they are committed; and, to conclude, what you lay to their charge.

We are now going to consider the situation where minor characters are fully developed, where they appear frequently and where they have a significant part to play with at least one of the major characters: we are are going to consider the **sub-plot**.

Sub-plots: an example

You may well have studied *A Midsummer Night's Dream* in Key Stage 3. There the central plot of the play concerns marriage and, most especially, three couples who eventually become happily married. The sub-plot of the play concerns characters who are known as the Rude Mechanicals and central among them is Bottom the Weaver.

Shakespeare wrote a whole series of plays about the history of England and in each of these the central plot concerns a king and his family and the part they play in history. *Henry IV Part One*, for example, is about the first part of the reign of King Henry IV, his son Prince Hal and the attempts of rebels, most significantly Harry Hotspur, son of the Earl of Northumberland, to remove him from the throne. The sub-plot contains a character who is generally considered to be one of Shakespeare's greatest creations, Sir John Falstaff. Falstaff is a huge man who frequents a fairly disreputable tavern in Eastcheap, London, with a group of debatable characters who live very much on the fringes of the law. Perhaps surprisingly, Prince Hal becomes one of his friends – there were rebellious teenagers even then! The sub-plot is about the education of Prince Hal and his preparation for kingship and, although he doesn't realise it, Falstaff helps Prince Hall distinguish right from wrong and helps him to understand how he must behave as a king.

Let us briefly consider the role of Falstaff and the rest of his group. We meet him with the Prince in the second scene of the play where he is introduced with Prince Hal's words:

> Thou are so fat-witted with drinking of old sack, and unbuttoning thee after supper, and sleeping upon benches after noon, that thou has truly forgotten to demand that truly which thou wouldst truly know.

They have a casual conversation before another of the Prince's companions, Poins, comes in and talk turns to a robbery which is being planned. After Falstaff has gone Poins and the Prince discuss how to make a fool of him. While we find Falstaff amusing we might well ask what the Prince is doing and it is very important that right in this first scene it is clear that he will get rid of Falstaff when the time is right. We then move on to the robbery and see Falstaff being ridiculed. Poins has taken his horse away and so he has to walk, something of which he is virtually incapable. We see, though, that he is able to laugh at himself, which is what keeps him so very likeable.

PRINCE HAL: Peace, ye fat-guts, lie down, lay thine ear close to the ground and list if thou canst hear the tread of travellers.

FALSTAFF: Have you any levers to lift me up again, being down?

The robbery takes place and Poins and the Prince take the money from the robbers. This gives the opportunity for an amusing scene when Falstaff exaggerates everything in an attempt to prove his bravery.

FALSTAFF: What's the matter? There be four of us here have ta'en a thousand pound this day morning.

PRINCE HAL: Where is it, Jack, where is it?

FALSTAFF: Where is it? Taken from us it is: a hundred upon poor four of us.

PRINCE HAL: What, a hundred, man?

FALSTAFF: I am a rogue if I were not at half-sword with a dozen of them two hours together.

Falstaff has ripped his own clothes, pretending that he fought furiously, but the truth comes out. So the sub-plot moves on, with Bardolph, Peto, the Hostess of the tavern and others helping to develop the situations and characters. The characters of the sub-plot become more involved with the main plot as the inevitable confrontation between the King's forces and the rebels approaches. Falstaff is a knight and it is therefore his

---

Examiner's tip

Whatever play you are studying, you should be able to differentiate between a main plot and a sub-plot.
- Note down the different threads of the plot, deciding which is the main plot and which the sub-plot. You will find that, although characters overlap, broadly speaking there will be one group which belongs to the main plot and another which belongs to the sub-plot.
- When you have outlined the sub-plot, write about the characters and their behaviour in detail.
- Explain the purpose and importance of the sub-plot.

responsibility to fight for the King and to provide soldiers. On the battlefield his customary cowardice is evident and he pretends to be dead while Prince Hal fights with Hotspur. It is only after Hotspur is dead that Falstaff gets up. He then compounds his cowardice by stabbing Hotspur's dead body and later claiming that he killed him. The Prince, however, cannot be angry: personal glory is not of importance to him.

Falstaff, the centre of this sub-plot, has often been cited as one of Shakespeare's greatest comic creations; his zest for life makes him appealing, however outrageous his behaviour.

Putting this into practice

In the last section we have examined minor characters and sub-plots. What follows now are two examination-style questions which invite you to bring your thoughts together:

- Choose several of the minor characters from the Shakespeare play you are studying and explain in detail their roles and the significance of these.

- Analyse in detail the sub-plot of your Shakespeare text, making sure that you examine the main characters of the sub-plot and explain how the sub-plot links with the main plot of the play.

Examiner's tip

- Remember that if you were really answering these questions for an examination you would be expected to write at least two sides of A4.
- You would also need to plan the answers carefully. You would need to avoid simply writing a list, dealing with one character at a time without linking them. You would also need to guard against too much re-telling of the story.

7.5 Picking out underlying themes

We have already dealt with the main plot and sub-plots. Plots and themes are not the same thing! A plot is the way in which a theme is interpreted. So, if we say the theme of *Romeo and Juliet* is 'the tragedy of young love' then it is interpreted through the story of Romeo and Juliet and the disaster of their love for each other.

In this section we will use several plays to show examples of underlying themes: *Much Ado About Nothing*, *Macbeth* and *Henry IV Part One*. Below is a list of some of the themes which we can find in these plays. They are not in any order; put the themes with the plays.

	Much Ado About Nothing	Macbeth	Henry IV Part One
ambition			
kingship			
love			
jealousy			
the supernatural			
personal rebellion			
justice			
irresponsibility			
fear			

Ambition is the fatal flaw in the characters of both Macbeth and Lady Macbeth and it is what ultimately leads to their deaths. You can trace the way in which their ambition drives them on until it is impossible for either of them to control the situation. It leads to Lady Macbeth's sleep-walking and possible suicide; it leads to Macbeth's fatalism at the end of the play.

The responsibilities of *kingship* underpin *Henry IV Part One*. King Henry came to the throne by usurping the former king and perhaps by being involved in some way with his assassination. Right from the beginning of the play he is concerned about his position as king and talks of visiting the holy land to purge himself. He talks of this several times, although he never does go there. Prince Hal recognises that one day he will have to take up the responsibilities of kingship and, in his time with Falstaff and the others, we find this preying on his mind. There is an important scene where he and Falstaff play at being king and son. What we do know from history is that Prince Hal did become a good king, although, unfortunately, he died young.

Love is clearly a theme in *Much Ado About Nothing*. Hero and Claudio have it and nearly lose it. Beatrice and Benedick claim they don't want it, fight against it but succumb to it. *Jealousy* is the potential destroyer of the love between Hero and Claudio.

The supernatural is clearly a major theme in *Macbeth*. It is explored in a variety of ways. The three witches, joined by Hecate, seem to control the destiny of Macbeth. The predictions they make seem unstoppable although Macbeth is determined to at least try and stop them coming true in the case of Banquo. There is inevitability in the fact that he will fail. In addition to the witches we have the ghost of Banquo who wreaks havoc at the feast – is it a ghost, is it a manifestation of a guilty conscience, is it imagination? There is the procession of spectres heralding what will happen to the kingship of Scotland.

Personal rebellion is a theme which is certainly explored through the character of Prince Hal. He is determined not to behave as his father wants him to. In this sense it could be argued that he is a very modern character, a very modern teenager.

Justice is a frequently recurring theme in Shakespeare's plays. In *Much Ado About Nothing* Don John, Borachio and Conrade are brought to justice even if it is by a rather unlikely group of law enforcers. In *Macbeth* justice is done as Macbeth and Lady Macbeth die. The same could be said as the rebellion is crushed and Hotspur is killed in *Henry IV Part One*. Justice is vital; Falstaff, in his absurdity, hankers after the role of Lord Chief Justice when, uncomprehendingly, he sees himself being advanced at the right time by Prince Hal.

Irresponsibility is clearly manifested by Falstaff and his cronies. For whatever reason, it is their intention to rob a group of pilgrims at Gadshill and, although it all comes out as a joke, clearly their irresponsibility is akin to illegality. The way in which Falstaff conducts his personal life is irresponsible, relying as he does on the goodness of others such as the hostess of the tavern, Mistress Quickly. The way in which he musters troops for the king's army is also irresponsible. The way in which he claims he killed Hotspur is, again, irresponsibility linked with falsehood.

Finally, *fear* is clearly a theme in *Macbeth*. Malcolm's and Donalbain's fear shows itself in their running away. Macbeth's attempts to control his fear are part and parcel of the reasons for his action.

You can go on teasing out how various themes are dealt with. What is important to remember is that the plot is the way in which themes are interpreted.

> **Examiner's tip**
>
> To get things clear in your mind, ask yourself the following question and then write the answer along the lines suggested:
> - What are the themes of the play you are studying? (You may well find that there is one dominant theme and a number of minor themes.)
> - List them.
> - Take each theme in turn and briefly show how the plot interprets that theme.

7.6 Shakespeare's language

Elizabethan language

Many students open a Shakespeare text and immediately decide that the language is impossibly difficult and that they can't understand it. Language is continually evolving and, inevitably, much has changed in the language since the sixteenth century. Having said that, though, much is the same. Look at this extract from one of Falstaff's speeches in *Henry IV Part One*:

> Lord, Lord how this world is given to lying! I grant you I was down, and out of breath, and so was he, but we rose both at an instant, and fought a long hour by the Shrewsbury clock.

Try this extract from a speech of Benedick in *Much Ado About Nothing*:

> I will go on the slightest errand now to the Antipodes that you can devise to send me on. I will fetch you a tooth-picker from the furthest inch of Asia.

You would not have to change very much to put either of these extracts into the sort of speech which you would naturally use.

Here are a few lines from *Macbeth*. Compare them with their modern versions:

> …Therefore to horse,
> And let us not be dainty of leave-taking,
> But shift away.

> *Let's go and get mounted up. We won't bother about saying goodbye, we'll just make a dash for it.*

> Stand not upon the order of your going
> But go at once.

> *Don't bother about who goes first, just go.*

> More needs she the divine than the physician.

> *A doctor won't do her any good, she needs to talk to a priest.*

> **E**xaminer's tip
>
> Work with a partner. One of you choose a few lines from your Shakespeare text; the other put them into the sort of language you use every day.

Differences and inconsistencies

You can pick up two editions of the same Shakespeare play and find that they are not quite the same. Why is this? If you have done any work on the life of Shakespeare you will know that, as well as being a writer, he was a practical man of the theatre, an actor. The probability is that many of the plays were written as the company was rehearsing and that changes were made throughout . As a consequence, when the plays were first performed, there was no clear printed version. It was probably some time later that the copies were tidied up and printed. In that tidying-up process odd things might have been changed a little more.

So we have what are called the **quarto versions** and **folio versions**, which are often slightly different. The main parts and especially the great speeches are always the same; the differences tend to be minor.

However, don't worry! It doesn't matter what edition of the play you are using.

Verse and prose

Look at your Shakespeare text and you will probably find that it is written in a mixture of prose and verse. If we take *Henry IV Part One* again you will find that the scenes in the King's court and those in the castles and camps of the rebel nobles are written in verse, while the scenes in the tavern are written in prose. The nobility speak in verse; the commoners speak in prose. This is not always the case, but you'll find that it is frequently so.

> **E**xaminer's tip
>
> - Examine your Shakespeare text and see how a mixture of prose and verse is used.
> - Can you see a pattern which will help explain why different styles are used at different times?

The iambic pentameter

The type of verse which Shakespeare used is known as the **iambic pentameter**.

Although much of the poetry which you study is in free-verse forms with irregular patterns of rhythm, equally, some of the poetry you see is in more formal patterns, with a regular and repetitive rhythm. Notice that what we are talking about at the moment has nothing to do with rhyme.

When you look at musical notation you probably find nothing odd in seeing rhythms expressed as a series of signs on a page. Nor is there anything strange in a conductor keeping the time of the rhythm with a series of beats of his baton. Similarly, it is perfectly reasonable that the rhythm of a piece of verse can be shown in a series of signs and beats.

7.6 Shakespeare's language

You probably know from the mathematical term 'pentagon' that any word with the prefix 'pent' has something to do with the number five. A pentameter has five heavy stresses or beats. An iambus is a description of a pattern of those stresses and the unstressed sounds in between.

In shorthand symbols an iambus is shown like this: **u /** (**u** is not stressed; **/** is stressed).

If you look at Shakespeare's verse you can use the shorthand symbols five times on each line: **u / u / u / u / u /**

If we apply this to one of Macbeth's great speeches the pattern would look like this:

    u / u / u / u / u /
Tomorrow and tomorrow and tomorrow

    u / u / u / u / u /
Creeps in this petty pace from day to day

There are irregularities. You may have noticed that there seems to be an extra syllable or sound left over at the end of the first line. Sometimes you can find lines where the emphasis is very firmly on the first syllable and in such cases the shorthand signs would be reversed: **/ u**. This is clearly for effect, making the beginning of the line very important.

> **Examiner's tip**
>
> Select a short speech from your Shakespeare text and see if it fits this idea of the iambic pentameter.

Rhyme

The most common place to find rhyme in Shakespeare's plays is at the end of a scene. A rhyming couplet is a very neat way to signal the end of a scene, or a particular part of it, effectively.

If we look at *Henry IV Part One* we can find scenes that end in this way.

Act One Scene Three

HOTSPUR: Uncle, adieu. O, let the hours be short
    Till fields, and blows, and groans applaud our sport!

Act Three Scene Two

KING HENRY: Our hands are full of business, let's away
    Advantage feeds him fat while men delay.

Act Five Scene Four

PRINCE HAL: Embowelled I will see thee by and by
    Till then in blood by noble Percy lie.

You will also see rhyme used for special effects. For example, the witches in *Macbeth* frequently speak in rhyme, as do various apparitions.

Act One Scene One

1ST WITCH: When shall we three meet again?
    In thunder, lightning or in rain?

2ND WITCH: When the hurly-burly's done,
    When the battle's lost and won.

3RD WITCH: That will be ere the set of sun.

In Shakespeare's comedies we frequently find songs which can almost be taken out of context as poems in their own right. Such a one is Balthasar's song in *Much Ado About Nothing*.

BALTHASAR: Sigh no more, ladies, sigh no more,
    Men were deceivers ever,
    One foot in sea and one on shore,
    To one thing constant never:
    Then sigh not so, but let them go,
    And be you blithe and bonny,
    Converting all your sounds of woe
    Into Hey nonny, nonny.

> **Examiner's tip**
>
> - Look at the ends of scenes in your Shakespeare text.
> - Are there any characters who speak in rhyme?
> - Are there any songs?
> - Write a short paragraph on the effectiveness of any of the above in your chosen play.

Chapter 7 Responding to Shakespeare

Examiner's tip

- Take one of the main speeches from your Shakespeare text and practise speaking it in different ways. When everyone else in the family is out, march around declaiming loudly and emphasising the verse. Then speak it quietly, without emphasis.
- Which do you think is more effective?

How to speak the words

The best advice is to look at the text and speak in sentences. We have talked about iambic pentameters and rhyme but that doesn't mean that you start reading Shakespeare like a jingle. The way in which it is written might say something about the way the words were spoken in Elizabethan England. Remember that theatres tended to be open-air. The members of the audience who stood in the open centre were probably not very well behaved, and a declamatory, loud style of speaking was probably required and effective.

Theatre is much more intimate today; television even more so. As a consequence, a quieter style of speaking is more effective – and this tends to reduce the emphasis on the verse.

Using quotations in your essays

When you are writing your GCSE essays remember to use apt quotations, i.e. illustrate your points by giving examples of Shakespeare's language.

For each major character in your Shakespeare play make sure that you have three or four short, apt quotations ready which you could use if needed.

In addition it would be useful to have ready a few short quotations to illustrate the themes of a play. For instance, a few quotations to illustrate the theme of witchcraft and the supernatural in *Macbeth*; some to illustrate the theme of kingship in *Henry IV Part One*; and others to illustrate the theme of love and mistrust in *Much Ado About Nothing*.

Examiner's tip

Don't forget to prepare quotations from your Shakespeare text.

Section 5 — Poetry

Chapter 8
Responding to poetry

Getting started

> I wandered lonely as a cloud
> That floats on high o'er vales and hills,
> When all at once I saw a crowd,
> A host, of golden daffodils;
> Beside the lake, beneath the trees,
> Fluttering and dancing in the breeze.
>
> *William Wordsworth*

> 'HE'S BEHIND YER!'
> chorused the children
> but the warning came too late.
>
> The monster leaped forward
> and fastening its teeth into his neck, tore off the head.
>
> The body fell to the floor
> 'MORE' cried the children
>
> 'MORE' 'MORE'
>
> 'MORE'
>
> *Roger McGough*

What is it that these two poems have in common? What could you deduce about poetry by reading either or both of them? Poetry is an essential part of GCSE courses in both English Literature and English. But many people come to poetry thinking that it is hard to understand and even harder to write about. Alternatively, they just think all poetry is sentimental. In the introduction to the poetry anthology *Touched with Fire* (Cambridge University Press, 1985), the editor, Jack Hydes, writes, 'Poetry is literature at its best.' If this is the case, then how should we read, study and respond to poetry if we are to enjoy it, the pinnacle of the art of writing?'

It may help to identify some basic features of poetry which it is important to come to terms with, whatever period of time, or poet, or type of poetry is being studied. We can say that poetry is usually:

- short;
- full of ideas expressed in a few words;
- made up of words and phrases carefully chosen and written;
- full of images and allusions;
- concerned with feelings and opinions.

It is a requirement of the National Curriculum that you study poetry written before 1900 and in the period after it. In their English Literature courses, as in the English courses which run alongside these, the examination boards have chosen pre-1900 poets from the list drawn up in the National Curriculum. Twenty-eight poets are mentioned in the Orders, four of whom must be studied in Key Stages 3 and 4. Students can either look at a variety of poems from a number of authors, or study in more depth the minimum number required. The National Curriculum Orders also expect twentieth-century poets with 'established critical reputations' to be studied.

In this chapter we shall look at ways of organising poetry in accordance with the examination syllabuses as well as ways in which poems can be studied. The poets, whose work is used as illustration, are those most often chosen in GCSE courses.

8.1 Looking at poets

One of the advantages of looking at several poems by a single writer is that you get a feel for the sort of things he or she writes about and ways in which the subject matter is handled. It is also helpful to find out something about a poet's life and times. Everyone's thoughts, feelings and writings are the product of experience. Living at a particular time may mean sharing some of the current beliefs and ideas; it may also mean reacting against them. It can be useful to know something about the life and times of the poets you study.

An example: William Wordsworth

William Wordsworth (1770-1850) was born and grew up in the Lake District. He went to Cambridge University but did not enjoy academic work. As a young man he spent a year in France, at the time of the French Revolution; he fell in love with a woman called Annette Valois who bore him a daughter. On his return to England he started to publish poetry. At first he was a supporter of the French Revolution and wrote in its favour. But when he began to see the violence of the Revolution he became disillusioned and depressed: you can see this in his poem *The Borderers* (composed 1796-7). Wordsworth received money through a legacy and that enabled him to settle with his sister in the west country, where he met and became friends with the poet Coleridge. After a period of time he settled in Grasmere, in Cumbria. In the 1800 edition of *Lyrical Ballads* Wordsworth added an introduction giving his thoughts on how poetry should be written; for this he was heavily criticised. In 1802 Wordsworth married. He wrote a great deal in the period up to 1814. He was appointed Stamp Distributor for Westmorland in 1813 (annual salary £400) and moved to Ambleside, where he lived for the rest of his life. Wordsworth settled into the role of a conservative public man, abandoning all the radicalism of his youth. He died in 1850.

These are only outline details, but they say something to us of Wordsworth's life and times. They do not, however, tell us how he felt about things; for this you must go to the poetry. Of his childhood he tells us,

> Fair seed-time had my soul, and I grew up
> Foster'd alike by beauty and by fear.

When he writes about his time as a student at St John's College, Cambridge, he tells us that he had,

> A feeling that I was not for that hour
> Nor for that place.

Of his time in France, and of his love affair, he writes as follows, changing both his own name and that of Annette Valois,

> A Town of small repute in the heart of France
> Was the youth's birth-place: there he vow'd his love
> To Julia, a bright Maid, from Parents sprung
> Not mean in their condition.

These three extracts come from Wordsworth's autobiographical poem, *The Prelude*. They add to what we know of him and the way he expresses his thoughts. Wordsworth has a reputation as a poet of Nature. As we have seen, he was born and lived most of his life in the Lake District. He believed that the experiences he had, which were at their strongest in his childhood, shaped him to be the person he was. The poem *I wandered lonely as a cloud*, composed in 1804, is typical of the way Wordsworth writes and feels.

I Wandered Lonely As a Cloud

I wandered lonely as a cloud
That floats on high o'er vales and hills,
When all at once I saw a crowd,
A host, of golden daffodils;
Beside the lake, beneath the trees,
Fluttering and dancing in the breeze.

Continuous as the stars that shine
And twinkle on the milky way,
They stretched in never-ending line
Along the margin of a bay:
Ten thousand saw I at a glance,
Tossing their heads in sprightly dance.

The waves beside them danced; but they
Out-did the sparkling waves in glee:
A poet could not but be gay,
In such jocund company:
I gazed – and gazed – but little thought
What wealth to me the show had brought:

For oft, when on my couch I lie
In vacant or in pensive mood,
They flash upon that inward eye
Which is the bliss of solitude;
And then my heart with pleasure fills,
And dances with the daffodils.

He describes the scene and develops it, giving as much detail as is necessary. He adds to the picture he is conjuring up in the reader's mind by the comparison, or simile, he draws in the second stanza. He compares the daffodils to the lake and its movement, and then returns to himself – 'I gazed – and gazed'. Then comes the final stanza. We are no longer beside the lake watching the daffodils; we are with him in a quiet room, and this simple but important scene is recalled. For Wordsworth, the recollection is the source of joy.

On the following page are two more short poems by Wordsworth. Of course, you could choose some others of your own. For each poem, identify:
- the subject matter;
- how it is treated;
- what it means to the poet;
- how the poem strikes you.

Chapter 8 Responding to poetry

To a Butterfly

I've watched you now a full half-hour,
Self-poised upon that yellow flower;
And, little Butterfly! indeed
I know not if you sleep or feed.
How motionless! – not frozen seas
More motionless! and then
What joy awaits you, when the breeze
Hath found you out among the trees,
And calls you forth again!
This plot of orchard-ground is ours;
My trees they are, my Sister's flowers;
Here rest your wings when they are weary;
Here lodge as in a sanctuary!
Come often to us, fear no wrong;
Sit near us on the bough!
We'll talk of sunshine and of song,
And summer days, when we were young;
Sweet childish days, that were as long
As twenty days are now.

There Was a Boy

There was a Boy; ye knew him well, ye cliffs
And islands of Winander! – many a time,
At evening, when the earliest stars began
To move along the edges of the hills,
Rising or setting, would he stand alone,
Beneath the trees, or by the glimmering lake;
And there, with fingers interwoven, both hands
Pressed closely palm to palm and to his mouth
Uplifted, he, as through an instrument,
Blew mimic hootings to the silent owls,
That they might answer him. – And they would shout
Across the watery vale, and shout again,
Responsive to his call, – with quivering peals,
And long halloos, and screams, and echoes loud.
Redoubled and redoubled; concourse wild.
Oh jocund din! And, when there came a pause
Of silence such as baffled his best skill:
There sometimes, in that silence, while he hung
Listening, a gentle shock of mild surprise
Was carried far into his heart the voice
Of mountain-torrents; or the visible scene
Would enter unawares into his mind
With all its solemn imagery, its rocks,
Its woods, and that uncertain heaven received
Into the bosom of the steady lake.

This boy was taken from his mates, and died
In childhood, ere he was full twelve years old.
Pre-eminent in beauty is the vale
Where he was born and bred: the church-yard hangs
Upon a slope above the village-school;
And through that churchyard when my way has led
On summer-evenings, I believe that there
A long half-hour together I have stood
Mute – looking at the grave in which he lies!

Examiner's tip
- Do not confuse knowledge about a poet with response to the poetry.
- Use what you know to help you understand.

Another example: R.S. Thomas

Ronald Stuart Thomas was born in 1913. He became an ordained clergyman of the Church in Wales in 1936 and worked as the rector (or vicar) of country parishes in Wales until he retired in 1978. He published his first volume of poetry in 1946 and many others followed subsequently. His poetry is coloured by the places where he lived and worked. Life in the Welsh countryside was hard and Thomas reflects this in his work. The churches where he worked often had small congregations and Thomas felt the difficulty of helping people understand the Christian faith. The pictures of Wales that he conjures up in his poems are often bleak: his views of the people with whom he lived and worked are also uncomplimentary. In the poem *They* he admits that, 'There is no love for such, only a willed gentleness'. As a poet he unites what he sees with his Christian belief, but we can sense that he works hard to keep his beliefs alive.

Here are two of R.S. Thomas' poems. Consider the ways in which you are helped to understand these poems, given what you know of the poet's life and profession.

Cynddylan on a Tractor

Ah, you should see Cynddylan on a tractor.
Gone the old look that yoked him to the soil;
He's a new man now, part of the machine,
His nerves of metal and his blood oil.
The clutch curses, but the gears obey
His least bidding, and lo, he's away
Out of the farmyard, scattering hens.
Riding to work now as a great man should,
He is the knight at arms breaking the fields'
Mirror of silence, emptying the wood
Of foxes and squirrels and bright jays.
The sun comes over the tall trees
Kindling all the hedges, but not for him
Who runs his engine on a different fuel.
And all the birds are singing, bills wide in vain,
As Cynddylan passes proudly up the lane.

Soil

A field with tall hedges and a young
Moon in the branches and one star
Declining westward set the scene
Where he works slowly astride the rows
Of red mangolds and green swedes
Plying mechanically his cold blade.

This is his world, the hedge defines
The mind's limits; only the sky
Is boundless, and he never looks up;
His gaze is deep in the dark soil,
As are his feet. The soil is all;
His hands fondle it, and his bones
Are formed out of it with the swedes.
And if sometimes the knife errs,
Burying itself in his shocked flesh,
Then out of the wound the blood seeps home
To the warm soil from which it came.

In this section we have chosen two poets whose work is mentioned in many syllabuses. In studying their writings we have suggested that there is something important to be gained by knowing about them and by reading several of their poems. There are many short accounts of poets' lives in reference books which are available in libraries. One of the most useful is *The Oxford Companion to English Literature* (Oxford University Press, 1990) edited by Margaret Drabble.

Chapter 8 Responding to poetry

8.2 Looking at themes

In Chapter 3 where we look at novels, themes are defined as ideas or beliefs that run through a novel or seem important to a novelist. When poetry is organised by themes this usually means aspects of life explored by poets in various ways and seen as a means of grouping poems together. A number of categories immediately suggest themselves: love, war, nature, death. Those who compile poetry anthologies are often more subtle than this, as can easily be illustrated by looking at some modern anthologies. Many of these are set works on GCSE syllabuses.

For the new English Literature examinations some examining boards (MEG, NEAB, WJEC) have compiled and published anthologies of their own. The *MEG Anthology*, for example, organises its selection of post-1900 poetry in three sections: Looking Back, The World Wars and Between, Brave New World. The *NEAB Anthology* (which covers English as well as English Literature) has five sections of poetry, in each of which there is both pre-1900 and twentieth-century writings. The sections are: Hearts and Partners, The Way We Live, Caught in Conflict, Words' Worth and Dancing in the Breeze.

The advantage of grouping poems together around a common theme is that, through comparison, it is possible to increase the reader's understanding and level of response. Such groupings, too, show very clearly the vast range of poetry that is worth reading and studying.

Putting this into practice

Here are two poems from the *NEAB Anthology*: they come from the 'Hearts and Partners' section.

Even Tho

Man I love
but won't let you devour

even tho
I'm all watermelon
and starapple and plum
when you touch me

even tho
I'm all seamoss
and jellyfish
and tongue

Come
leh we go to de carnival
You be banana
I be avocado

Come leh we hug up
and brace-up
and sweet one another up

But then
leh we break free

And keep to do motion
of we own person/ality

Grace Nichols

Stop All the Clocks, Cut Off the Telephone

Stop all the clocks, cut off the telephone,
Prevent the dog from barking with a juicy bone,
Silence the pianos and with muffled drum
Bring out the coffin, let the mourners come.

Let aeroplanes circle moaning overhead
Scribbling on the sky the message He is Dead,
Put crêpe bows round the white necks of the public doves,
Let the traffic policemen wear black cotton gloves.

He was my North, my South, my East and West,
My working week and my Sunday rest,
My noon, my midnight, my talk, my song;
I thought that love would last forever: I was wrong.

The stars are not wanted now: put out every one;
Pack up the moon and dismantle the sun;
Pour away the ocean and sweep up the wood.
For nothing now can ever come to any good.

W.H. Auden

Look at the poems in detail and consider the following.

■ Are the two poems well chosen for this section dealing with love and the effect it has on people? How is this theme dealt with in the two poems?

Here are some ideas; check your own thoughts against these.

Even Tho
- a short but direct poem, written in dialect
- spoken by a woman about the man she loves
- he loves her too
- he excites her, she finds contact with him exciting
- she wants to spend time with him
- she does not want either of them to lose their independence
- they must be able to 'break free'

Stop All the Clocks, Cut Off the Telephone
- a poem about death, the death of someone the poet loved
- the poet is totally overcome by this loss
- nothing has any meaning or purpose any more
- all modern means of communication are to be silenced – the poet wants to mourn
- all the beauty of the world is worth nothing
- there is no future

It is not only love that leads poets to write; they write about hatred, violence and war too. The First World War led to a great outpouring of poetry, poetry that is now frequently studied in depth. The war shocked people of its own generation. They thought that wars were soon over and gave a wonderful opportunity for young men to prove themselves. Military service, marching in smart uniforms, martial music – all of these had a certain glamour. Men believed that what they were doing was right and that they would win. You can see this confidence in Thomas Hardy's poem, *Men Who March Away*, written in 1914.

Men Who March Away

(Song of the Soldiers)

What of the faith and fire within us
    Men who march away
    Ere the barn-cocks say
    Night is growing gray,
Leaving all that here can win us;
What of the faith and fire within us
    Men who march away?

Is it a purblind prank, O think you,
    Friend with the musing eye,
    Who watch us stepping by
    With doubt and dolorous sigh?
Can much pondering so hoodwink you!
Is it a purblind prank, O think you,
    Friend with the musing eye?

Nay. We well see what we are doing,
    Though some may not see –
    Dalliers as they be –
    England's need are we;
Her distress would leave us rueing:
Nay. We'll see what we are doing,
    Though some may not see!

In our heart of hearts believing,
    Victory crowns the just,
    And that braggarts must
    Surely bite the dust,
Press we to the field ungrieving,
In our heart of hearts believing
    Victory crowns the just.

Hence the faith and fire within us
    Men who march away
    Ere the barn-cocks say
    Night is growing gray,
Leaving all that here can win us;
Hence the faith and fire within us
    Men who march away.

Thomas Hardy

But the reality of war was something very different. Amongst those who wrote about their experiences in the trenches and on battlefields, about being injured themselves as well as witnessing death around them every day, was **Wilfred Owen**. In *Exposure* he writes of the conditions the soldiers faced each day – the fear, suffering and tedium of it all. Wilfred Owen was killed in 1918.

Exposure

Our brains ache, in the merciless iced east winds that knive us...
Wearied we keep awake because the night is silent ...
Low, drooping flares confuse our memory of the salient...
Worried by silence, sentries whisper, curious, nervous,
    But nothing happens.

Watching, we hear the mad gusts tugging on the wire,
Like twitching agonies of men among its brambles.
Northward, incessantly, the flickering gunnery rumbles,
Far off, like a dull rumour of some other war.
    What are we doing here?

The poignant misery of dawn begins to grow...
We only know war lasts, rain soaks, and clouds sag stormy.
Dawn massing in the east her melancholy army
Attacks once more in ranks on shivering ranks of grey,
    But nothing happens.

Sudden successive flights of bullets streak the silence.
Less deadly than the air that shudders black with snow,
With sidelong flowing flakes that flock, pause, and renew,
We watch them wandering up and down the wind's nonchalance,
    But nothing happens.

Pale flakes with fingering stealth come feeling for our faces –
We cringe in holes, back on forgotten dreams, and stare, snow-dazed,
Deep into grassier ditches. So we drowse, sun-dozed,
Littered with blossoms trickling where the blackbird fusses.
    Is it that we are dying?

Wilfred Owen

> **Examiner's tip**
>
> - When studying a poem consider what it has to say for itself. Do not let the 'theme' take over from your personal opinions and response.
> - It always helps to compare poems on a similar topic: the differences can help your understanding a great deal.

In studying these poems ask yourself:
- What experiences led to the poems?
- What are the beliefs of the soldiers in the two poems?
- What does each poem tell its readers about war?
- Very simply, how are the two poems different?

8.3 Types of poem

It is possible to look at, and group, poems in a third way. There are recognised forms which some poets follow in their writing. Broadly speaking these fall into two groups: in the first there is a clear format of lines, length and of rhyming scheme; in the second the group is defined by the treatment of its subject matter.

Examples of the first are:
- sonnet
- limerick
- haiku

Examples of the second are:
- ode
- ballad
- monologue
- narrative

In this section we shall look at one example from each list, chosen because it features in some GCSE schemes.

The sonnet

The most famous sonnet writer in the English language is Shakespeare. The sonnet is a fourteen-line poem, written in one of two forms:
- The **English**, or **Shakespearean**, **sonnet** has three four-line verses, followed by two lines (a couplet). The rhyming scheme here is usually *ababcdcdefefgg*, though there are some variations on this.
- The **Italian**, or **Petrarchan**, **sonnet** is arranged in two sections of eight lines (the octet) and six lines (the sestet). There is usually a difference, or 'turn' to be noticed after the first eight lines, although this change may be delayed. Milton and Wordsworth both made this a feature of their sonnets. There is also a noticeable pattern of rhyme: usually it is *abbaabba: cdecde*.

Putting this into practice

Here are two sonnets: the first by Shakespeare, the second by John Milton. Shakespeare writes of love and passing beauty; Milton of his own blindness.

> Shall I compare thee to a summer's day?
> Thou art more lovely and more temperate:
> Rough winds do shake the darling buds of May,
> And summer's lease hath all too short a date:
> Sometimes too hot the eye of heaven shines,
> And often is his gold complexion dimm'd;
> And every fair from fair sometime declines,
> By chance, or nature's changing course, untrimm'd;
> But thy eternal summer shall not fade,
> Nor lose possession of that fair thou owest;
> Nor shall Death brag thou wander'st in his shade,
> When in eternal lines to time thou growest;
>   So long as men can breathe, or eyes can see,
>   So lives this, and this gives life to thee.
>
> *William Shakespeare*

> When I consider how my light is spent,
>   Ere half my days, in this dark world and wide,
>   And that one Talent which is death to hide,
>   Lodg'd with me useless, though my Soul more bent
> To serve therewith my Maker, and present
>   My true account, least he returning chide,
>   Doth God exact day-labour, light deny'd,
>   I fondly ask; But patience to prevent
> That murmur, soon replies, God doth not need
>   Either man's work or his own gifts, who best
>   Bear his milde yoak, they serve him best, his State
> Is Kingly. Thousands at his bidding speed
>   And post o're Land and Ocean without rest:
>   They also serve who only stand and waite.
>
> *John Milton*

Now look carefully at the two sonnets and consider the following:

- How does the form of the sonnet help each poet to develop his argument? How does the final couplet allow a fitting climax in each case?

In *Shall I compare thee to a summer's day?* Shakespeare is using a mental picture of spring and summer as something against which to compare his loved one. He makes us think of fine and beautiful days, but also about how a beautiful day can change quickly: 'Rough winds' or the sun obscured by clouds can easily mar a fine day. He goes on to say that Nature is all about change, that nothing stays the same. He includes all this in the first eight lines of the poem. He moves on, using these ideas, to claim that the one he loves will always remain untarnished. He talks of 'eternal summer' and of lasting qualities that will outshine death. His thoughts come to a confident conclusion in the last couplet of the poem: it is through the lines of his sonnet that his loved one's beauty will be remembered.

Milton's sonnet *When I consider how my light is spent* is arranged in a slightly different way. He writes from personal experience about his blindness. He explores his thoughts, wondering how he may best serve God and what account he can give God of the way he spends his life. Gradually, he too works towards a climax or final thought that answers his own question: 'They also serve who only stand and waite.'

The narrative

From the second list above we have chosen the narrative, a poem that tells a story. By this we mean not only that there is subject matter, but also that a real story unfolds in poetic form. Some of the great literature of ancient Greece and Rome comes in this form: Virgil's *Aeneid* tells the story (in twelve poetic books) of the hero Aeneas' flight from Troy, his travels and adventures until he founds the great city of Rome. Following this tradition, Milton wrote *Paradise Lost* to present the Christian view of God's fight against Satan: the creation and subsequent corruption of the human race. Wordsworth's *Prelude* is a narrative of his own life.

These great works form the tradition of the narrative poem, but those set or recommended in GCSE courses are not so long. Amongst them are two by Tennyson (1809-1892), *The Lady of Shalott* and *Morte d'Arthur*. Others include *How They Brought the Good News from Ghent to Aix* by Robert Browning, *Lochinvar* by Sir Walter Scott, T.S. Eliot's *Journey of the Magi*, Wilfred Gibson's *Flannan Isle* and John Masefield's *Reynard the Fox*.

Putting this into practice

Below is Robert Browning's poem *How They Brought the Good News from Ghent to Aix*.

> I sprang to the stirrup, and Joris, and he;
> I galloped, Dirck galloped, we galloped all three;
> 'Good speed!' cried the watch, as the gate-bolts undrew;
> 'Speed!' echoed the wall to us galloping through;
> Behind shut the postern, the lights sank to rest,
> And into the midnight we galloped abreast.
>
> Not a word to each other; we kept the great pace
> Neck by neck, stride by stride, never changing our place;
> I turned in my saddle and made its girth tight,
> Then shortened each stirrup, and set the pique right,
> Rebuckled the cheek-strap, chained slacker the bit,
> Nor galloped less steadily Roland a whit.
>
> 'Twas moonset at starting; but while we drew near
> Lokeren, the cocks crew and twilight dawned clear;
> At Boom, a great yellow star came out to see;
> At Duffeld, 'twas morning as plain as could be;
> And from Mecheln church-steeple we heard the half-chime,
> So, Joris broke silence with, 'Yet there is time!'

Chapter 8 Responding to poetry

At Aershot, up leaped of a sudden the sun,
And against him the cattle stood black every one,
To stare thro' the mist at us galloping past,
And I saw my stout galloper Roland at last,
With resolute shoulders, each butting away
The haze, as some bluff river headland its spray:

And his low head and crest, just one sharp ear bent back
For my voice, and the other pricked out on his track;
And one eye's black intelligence, – ever that glance
O'er its white edge at me, his own master, askance!
And the thick heavy spume-flakes which aye and anon
His fierce lips shook upwards in galloping on.

By Hasselt, Dirck groaned; and cried Joris, 'Stay spur!
Your Roos galloped bravely, the fault's not in her,
We'll remember at Aix' – for one heard the quick wheeze
Of her chest, saw the stretched neck and staggering knees,
And sunk tail, and horrible heave of the flank,
As down on her haunches she shuddered and sank.

So, we were left galloping, Joris and I,
Past Looz and past Tongres, no cloud in the sky;
The broad sun above laughed a pitiless laugh,
'Neath our feet broke the brittle bright stubble like chaff;
Till over by Dalhem a dome-spire sprang white,
And 'Gallop' gasped Joris, 'for Aix is in sight!'

'How they'll greet us! and all in a moment his roan
Rolled neck and crop over, lay dead as a stone;
And there was my Roland to bear the whole weight
Of the news which alone could save Aix from her fate,
With his nostrils like pits full of blood to the brim,
And with circles of red for his eye-sockets' rim.

Then I cast loose my buffcoat, each holster let fall,
Shook off both my jack-boots, let go belt and all,
Stood up in the stirrup, leaned, patted his ear,
Called my Roland his pet-name, my horse without peer:
Clapped my hands, laughed and sang, any noise, bad or good,
Till at length into Aix Roland galloped and stood.

And all I remember is – friends flocking round
As I sat with his head 'twixt my knees on the ground;
And no voice but was praising this Roland of mine,
As I poured down his throat our last measure of wine,
Which (the burgesses voted by common consent)
Was no more than his due who brought good news from Ghent.

Study the poem carefully and consider the following:

■ What story is being told here? Does the story gain from being in a poetic form? What are the advantages of poetry over prose in this case?

You will probably decide that poetry adds excitement to the story of a race against time. Three riders are urging their horses on to reach Aix with the vital news. The time is short and the rhythms of the poem imitate the galloping of the horses. The story is powerful, too, for there are three riders, then two and then one only who makes the journey all the way. Each stanza (verse) takes us a little further into the story, with an important development in each one. If you look carefully you will see that each stanza is one complete sentence, moving forward and telling us the next part of the story. It is difficult to imagine the story being so exciting without the rhythm and rhyme of the poem.

8.4 The use of language in poetry

We have now looked at various ways of grouping poems. We have considered poets, themes and types of poems. We have left until last what should be obvious as you read any of the selected poems – the particular way in which a poem is written. Often it is this which gives it special effectiveness. It is because so many people find the way that, say, Owen writes about the war or Shakespeare about love, Wordsworth about nature or R.S. Thomas about the Welsh, so very special and memorable that these writers are regarded as great poets.

If you look at a GCSE syllabus you will find aims such as:

Candidates should be able to appreciate the ways in which authors achieve their effects.

and Assessment Objectives such as:

Explore how language, structure and forms contribute to the meanings of texts.

In poetry there are special opportunities to do these things. If you cannot see immediately what to do, then a checklist is very useful. In considering the writing of a poem, you should look at:

- rhyme
- rhythm
- comparisons and imagery
- choice of words
- feeling or mood

Imagery is so important in poetry that many different types have been recognised and named. The main technical terms that you should know and use are:

- simile
- metaphor
- personification
- alliteration
- hyperbole
- litotes
- oxymoron

The question you should always ask yourself is: 'How does what I notice make the poem effective or vivid?' Remember that whatever you say should show how the poem has made an impact on you.

> **Examiner's tip**
>
> Be ready to use technical language, but only as a tool. There is nothing to be gained from finding, say, a metaphor if you cannot say how it is effective.

Putting this into practice

■ Look back at some of the poems in this chapter. Which 'devices' listed above would you say help them to gain their effects?

Here are some of the replies you might give:

- In *Men Who March Away* the poem gains effectiveness through its regular rhythm: it reads like a song chanted by marching men. It begins with questions that the men themselves and their critics might ask; it then gives answers to these questions. As the marching men dismiss their critics there is a sense of building up to a climax which finds expression especially in the repeated phrase 'Victory crowns the just'. The poem ends where it began, with the men making sacrifices. They are described as men with 'fire' within them: this suggests that they are passionate and committed to what they are doing – there is nothing half-hearted about them.

- In *Exposure* Wilfred Owen tells us something of the experience of war. The mood of the poem is sombre, finding expression in quiet sounds and slow-moving lines. The poem begins powerfully, describing the physical suffering of the men: the winds are 'merciless' and they 'knive'. These two words suggest a cruelty in nature which mirrors the inhumanity suffered by the soldiers. 'Wearied' and 'Worried' set the tone and mood of the whole poem. The poet writes about the senses and in the second stanza it is sight

Chapter 8 Responding to poetry

and sound that make their impact: the 'mad gusts' are compared to the 'agonies of men'. Here the poet clearly has a picture in his own mind of the men caught in the barbed wire, suffering brutal deaths. Often in poetry human action is compared to what happens in nature; here there is a reversal – the sound of the wind reminds the poet of the cries of dying men. This second stanza builds up to a rhetorical question – 'What are we doing here?' We can only share in the soldiers' perplexity and confusion.

- When Shakespeare writes of his love he wishes to praise his lady's beauty. He uses the tradition of comparing a woman's beauty to something in nature – here to a wonderful summer's day. But he does not start his sonnet in this way; instead he dismisses the beauty of the summer as an inadequate comparison. He points out the imperfections in nature while still showing us in memorable phrases, its beauty – 'the darling buds of May', 'summer's lease' – and he refuses to idealise the summer, for sometimes it rains and the clouds cover the sky. By comparison, he insists, the one he admires and loves has a permanence in the memories and praises of men. The whole sonnet is closely written, tying in a picture of a glorious summer with the beauty that is so potent for the writer. The poem turns on our awareness of the effects of time; of what changes and what is permanent.

Examiner's tip

- Let the poem make an impact upon you. Think of the language, the choice of words and the mood.
- Explain in a direct way how you come to hold the views you have.

Section 6 Coursework

Coursework skills

Approaches to coursework

Coursework is worth 30% of your final marks for this examination and is, obviously, the 30% where you have most control. You can plan carefully and take more time over coursework tasks than you possibly can over your examination answers. You can draft and re-draft and you can take care over your presentation. Let's take each point in turn and consider it.

1 Planning

It is sensible not to leave coursework until the last minute and it should certainly be completed before your revision schedule starts. It may be that, in your lessons, each of your coursework texts will be treated as a unit, and the culmination of the study of the text will be completing the piece of coursework. (Equally you may well complete several tasks on the text, each of which would be suitable for coursework and you will be able to select the best one.) Make sure, whenever you reach the moment to approach a piece of coursework, that you are organised with the text and with your notes as these will form the basis of your writing.

You may well be given a deadline by your teacher. Make sure that you plan towards that deadline. Don't leave everything to the last minute. You may plan your writing and show the plan to your teacher to ask for general comments on your proposed approach. Plan your time and you will have time to write a first draft which you might show either to your teacher or possibly to one of your parents for comments. This will clearly be impossible if you wait until the last minute. Whatever you do, don't miss the deadline which has been set. Otherwise you will find yourself working on the coursework for one text while you are meant to be concentrating on the next piece of work and that will not help you at all.

2 Drafting and re-drafting

This is a very important process but it is also important to understand exactly what is allowed and what is not allowed in the process. Once you have been given the task, the first thing you should do is plan your approach. Let us suppose that you have been set the following essay title after studying *Julius Caesar*.

- 'Machiavel or passionate idealist' – which of these descriptions most aptly describes Mark Antony?'

Clearly the first thing to do is to make absolutely sure that you understand the terms which are used in the question. What is a 'Machiavel'? How would you describe in your own words a 'passionate idealist'? Are you sure that you know what the word 'aptly' means. Once you have made sure you understand the question then you can go to your notes and make a broad judgement based on your own views of Mark Antony. Remember that in literature there is very rarely a right or a wrong answer and you might well have a different view from someone else. So long as you can justify your opinion clearly and sensibly you have nothing to worry about.

Having reached a broad view then you can think through and make notes in detail to show how you arrived at and can justify that view. From these notes you can then write your essay plan. At this stage, as we have suggested above, you might show your plan to your teacher or to another member of the class to seek their opinion.

You are now ready to write your first draft. Remember that in coursework there is no intrinsic value in length. You obviously have to write enough to answer the question but no purpose is served by making the same point over and over again.

When you have written your first draft you should show it to someone to seek their opinion. That opinion should be expressed in general terms. For instance, it might be suggested that you have said little about Mark Antony's relationship with Octavius Caesar and could consider looking at that aspect of the play a little more fully. Similarly, it might be suggested that a few quotations from the funeral oration would clarify several of your points. Comments might even be more general, perhaps about your writing style rather than the content of your essays. For instance, you may have made a number of spelling errors or your sentences might be carelessly faulty in structure. Whatever is said to you should be in general terms. Whether you act on all the advice which you are given at this stage is entirely up to you. It might be that you disagree with the views of your adviser. Just be sure that you consider all advice carefully and, if you choose to reject it, you must be sure of what you are doing.

You are now in a position to write your second and probably final draft.

3 Presentation

At this stage think about your presentation and your handwriting. There is nothing more frustrating for an examiner, or for a teacher for that matter, than to have problems reading what has been written.

Below is one student's answer to the coursework question on the character of Mark Antony. The essay was word-processed and was presented very neatly.

Read the essay through carefully and see what you think of it. You may have studied *Julius Caesar* in Key Stage 3, you may not have studied it at all, but you will nevertheless be able to assess it as a piece of writing. Does it address the question well? Is it clearly expressed? Does it lead logically to its conclusion? Would you have used more quotations? Would you have made any other points?

The teacher who marked the essay was pleased with it and termed it 'terse and convincing'. It was considered a successful piece of coursework.

Mark Antony is certainly passionate about his cause, but this cause can hardly be described as an ideal. In his soliloquy in Act Three Scene One, he sets out his objective — to avenge Caesar's assassination. This takes precedence over the welfare of Rome and its people, and Antony is prepared to plunge Rome into a bloody war if that is what is necessary to defeat the conspirators.

Antony presents himself, first to the conspirators and then to the Roman crowd, as a loving friend of Caesar, grieving over his death, but prepared to accept Brutus's explanation that it was necessary 'for the good of Rome'. In this guise, he obtains permission from Brutus to speak at Caesar's funeral, on the condition that he does not blame the conspirators.

Brutus speaks before Antony, and in his speech he explains to the crowd the reasons for the assassination. However, it can be seen that the crowd does not respond to Brutus's republican ideal. It is doubtful if they understand it. This is shown clearly by the shout of 'Let him be Caesar!' Although the crowd has been converted to Brutus, it has not been converted to his republicanism. Quite simply, they do not understand the argument. Brutus seems to have won popular support, but this support is easily won and lost.

Brutus's explanation for the assassination is coherent and well-argued, but it is wasted on the crowd. Perhaps the most effective part of his speech is when he asks, 'Who would be a bondman? Who would not be a Roman? Who does not love his country?' This touches the people's emotions, but Brutus prefers to appeal to their reason. This is where Antony is well ahead of Brutus — he doesn't even try to reason with the crowd because he knows that they will not be moved by rational argument.

Although Antony begins his funeral speech (Act Three, Scene Two, line 70+) with 'I come to bury Caesar, not to praise him', the first part of his oration is dedicated to extolling Caesar's virtues. These virtues (loyalty, military skill, compassion) are not incompatible with ambition, and refusing the crown might well have been part of a long-term plan. Nonetheless, Antony uses these examples to 'prove' that Caesar was not ambitious. After each example, he interrupts himself, and reminds the crowd that, although it may appear to them as though Caesar was not guilty of ambition, Brutus has said that he was, and Brutus can be trusted — he is 'an honourable man'. Even the Roman crowd can work out the implications if it can be proved (to their satisfaction at least) that Caesar was not ambitious.

Antony knows how to touch an audience. By saying, 'My heart is in the coffin there with Caesar', he is not actually improving his case in any way. It is not the type of statement that Brutus would make, whether he felt like that or not. It is by making sure that the crowd know that he is mourning for Caesar, that he is forwarding himself as a possible successor. He says that he loved Caesar, and appreciated all of his qualities. If the crowd can be convinced that Caesar was a good ruler, they will not support the man who overthrew him. There is a vacancy, and by aligning himself with all that Caesar stood for, Antony has made sure that he is the first in line. Although he is at present concerned with revenge, Antony is determined to be the leader of this 'opposition', and ultimately the leader of Rome. Antony would not need to amass popular support if his sole ambition was to avenge the assassination of Caesar. A small band of followers would surely be adequate to arrange the return assassination of Brutus, as it was for the killing of Caesar. It is incredible that Antony would go to all the unnecessary trouble of rousing the Roman people to his cause if he were then to relinquish the power that he had gained by doing so.

When Antony resumes his oration (line 118+) he is well into his stride. He can already feel the crowd on his side, and now he reveals that he has some information that would turn the people against the conspirators. But, of course, he would not do that — Brutus and Cassius are honourable men. In fact, he would rather wrong 'the dead' (Caesar), the people and himself, than do any wrong to Brutus. Antony identifies himself with Caesar and the people of Rome, but the conspirators are set apart from them. Solidarity between Antony and the people is thus established.

Antony now produces his trump card, Caesar's will. However, he still refuses to say or do anything against Brutus, including reading the will. This, of course, tells the crowd that there is something quite damaging to Brutus in the will, even if it be only a proof of Caesar's virtue. Antony is effectively saying, 'I could quite easily turn you against Brutus, if I was only to tell you the whole story — but I won't, because Brutus is an honourable man.' The crowd is left to wonder whether Brutus really is as honourable as Antony persists in telling them he is. Antony spends quite a while whetting the crowd's appetite for the will. 'It is not meet you know how Caesar loved you', he says. Finally, he allows the crowd to 'compel' him to read the will, but before that comes another piece of drama, stronger than 'my heart is in the coffin there with Caesar': the revealing of Caesar's body. Now Antony has become bold, and for the first time he does say something openly against Brutus: 'Brutus, as you know, was Caesar's angel', but this did not stop Brutus from participating in the assassination. Antony does not need to say that this is not the action of an honourable man.

Antony's final deception is a blatant lie. It is obvious that he has been cleverly manipulating the crowd since the start of the speech, but still he presents himself as the ordinary man, mourning his friend. He compares himself with Brutus, and says that Brutus could present the case much better than he could: Brutus would be able to manipulate you, Brutus would stir your blood — Antony is using a typical Machiavel trick, presenting himself as an ordinary, straightforward, honest man in contrast to his scheming counterpart.

Antony spends the entire speech castigating Brutus and dismantling his 'honourable' status. Throughout the oration he persuades the people that Brutus is dishonourable, that he is a great enemy of Rome. However, at the end of the play, when Brutus lies dead, Antony says 'This was the noblest Roman of them all.' Antony therefore compromised his personal integrity by making accusations which he knew to be totally false — in order to gain power. On the evidence of his funeral speech and its direct aftermath, I do not believe that the avenging of Caesar's assassination was Antony's ultimate objective. If it were, and Antony only wanted power as a means to an end, that of carrying out Caesar's wishes, he would not have tried to defraud the people regarding the contents of the will (Act Four, Scene One, lines 6–9). It is in this fourth Act that Antony is most clearly seen as a Machiavel. At this point, power is held jointly by Octavius, Lepidus and Antony himself, and Rome is now at war with Brutus and the remaining supporters of the conspiracy. However, Antony is still unsatisfied. Despite the fact that this leadership is as determined as he is to crush the rebels, he still wants more power, and he and Octavius begin to devise a plan aimed at depriving Lepidus of his share of power. These are not the actions of the man who, in his Act Three, Scene One soliloquy, appeared to seek only a just revenge for the killing of Caesar.

I therefore conclude that, while Antony may have been initially driven by his desire to see Caesar's assassination avenged, most of the evidence points to him being an unscrupulous Machiavel.

Types of coursework task

It is essential that the coursework tasks you are set are clear and that they challenge you; the success of coursework depends in part on the quality of the tasks that you are set. If you are not clear about a task then you must ask until you are absolutely sure. Above we talked about making sure you know what the words of the question mean. You can do that for yourself but if you are not clear about the focus of the task then finding out about individual words might not help you.

- Your task might focus on individual characters as the example we have already used does.

- Your task might focus on one or more of the themes of the text. For instance, you might be asked to write about the theme of the supernatural in *Macbeth*.

- Your task might focus on the writing style. For instance you might be asked how Dickens creates the atmosphere at the beginning of *Great Expectations*.

- Your task might focus on the plot. For instance you might be asked how effective the plot of *Z for Zachariah* is – does the story-line take you with it?

- Your teacher might ask you to pick up on one or more of the requirements of the National Curriculum by asking you to compare two different pieces of writing. For instance, you might be asked to compare a nineteenth-century poem about war with a twentieth-century poem on the same subject.

- Your teacher might put a question together in such a way that you have to consider the cultural background of the text. For instance, in *Far from the Madding Crowd* by Thomas Hardy, we are looking much of the time at people working on farms. It is a little unusual that Bathsheba is one of the farmers; Gabriel loses everything and has to offer his services at a hiring fair, which was quite common at that time; Bathsheba hires him and, because of the culture of the time, their relationship is considerably affected.

- You might be asked to look at the historical setting of a text. For instance, you might be asked to consider Shakespeare's *Henry V* and the characters in their historical setting.

Below are ten examples of tasks, together with a commentary on the focus of each of them. You may not have studied the books referred to in these titles, but you will find that often you will be able to adjust one of the tasks to one of your books.

- Michael Henchard in Thomas Hardy's *The Mayor of Casterbridge* is obviously a singular man, but are there more of the qualities of a hero or of a villain in his character?
  – *is asking you to look at the central character in detail.*

- How do you feel the poets of World War One (Owen, Sassoon, Brooke) attempted to repudiate government propaganda?
  – *is asking you to look at the historical background against which these poets were writing; it is also asking you to deal with more than one poet and thus make a comparison.*

- Who in Shakespeare's *Macbeth* do you consider should take the larger share of the guilt for the murder of Duncan: Macbeth or Lady Macbeth?
  – *is asking you to look at one of the main events of the play and the parts played in it by the two central characters; it is also asking you to make a judgement about the characters by comparing them.*

- 'Fair is foul and foul is fair.' Discuss examples of illusion, ambiguity and uncertainty in Shakespeare's *Macbeth* and show their effects on the play.
  – *is asking you to examine one of the major themes of a play.*

- Write an imaginary letter in response to Robert Browning's poem *My Last Duchess*.
  – *is asking you to make an empathic response to a poem; is also indirectly asking you to consider a style of writing suitable for that response, which might lead you to consider the historical setting.*

- Write a detailed commentary on the poem *Dulce et Decorum Est* by Wilfred Owen.
  – *is asking you for a straightforward analysis of a poem.*

- Write about the pressures on the different members of the family in *Spring and Port Wine* by Bill Naughton.
  – *is asking you to look at a group of characters in a play and to analyse their relationships.*

- Show the part played by the relationship of Winston and Julia in George Orwell's *Nineteen Eighty-Four*.
  – *is asking you to look at two characters in a novel and their relationship; in doing so is also asking you to focus on the theme of allowed relationships which is central to the novel.*

Coursework skills

> **E**xaminer's tip
>
> When you are approaching a task ask yourself what type of task it is – what is its focus?

- 'The world of the ranch is tough and lonely; there is no place for friendship and no place for women.' Discuss this quotation from *Of Mice and Men* by John Steinbeck.
  – *is asking you to look at the setting of a novel and to comment on it; is also asking you to consider the themes of the novel and the relationships between characters.*
- How does Shakespeare capture the audience's attention in Act One Scene One of *Romeo and Juliet*?
  – *is asking you to look at style and technique.*

Marking coursework

Initially your coursework will be marked by your teacher, using criteria which will have been agreed by the examination board whose examination you are taking.

The criteria

Your teacher will be looking to see that you have written a *coherent* response to the task set and that you have *commented* on the text; that you have *drawn conclusions* and that you have expressed a *personal opinion*; that, where relevant, you have used *quotations* to illustrate your points; and that you have demonstrated an understanding of the *language, structure* and *form* of the text.

Where you are writing about plays your teacher will want to see that you have understood how a play works and that you can demonstrate *understanding of character and theme*. You may also need to show that you understand different types of play: *comedy and tragedy*.

Where you are writing about prose you may be asked to show that you have an *overview* of the whole text and, perhaps, an understanding of its *social, cultural or historical background*.

Where poetry is concerned you may be asked to demonstrate your understanding of how poetry is structured and you will almost certainly have to write about *style and imagery*.

To achieve the highest grades your teacher will be looking for *detailed personal theories* and *originality of thought*; for arguments that are *complex* and *interesting to the reader*; for the ability to make *comparisons* between texts and evidence of *critical awareness*.

Procedures which will be followed

- Your teacher will mark your coursework using the criteria agreed by the examination board.
- The English department in your school will then 'internally moderate' all the marks. This means that marks given by all the teachers in your school will be compared to make sure that everyone is marking to the same standard. Usually the Head of English takes charge of this procedure.
- The examination board will then 'externally moderate' a sample of coursework from the school. This means that the standards of your school will be compared with the agreed standards of the board and, if any adjustments are necessary, they will be made. The procedures of the different examination boards are not absolutely identical, but they will all produce the same end result.
- The end result will be that your coursework is awarded the correct number of marks within the right grade.

> **E**xaminer's tip
>
> Make sure that you know the criteria which are being used to mark your coursework and make sure that you meet the requirements of those criteria at the highest grades when you are writing.

Marking a coursework essay: try for yourself

Below is a short piece of coursework. It is an analysis of a very well known poem, *Dulce et Decorum Est* by Wilfred Owen, a young poet at the time of the First World War. You will find the poem in full on page 21.

Ask your teacher if you can have a copy of the criteria which have been supplied by your examination board. Read the essay, look at the criteria and use your judgement in applying the criteria. What would you say about this piece of writing? What grade and mark would you award it?

Dulce et Decorum Est by Wilfred Owen

In the first stanza, Owen is describing the physical condition of the soldiers who were being portrayed back in Britain as great heroes. They are, in fact, anything but heroic — they are 'bent double', and 'knock-kneed', and coughing. They resemble 'old beggars ...hags': the war has destroyed them, from fit, young men to exhausted, diseased men. This stanza is devoted to exposing the men's plight, and accordingly it has a slow thoughtful rhythm which could even be described as weary. The men had lost their boots, but still had to continue walking with none, and their feet are covered in blood ... they are lame, blind — in short, nearer dead than alive. This is very closely related to the title, Dulce et Decorum Est, because these men are certainly not living in beautiful, honourable or fitting conditions.

The second stanza describes the mustard gas attack. The men are almost too tired to move, but they still find some energy from somewhere with which to fit their helmets. It is the helmets which are described as clumsy, but it is really the soldiers who are too fatigued to fit them on properly. Again this relates to the title — they can hardly be described as heroes. The dying man is 'yelling out and stumbling', and 'floundering' — hardly a dignified or fitting death. Nor is he even dying for his country, for England has gained nothing from his sacrifice. This stanza is an action stanza, and it is fast and breaks the slow rhythm of the first stanza just as the mustard gas broke up the men's marching. The first stanza is slow and fatalistic, the second fast and desperate.

Mustard gas is slightly green — if it is concentrated to make a deadlier killer it is then darker green. It kills by burning away the lungs — and so Owen sees the soldier 'under a green sea, drowning'. As with under-sea drowning, he knew he was going to die, died painfully and could do nothing about it. Not an honourable or fitting death at all.

The third stanza, only two lines, is a powerful, haunting one. 'In all my dreams' shows that Owen would never be able to forget the murder of his comrade, the killing of whom he could do nothing about, or the way that he hopelessly plunged at him as he died. It shows how war not only destroys those who die, whether honourably, for their country or whatever, but also those kept alive who are mentally scarred forever.

The fourth and last stanza is a bitter accusation against the writers back in England who glorify war and quote the title of the poem gleefully. He asks them, many of them middle- and upper-class women who would never experience war and its horrors, to imagine themselves in his position. He describes, with chilling clarity, the way the dead man was dealt with — his corpse flung on a waggon, probably with a load of other junk. To throw a body on a wagon is not an accepted way of treating the dead in a regular situation. However, in war, lives become very cheap and any 'decorum' (English or Latin meaning!) goes out of the window, yet again exposing the myth. If it is so great to die in war, why are the dead treated so badly?

Owen describes the man with accuracy and it is gruesome. 'White eyes writhing in his face' — 'hanging face' — this is what dead soldiers are

> really like, not some mythical hero. His lungs bleed badly and he still 'gargles' his own blood.
>
> Some similes are slightly obscure. 'face like a devil's sick of sin' — what is a devil who doesn't sin? A soldier who doesn't kill; maybe a dead soldier? — who, after all, is no use to anyone, whether he was a hero or not. He says 'vile, incurable sores on innocent tongues' — another affliction for a soldier, another disease? The poem does seem to lose its way in the last stanza, perhaps because Owen's own strong feelings get in the way of good poetry. However, it ends strongly. There is a heavy irony on 'My friend' — the people he is accusing are certainly not his friends. 'If you knew what you encourage', he says, 'you would not be so quick to send young men off to die, or to drum it into children that it is something good to die in war.'
>
> 'Dulce et decorum est', he says, is 'the old Lie'. Not just any lie, but the Lie, the one which had sent countless millions to death beforehand and was doing so at that time when he was writing.

I wonder if you have been generous or harsh with the essay or whether you agree with the teacher who originally marked it! It was described as 'concise and perceptive'. The candidate has taken us through the poem in detail commenting on significant points. The imagery has been mentioned and the writer is clearly able to evoke the atmosphere of the battlefield. There is personal comment and the writer is able to justify to us the title of the poem. The essay was originally awarded an A grade and, although it would not be at the top of that grade because it fails to develop some points, that is the band in which it fits. There is an analysis and evaluation of the poem, the poem is interpreted and there is a personal response. Quotation is used effectively, consistently and imaginatively.

Follow these procedures and you will have made sure that you will gain the highest marks possible!

Section 7   The examination

Examination questions

Different types of question

We can now look at examples of questions drawn from the specimens that have been published by the examination boards.

Questions testing critical response and interpretation

Here are two examples of questions about different Shakespeare plays:

- Romeo has been described as brave by some critics and foolish by others. Discuss these opinions and give your own.

    SEG (specimen)

- Basing your answer on a close reading of the play, consider whether there is, in your opinion, any justification for the conduct of Lady Macbeth.

    SEG (specimen)

In the first question you are expected to write about Romeo's character. But this is not to be done in a general way, as if the question were 'Write a character study'. The way the discussion is to be carried on is to consider two different views: is Romeo brave or foolish? The question implies that there is evidence in the play to support both of these possible opinions. A good answer will show Romeo's actions in key scenes and come to a conclusion about them. A candidate's personal and final view about Romeo (whatever it is) will be important. But there isn't a right answer.

All this might be understood from the question. The published mark scheme indicates, too, that the candidate must not lose sight of the fact that Romeo is a character in a play, not a 'real' person. So structure and form, as well as Romeo's 'words and actions', are important too.

The question about Lady Macbeth is direct. Is there anything that can be said to justify what she does? Obviously, in answering the question, there must be a clear understanding of her part in the play. Why she does things must be pointed out and the reasons for her behaviour need to be considered. Again, the candidate's own opinions are important, but they must be based firmly in the play. The words 'close reading of the play' are very important in the question.

WJEC has similar questions to those above. One question set, for example, is on Harper Lee's *To Kill a Mockingbird*.

- Write about the relationship between Jem and Scout. Show how and why it changes and how it is presented throughout the novel.

    WJEC (specimen)

The second sentence in this question defines what has to be done. 'Show' means refer to important events that happen in the novel concerning Jem and Scout. 'Why' means give reasons for the changes and developments that have been referred to. 'Presented' means think about the writer: why she puts things like this, in this order; why her characters speak and think as they do. The published mark scheme expects A/A★ candidates to provide 'abundant evidence of assimilation of stylistic devices'.

Examination questions

Role-play questions

Some boards also set questions which ask for the candidate to write 'in role'. This involves showing an understanding of character: for example, by giving his/her account of something important.

■ Imagine you are Aunt Alexandra at the end of the novel [*To Kill a Mockingbird*]. You think back over events. Write down your thoughts and feelings. Remember how Aunt Alexandra would speak and behave when you write your answer.
WJEC (specimen)

In a question like this the candidate can show an understanding of Aunt Alexandra by expressing ideas and opinions that the character we have seen in the novel would have. In addition, the ability to express these in her words and in situations she might be in, would add to the quality of an answer. Consistency with the character in the novel is a very important quality in such answers.

Questions on comparisons and relationships

The third National Curriculum Assessment Objective in English Literature (relationships and comparisons) is explicitly tested in GCSE examinations. MEG has questions of this type, based on poems in the *MEG Anthology*.

■ How would you compare the supernatural elements in *The Choirmaster's Burial* by Thomas Hardy and those in *Horses* by Edwin Muir. What does this supernatural description add to the poems, do you think?
MEG (specimen)

■ Compare the poets' attitude to war in *two* poems in this selection. How did the language of these poems affect your own feelings about war.
MEG (specimen)

In the first question the grounds for comparison are made clear. An answer must focus on the important area of the supernatural in these two poems. What is similar? What is different about the ways in which the supernatural is presented? There is plenty of opportunity here to look at language and the form of the poems too.

In the second question there are more opportunities for personal choice by the candidate. War in two poems defines the subject matter: the choice of which two poems is entirely up to the person answering the question but, at the same time, a wise choice will help in the putting together of a successful answer.

Questions on social, historical and cultural factors

MEG also has questions about 'social, cultural and historical' factors; all other boards leave these areas to coursework.

■ In *The Withered Arm* [by Thomas Hardy] Rhoda Brook has many difficulties to face. How well does she cope with them, given the way people would feel about her situation at the time?
MEG (specimen)

■ The characters in the novel [*Pride and Prejudice*] have strong reactions to Lydia's behaviour. As a modern reader of this novel are you shocked or amused by her? You should refer to the social and historical background of the novel in your answer.
MEG (specimen)

In each of these questions we see an extra dimension to GCSE questions. In the first question the candidate must discuss the opinions people would be likely to have of a woman in Rhoda's position at the time the story is set. The idea here is that we can only fully appreciate her actions and her difficulties if we understand certain ideas about male/female relationships and about marriage. A similar area is chosen for the question on *Pride and Prejudice*, with a suggestion that an answer should compare the contemporary attitude to Lydia's behaviour with a modern one.

Different types of question

Passage-based questions

Finally, all examination boards set questions on extracts printed on the examination paper itself. These are of two kinds: passages from set books and 'unseen' passages.

NEAB has questions on prose set books, using short extracts or what we might call 'extended quotations'. The following question is on an extract from *Of Mice and Men* by John Steinbeck.

- Read the passage printed below and answer *all* parts of the question that follows.

- The passage is taken from near the beginning of Chapter 3 where George is thanking Slim for giving Lennie one of his pups.

> George looked over at Slim and saw the calm, god-like eyes fastened on him. 'Funny' said George. 'I used to have a hell of a lot of fun with 'im. Used to play jokes on 'im 'cause he was too dumb to take care of 'imself. But he was too dumb even to know he had a joke played on him. Why, he'd do any damn thing I tol' him. If I tol' him to walk over a cliff, over he'd go. That wasn't so damn much fun after a while. He never got mad about it, neither. I've beat the hell outa him, and *he coulda bust every bone in my body jus' with his han's* but he never lifted a finger against me'. George's voice was taking on the tone of a confession. 'Tell you what made me stop that. One day a bunch of guys was standin' around up on the Sacramento River. I was feelin' pretty smart. I turns to Lennie and says: "Jump in." An' he jumps. Couldn't swim a stroke. He damn near drowned before we could get him. An' he was so damn nice to me for pullin' him out. Clean forgot I told him to jump in. Well, I ain't done nothing like that no more.'
>
> 'He's a nice fella,' said Slim. 'Guy don't need no sense to be a nice fella. Seems to me sometimes it jus' works the other way around. *Take a real smart guy and he ain't hardly ever a nice fella.*'

(a) These questions are all based on the passage. Spend half your time on (a).
  (i) Explain clearly why you think George changes from having a 'hell of a lot of fun' with Lennie (line 2) to 'I ain't done nothing like that no more' (line 13). Look at the two italicised sections (lines 7 and 15/16).
  (ii) Explain how the first italicised section prepares us for an event later in the chapter.

(b) These questions are on the text as a whole. Spend half your time on (b).
  (i) What evidence can you find in the novel to show that Lennie is 'a nice fella' but not 'a real smart guy'?
  (ii) Compare Lennie with *one* character who is 'smart' but 'hardly ever a nice fella'.

NEAB (specimen)

The passage is used here in two ways. First, question (a), to focus an answer on specific points in the passage itself which show things about George's attitude to Lennie. Secondly, question (b), as a springboard for considering other aspects of the same novel.

MEG passage-based questions are different. In them there are longer extracts from literature and usually the answer is based entirely upon the extract. This does not mean, of course, that these extracts should be tackled unseen. A sound knowledge of the text will help in the understanding of what is read. The following question is on an extract from *Dr Jekyll and Mr Hyde* by Robert Louis Stevenson.

- A good horror story is meant to shock you. What are your feelings as you read through this extract? How has the way it is written helped to create these feelings?

MEG (specimen)

Examination questions

Examiner's tip

Find out what types of question there will be in your examination. Practise the skills that they will be testing.

> 'And now,' said he, 'to settle what remains. Will you be wise? will you be guided? will you suffer me to take this glass in my hand, and to go forth from your house without further parley? or has the greed of curiosity too much command of you? Think before you answer, for it shall be done as you decide. As you decide, you shall be left as you were before, and neither richer nor wiser, unless the sense of service rendered to a man in mortal distress may be counted as a kind of riches of the soul. Or, if you shall so prefer to choose, a new province of knowledge and new avenues to fame and power shall be laid open to you, here, in this room, upon the instant; and your sight shall be blasted by a prodigy to stagger the unbelief of Satan.'
>
> 'Sir,' said I, affecting a coolness that I was far from truly possessing, 'you speak enigmas, and you will perhaps not wonder that I hear you with no very strong impression of belief. But I have gone too far in the way of inexplicable services to pause before I see the end.'
>
> 'It is well,' replied my visitor. 'Lanyon, you remember your vows: what follows is under the seal of our profession. And now you who have so long been bound to the most narrow and material views, you who have denied the virtue of transcendental medicine, you who have derided your superiors – behold!'
>
> He put the glass to his lips, and drank at one gulp. A cry followed: he reeled, staggered, clutched at the table and held on, staring with injected eyes, gasping with open mouth; and as I looked there came, I thought a change – he seemed to swell – his face became suddenly black, and the features seemed to melt and alter – and the next moment I had sprung to my feet and leaped back against the wall, my arm raised to shield me from that prodigy, my mind submerged in terror.
>
> 'O God!' I screamed, and 'O God!' again and again; for there before my eyes – pale and shaken, and half fainting, and groping before him with his hands, like a man restored from death – there stood Henry Jekyll!
>
> What he told me in the next hour I cannot bring my mind to set on paper. I saw what I saw, I heard what I heard, and my soul sickened at it; and yet, now when that sight has faded from my eyes, I ask myself if I believe it, and I cannot answer. My life is shaken to its roots; sleep has left me; the deadliest terror sits by me at all hours of the day and night; I feel that my days are numbered, and that I must die; and yet I shall die incredulous. As for the moral turpitude that man unveiled to me, even with tears of penitence, I cannot, even in memory, dwell on it without a start of horror. I will say but one thing, Utterson, and that (if you can bring your mind to credit it) will be more than enough. The creature who crept into my house that night was, on Jekyll's own confession, known by the name of Hyde and hunted for in every corner of the land as the murderer of Carew.
>
> HASTIE LANYON

Some English Literature examinations have passages not previously seen by the candidate so as to test the ability to read and respond without the opportunity to discuss with others or consider the passage over a period of time.

Writing literature essays

What you know, understand and can do will be shown in the way that you write, both in coursework and in the examination itself. Writing is a very personal thing but there are important points to consider when writing about literature.

❶ The starting point for a piece of writing is a question or a task. The essential here is that the topic to be written about is clearly defined. A question such as, 'Write all you know about Macbeth' would not be helpful at all – it gives no indication of what is expected of the writer.

Writing literature essays

❷ Plan an outline of the material in the text that will help you provide an answer. Very often you will need to identify 'key' episodes or features that will help you. So if you are asked about Macbeth killing Duncan, you will want to choose, say, the witches' prophecies, the title of 'Cawdor', Malcolm named as heir, Lady Macbeth in conversation with her husband.

❸ Next, what is really being asked of you? Important words in the question will assist here: 'Explain', 'Account for', 'Why?', 'What do you think?' and many others will show what it is you are to do with the evidence you have to hand.

❹ An answer will now begin to emerge. Remember that it must take the reader through your own opinions and thoughts in a logical way. An introduction, the development of a point of view and a conclusion will all be needed. There must be a balance between your views and evidence to support them.

❺ Make sure that you cover all aspects of the question or task. An unbalanced answer will not usually be eligible for the full range of marks.

❻ Finally, remember that literature (particularly novels, stories and plays) is usually concerned with change and development. If things stay the same they don't usually interest us. So, in an answer ask whether you have developed a set of ideas which relate to the changes in what you have read.

Examiner's tip

Be clear what argument you are going to put forward. Never write 'all you know'.

Putting this into practice

In this section we are going to look at two answers to a GCSE question on *Animal Farm* by George Orwell. The two essays have been written by examination candidates. The question set was:

- Imagine that, after being driven from Animal Farm, Snowball writes his memoirs about his time there. Write them for him.

MEG

> Now that I have been chased away from Animal Farm, I suppose that the windmill will go ahead without me.
>
> I put so much effort into those plans. I had never denied that building it would be a hard job, but I knew we could have achieved it together, as a team.
>
> Napoleon has never come up with any ideas of his own, and yet, everything I come up with he passes off by saying, 'It will come to nothing.'
>
> I found full plans for innovations and improvements, which if we had put into practice would have greatly improved our standard of living, and work efficiency. Napoleon just wasn't interested in any of it.
>
> The truth of the matter is obvious to me, Napoleon just can't handle the fact that I am better at improving the farm than he is.
>
> Surely, that is the reason I have been driven away.
>
> The windmill must have been the final straw for Napoleon. He knows that I always give a better speech, and that I manage to get the rest of the animals on my side. Who wouldn't welcome electricity to light the barns and keep us warm and run electrical machinery, except Napoleon, who wasn't happy because he didn't make the plan. He wasn't being praised by the other animals, as I was.

Examination questions

> Only when the plans were completed did Napoleon decide I was no longer needed, and set those terrifying dogs on me.
>
> Now I know the truth about Napoleon, and I see that I was a threat to him because I was striving for better quality of living and an equal way of working. Napoleon however doesn't want to be equal, he wants to be on top, he wants to be needed by the other animals. He does this by making all the decisions that affect the farm, so that the animals look up to him.
>
> The farm will collapse with him as leader, and the animals are no better off than they were with Farmer Jones.

Here is a second answer to the same question.

> I will never forget the night when Old Major announced his dream to the other animals. When he first sang 'Beasts of England', what an amazing moment that was. Unforgettable. Now I hate the thought of that song. Not the actual song, but the memories that go with it. It was such an exciting time. Even when Old Major died we weren't sad. We were happy and excited about fulfilling his dream, something that would have made him very proud.
>
> The rebellion itself is another great memory. The feeling of pure ecstasy when Mr Jones was chased out of the farm. We knew at that moment, all of the animals, that we would really make Old Major's dream come true. Such a satisfying feeling for me, and I'm sure for all the animals, was when we threw the remains of our horrid times with Mr Jones down the well or onto the fire that we made. Every time we sang 'Beasts of England', especially on the night of the rebellion, was a magical experience.
>
> We just couldn't believe what had happened on the farm until the next morning when we all went on top of the knoll. We looked at the farm, its fields and buildings, and we realised that it was all ours! Not a human in sight. I can remember being quite anxious about going into the farmhouse where Mr and Mrs Jones lived. Napoleon and I went in first, when all the animals went in. It was quite an experience as I had never seen anything like it before in my life.
>
> I can remember vividly my feeling of pride when I changed the name of the farm to Animal Farm. It simply reinforced the fact that we had got rid of humans from our lives, and could now live in comfort. It would not be for much longer though.
>
> The harvest was fantastic. It was very hard work but we worked with a pleasure we had not felt before, because we knew that we would reap the rewards. This was the feeling, for me at least, as well as the others, that went on all through that summer. We all worked so well together and everyone did their share. I tried to set up several committees to make the most of the skills that certain animals had and generally to make them better animals for it. Napoleon didn't think these were a good idea and for the first time since the rebellion we disagreed on something. It would not be the last.

Writing literature essays

> *Looking back to when the other pigs and I had that milk from the cows when the other animals didn't have any, I can see that we really weren't being fair and we were even breaking a commandment. I am regretful of this now.*
>
> *One of the best days of my time on the farm was the Battle of the Cowshed. It wasn't just that we defeated the humans, it also proved that we were very serious about the running of our farm when the farmers just laughed at us. It was one of the proudest moments of my life when I was declared an 'Animal Hero, First Class'.*
>
> *One of the worst days of my life, in contrast to this, was when Napoleon's dogs chased me out of Animal Farm. We didn't agree about the plans for the windmill, Napoleon and I. He thought it would take too much time and effort to build but I disagreed, saying it would save a lot more work in the long run. I didn't realise how much Napoleon must have disliked me until he sent his dogs to kill me. I only just made it out of the farm in time. Okay, we had argued about the committees and the windmill, both of which I thought would make life on the farm even better, but this is surely no reason to want one of your supposed best friends to die? I can never forgive him for that. I don't want to forget about the good times I've had on Animal Farm, how happy we all were. Unfortunately, those memories are cancelled out by the events of my last days on Animal Farm. It just goes to show that you can't trust anyone these days, not even those who you thought of as friends and comrades.*

Which of these is the better answer?

To decide this you must first ask what it is that the question is really testing. This must include knowledge of the events in the novel concerning Snowball and his expulsion. His role and the sort of character he is must also be considered. Then, we are asked to put a perspective on events up to the time of Snowball's expulsion and to decide how Snowball would have felt about it. Finally, thought must be given to expression and to the way memoirs would sound.

The first writer confines himself to the argument over the windmill. Snowball, he knows, regarded the windmill as very important and worked hard on it. The plans weren't accepted, he says, because of Napoleon's opposition. It would be good if the writer would tell us why the plans will now probably go ahead. Looking back, this Snowball sees the contest over the windmill as a clear indication of Napoleon's ambitions and his ruthlessness.

The second writer takes a much fuller view. The ideals of the revolution and its accomplishment are important. Snowball's feelings are made clear. The development of all this and the success of the animals are a cause of pleasure. There is reference here to the ideals and some of the ways in which these were betrayed. All this leads us nicely into the power struggle with Napoleon and Snowball's expulsion.

Each of these has clear merits and probably show us a grade C for the first essay and a grade B for the second. What, perhaps, is surprising is that Snowball sounds so controlled and reasonable in each of them. A more successful answer would surely explore the deep disappointment of Snowball, his fears for the future, and even the plans he might have.

Examiner's tip

Consider carefully what is involved in a question. Identify the immediately important but also consider what would give real quality to an answer.

Examination questions

Try for yourself!

Here are some types of question that you might like to fit to any of the novels (or short stories), plays or poems that you know well or are studying.

Prose

- .... is an important character in this book. What are his/her main features? How do you react to him/her?

- .... is a hero/villain. How is he/she presented in the novel?

- ....'s character changes throughout the novel. Is this for better or for worse?

- Why does .... behave as he/she does?

- Imagine you are .... at an important point in the novel (or at the end). How would you explain what is happening and your reactions?

Poetry

- Compare the way .... is presented in two different poems.

- What different views about .... are to be found in two of the poems you have been studying?

- How does the treatment of .... differ in these poems?

- What do you notice about the approach and ways of expression in two poems on the subject of ....?

- Compare the ways in which writer A and writer B present their poems on the subject of ....

Drama

- Evil is an important force in this play. In what ways is it presented?

- Is the ending of the play appropriate? Have we been prepared for it in what has gone before?

- The author uses surprises in this play. Consider the effect of these on your reactions to what is happening.

- Can the actions of .... be justified in this play?

- How would you want to produce scene – to make it effective on stage?

All of these questions will help you think about the texts you study. Practise the skills of selecting relevant illustration from the text and using it to support and illustrate your own answer.

Examiner's tip

You can make the best of your ability and knowledge if you:
- grasp the main idea of the question;
- work out what you really want to say;
- use good reference or quotation – never too long, but always to the point.

Avoid:
- telling the story;
- writing all you know in the vague hope that the examiner will sort it out.

Always:
- keep a close watch on time;
- answer all the questions;
- make sure you follow instructions carefully.

Glossary

A list of terms which you might come across in your studies of English Literature and which you might want to use in your own writing.

Alexandrine	A line of poetry which has six regular patterns of sound (feet), usually in an iambic pattern (u/).
Allegory	An extended metaphor used to convey an idea.
Alliteration	Repetition of the same consonant sounds to produce a particular effect. It is used especially in poetry.
Alliterative	The adjective from alliteration.
Ambiguity	Something which has more than one possible meaning.
Ambiguous	The adjective from ambiguity.
Anachronism	Something which is inappropriate in terms of time. In *Julius Caesar*, for instance, there is reference to a clock striking. Although Shakespeare would have heard clocks striking, the Romans didn't have such clocks. Shakespeare didn't bother about the accuracy of details of this type.
Analysis	Examination of a text in detail and drawing conclusions about it.
Anticlimax	When a story builds towards what seems to be a moment of importance but which turns out to be insignificant.
Antithesis	Words arranged so that they contrast in a deliberately balanced way.
Apron stage	The part of the stage which juts out into the audience in front of the proscenium arch. Actors performing on the apron are very close to the audience.
Assonance	In poetry, when vowel sounds rhyme but not the consonant or hard sounds which go with them.
Audience	A group of people watching a play; the readers of a work of prose or poetry. A writer may vary his or her style of writing according to the particular audience in mind.
Ballad	A type of simple, straightforward narrative poem, telling a story whose origins are usually in folk tales or historical mythology.
Blank verse	Verse which does not rhyme but which has a regular rhythm. The majority of Shakespeare's plays are written in a very common form of blank verse known as the iambic pentameter.
Caesura	A pause in the middle of a line of verse.
Caricature	Comic exaggeration of character, for instance as found frequently in Dickens.
Characterisation	The ways in which a writer uses language to build up and reveal character e.g. through speech, description of appearance, actions, etc.
Chorus	A character in a play who has no part in the action but who comments on what is happening, e.g. the Chorus in *Henry V*.

Glossary

Cliché	A phrase or an idea which is overused.
Climax	The most important point in a text. The majority of texts build up to a climax at the very end but some have a series of climaxes throughout.
Comedy	A play or other work which is amusing. In the case of Shakespeare's comedies, they also tend to end with one or more marriages.
Context	What goes before a particular passage and what comes after. Things are often easier to understand when they are put in context.
Couplet	A pair of lines which rhyme and which are completely self-contained.
Crisis	A turning point, especially in a play.
Criticism	Analysing and appraising a text or part of a text in a detailed way. A criticism can be either favourable or unfavourable.
Dénouement	A French word which literally means 'unknotting'. In literature it is used to indicate the unravelling or sorting out of a complicated plot at the end of the story.
Dialogue	Speech between two or more characters.
Dramatic irony	When a character in a play says something without realising its full importance. The audience may well know far more than the character and understand the full importance of what is being said.
Elegy	A poem lamenting the dead.
Elegiac	The adjective from elegy, describing writing of a sad or melancholic kind.
Empathy	Entering fully into the world of the text and showing understanding of and feeling for the characters and situation.
Episode	A coherent and virtually complete part of a longer narrative. Can be a chapter, a scene or a longer section of a work.
Euphemism	A description in gentle or inoffensive words of something which is unpleasant. There are, for instance, a number of euphemisms for the idea of death.
Fable	A short story which is designed to teach a lesson and which uses animals as symbols. *Animal Farm* is a fable.
Farce	A play where the characters are made to look ridiculous to the audience.
Figures of speech	Expressions which are not to be understood literally; the words have a different meaning from usual.
Foot	In poetry, a group of syllables which have a fixed pattern; it can be compared to a bar in music.
Free verse	A type of verse which does not have a particular rhyme scheme or a regular rhythm.
Genre	A particular style of writing, e.g. prose, poetry, drama.
Hero/heroine	The central character in a work of literature.
Hyperbole	Extreme exaggeration for effect.
Iambus	In poetry, a type of foot where an unstressed syllable is followed by a stressed syllable. Shakespeare generally wrote in iambic pentameters.
Imagery	A general term used to describe the creation of a picture in the mind. The most common types of imagery are similes and metaphors.

Glossary

Litotes	Understatement where something is affirmed by using a negative with its opposite.
Lyric(al)	Poetry which is musical and has the qualities of a song. (At one time poems were commonly sung, accompanied by a lyre.)
Melodrama	A play with song, designed to have popular appeal. Plot is simple with easily recognisable good and bad characters. The most well-known melodramas, like *Sweeney Todd*, were written in the nineteenth century.
Metaphor	A type of imagery where the qualities of one thing are suggested by association with something else.
Metre	In poetry, the rhythm or beat comes from the number of syllables in a line.
Mood	The tone or atmosphere of a piece of writing. Adjectives and adverbs in particular are used to create mood.
Narrator	The teller of a story. The narrator may also be a character in the action.
Novel	Fictional prose writing of considerable length; the plot generally revolves around a group of people, often in a contemporary situation.
Onomatopoeia	The use of actual or invented words whose sound conveys the meaning. Words like 'crash' and 'bang' are simple examples.
Onomatopoeic	The adjective from onomatopoeia.
Oxymoron	Contradictory or incongruous ideas placed together for effect.
Paraphrase	Putting a passage into your own words.
Parody	A type of writing where a particular style is imitated with intent to ridicule the original.
Pentameter	A line of verse which has five feet.
Personification	A kind of metaphor where the writer treats an inanimate thing as if it is a person and gives it human characteristics.
Plagiarise	Taking someone else's ideas and words and trying to pass them off as your own.
Plot	The outline plan of a play or a novel.
Proscenium	The archway in a theatre which divides the stage from the audience.
Prose	A type of writing which is continuous and does not have the patterns of poetry, e.g. the novel or the short story.
Protagonist	The central characters in a work of literature.
Quatrain	A group of four lines of poetry creating a stanza.
Rhetoric	A declamatory type of language used to persuade or influence.
Rhyme	In poetry, words placed in a particular relationship, usually at the ends of lines, and having the same sound.
Rhythm	The regular pattern, the metre, or the beat of lines in poetry.
Semantics	The study of the meanings of words.
Simile	A type of imagery where something is described effectively by making a comparison. All similes are introduced by 'like' or 'as', e.g. 'he ran as fast as the wind'.
Soliloquy	When a character speaks his or her thoughts out loud while alone on stage; this occurs frequently in Shakespeare. A well-known example is when Macbeth makes his speech beginning, 'Is this a dagger which I see before me?'

Glossary

Sonnet	A highly structured poem which has fourteen lines and a very definite rhythm and rhyming pattern.
Stanza	In poetry, a group of lines arranged in a regular and repetitive pattern. There are normally at least four lines in a stanza.
Style	The particular way in which a writer writes. A writer may adopt different styles of writing for different purposes.
Theme	The central idea of a work, e.g. 'young love' in Shakespeare's *Romeo and Juliet*. A work may have several themes.
Tragedy	A work of literature which ends with the death of the central character, often brought about by his or her 'fatal flaw'. Othello, for example, brings about his own destruction because he is unable to control his jealousy.
Verse	The rhythmical pattern of poetry; sometimes used interchangeably with 'stanza'.
Voice	The sense of a writer's presence in his or her work.

Index

Note: The pages in bold figures refer to glossary definitions

A

Achebe, Chinua: *Things Fall Apart* 36
Adventure of the Speckled Band, The (Conan Doyle) 56, 60
Albee, Edward: *The Zoo Story* 85-92
Alexandrine **161**
allegory **161**
alliteration/alliterative 18, **161**
ambiguity/ambiguous **161**
anachronism **161**
analysis **161**
Animal Farm (Orwell) 36
    essay on 157-9
    response to 54
    themes 31, 48
anticlimax **161**
antithesis **161**
apron stage 97, **161**
assonance 18, **161**
Auden, W.H.: *Stop All the Clocks, Cut Off the Telephone* 137
audience **161**
Austen, Jane
    Emma 35
    Mansfield Park 33-4
    Pride and Prejudice 29-30, 32, 35, 154

B

ballad **161**
Barbara of the House of Grebe (Hardy) 56, 57-60
Behn, Aphra: *The Willing Mistress* 20
blank verse **161**
Bolt, Robert 35
Brighouse, Harold: *Hobson's Choice* 24
Brontë, Charlotte, Emily and Anne 25, 34
Brook, Rupert 22, 149
Browning, Robert
    How They Brought the Good News from Ghent to Aix 141-2
    My Last Duchess 149

C

caesura **161**
caricature **161**

characters
    characterisation **161**
    drama *see under* drama
    major 45
    minor *see* minor characters
    novels 24, 41-8, 54-5, 149
    study 42-5
Choirmaster's Burial, The (Hardy) 154
chorus **161**
cliché **162**
climaxes 78-80, **162**
comedy 101-9, 129, **162**
comparisons 18-26
    drama 23-4, 25-6
    poetry 19-22
    prose 24-6
    questions 154
Conan Doyle, Arthur 37
    Adventure of the Speckled Band, The 56, 60
context **162**
couplet **162**
coursework 145-52
    drafting and re-drafting 145-6
    marking 150-2
    planning 145
    presentation 146-8
    task types 148-50
crisis **162**
critical response questions 153
criticism **162**
cultural background *see* historical
Cynddylan on a Tractor (R. S. Thomas) 135

D

Delaney, Shelagh *see Taste of Honey, A*
dénouement **162**
detective fiction 37;
    see also Conan Doyle
dialogue **162**
Dickens, Charles 36, 161
    see also Great Expectations
Douglas, Keith 36
Dr Faustus (Marlowe) 93-7
Dr Jekyll and Mr Hyde (Stevenson) 155-6
drama 18
    pre-1900 93-114
    in 20th century 64-92

characters 23-4, 25, 81, 94-5, 97, 114, 121, 149, 153;
  see also minor characters *below*
climaxes 78-80
comedy 101-9
comparisons 23-4, 25-6
endings 72-8
language and style 82-5, 95-7, 110-14, 127-30
minor characters and sub-plots 45, 82, 119, 120, 122-6
one-act plays 85-92
openings 65-72
plots 93, 97-100, 110, 149
themes 23-4, 25, 82, 94, 126-7, 130, 149
dramatic irony **162**
Dulce et Decorum Est (Owen) 21, 149
  essay on 150-2

E

Educating Rita (Russell) 64-5
  characters 81
  ending 76-8
  exam question 85
  language 83
  opening 70-2
  plot 82
  themes 24
Election, The (Mitford) 28-9
elegy and elegiac **162**
Eliot, T.S. 141
Elizabethan language 127-8
Emma (Austen) 35
empathy **162**
endings of plays 72-8
England, Barry: *Conduct Unbecoming* 36
episode **162**
essays 156-9;
  see also comparisons
euphemism **162**
Even Tho (Nichols) 136-7
examination 153-9
  essays 156-9
  question types 153-6
Exposure (Owen) 138-9, 143-4

F

fable **162**;
  see also *Animal Farm*
farce **162**
figures of speech **162**
foot **162**
form *see* structure and form
Forster, E.M. 36

G

genre **162**
Gibson, Wilfred 141
Great Expectations (Dickens)
  characters 24, 45
  narrator 50
  plot 41
  response to 53
  themes 24, 31-2, 36, 48

H

Hamlet (Shakespeare) 23, 123
Hardy, Thomas 34
  Barbara of the House of Grebe 56, 57-60
  Choirmaster's Burial, The 154
  Far from the Madding Crowd 149
  Men Who March Away 137-8, 143
  Son's Veto, The 37-9
  Withered Arm, The 154
  see also *Mayor of Casterbridge, The*
Henry IV Part One (Shakespeare) 126-8, 129, 130
Henry V (Shakespeare) 35
hero and heroine **162**
historical, social and cultural background 27-39
  exam questions 154
Hobson's Choice (Brighouse) 24
Hopkins, Gerard Manley 22
Horses (Muir) 154
How They Brought the Good News from Ghent to Aix (Browning) 141-2
Huxley, Aldous: *Brave New World* 37
hyperbole **162**

I

I Wandered Lonely As a Cloud (Wordsworth) 23, 131, 133
iambic pentameter 128-9
iambus **162**
imagery **162**
Importance of Being Earnest, The (Wilde) 35, 93, 109-14
Inspector Calls, An (Priestley) 34, 64-5
  climaxes 79-80
  ending 72-4
  exam question 85
  language 83-4
  opening 65-8
  plot 82
  themes 24
interpretation questions 153
irony, dramatic **162**

Index

J
James, P.D. 37, 60
Julius Caesar (Shakespeare) 145, 146-8, 161

L
language
    drama 82-5, 95-7, 110-14, 127-30, 161
    poetry 143
Lawrence, D.H. 34
    Tickets, Please 56, 61-2
Lee, Harper *see To Kill a Mockingbird*
Life Drawing (MacLaverty) 56, 62-3
litotes **163**
Luke, St, Gospel of 31
lyric/lyrical **163**

M
Macbeth (Shakespeare)
    characters 23, 120-2, 149, 153
    essay plan on 156-7
    exam question on 153
    language 128, 129
    one scene from 116-19
    plot 120, 149
    soliloquy 163
    themes 126-7, 130, 149
McGough, Roger 131
MacLaverty, Bernard: *Life Drawing* 56, 62-3
major characters 45
Mansfield Park (Austen) 33-4
marking coursework 150-2
Marlowe, Christopher: *Dr Faustus* 93-7
Marvell, Andrew: *To His Coy Mistress* 19, 20
Masefield, John 141
Matthew, St, Gospel of 27
Mayor of Casterbridge, The (Hardy)
    characters 24, 42-4, 45, 149
    themes 32, 48
melodrama **163**
Men Who March Away (Hardy) 137-8, 143
Merchant of Venice, The (Shakespeare) 25, 26, 123
metaphor 18, **163**
metre **163**
Miller, Arthur: The Crucible 35
Milton, John 141
    When I consider how my light is spent 140-1
minor characters and sub-plots 45, 82, 119, 120, 122-6
Mitford, Mary Russell: *The Election* 28-9
mood **163**
Much Ado About Nothing (Shakespeare)
    language 128, 129
    minor characters and sub-plots 123-5
    themes 126-7, 130
Muir, Edwin: *Horses* 154
My Last Duchess (Browning) 149

N
Naming of Parts (Reed) 22
narrative/narration
    narrator **163**
    novels 24, 41, 50
    poetry 141-2
Naughton, Bill: *Spring and Port Wine* 149
Nichols, Grace: *Even Tho* 136-7
Nineteen Eighty-Four (Orwell) 24, 36, 149
novels 40-55, **163**
    characters 25, 41-8, 54-5, 149
    plot 40-1, 54
    reading log 54-5
    response to 53-4, 55
    setting 49-50, 55, 150
    style, form and structure 50-1, 55
    themes 25-6, 31-2, 36, 48, 51-3, 55, 150

O
Of Mice and Men (Steinbeck) 36
    characters 46-8
    exam question 155
    plot 40, 41
    reponse to 54
    setting 150
    themes 36, 48, 150
one-act plays 85-92
onomatopoeia **163**
openings of plays 65-72
Orwell, George
    Nineteen Eighty-Four 25, 36, 149
    see also Animal Farm
Osborne, John 65
Owen, Wilfred 36
    Exposure 138-9, 143-4
    see also Dulce et Decorum Est
oxymoron 18, **163**

P
paraphrase **163**
parody **163**
passage-based questions 155
pentameter **163**
personification **163**
plagiarise **163**
plays *see* drama
plots **163**
    drama 93, 97-100, 110, 149
    novels 40-1, 54
    see also minor characters and sub-plots
poetry 18, 131-44
    comparisons in 19-23
    in drama 95-7
    language of 143
    themes in 136-9
    types of 139-42

Index

Prelude (Wordsworth) 132-3, 141
presentation of coursework 146-8
Pride and Prejudice (Austen) 29-30, 32, 35, 154
Priestley, J.B. see *Inspector Calls, An*
proscenium **163**
prose 18, **163**
   comparisons 24-5
   see also novels; short stories
protagonist **163**

Q

quatrain **163**
quotations 130

R

racial prejudice 36, 49-50
reading log 54-5
Reed, Henry 36
   Naming of Parts 22
relationship questions 154
response to novels 53-4, 55
rhetoric **163**
rhyme 18, 129, 140, **163**
rhythm 18, 128-9, **163**
role-play questions 45-8, 154
Roll of Thunder, Hear My Cry (Taylor) 36, 49-50
Romeo and Juliet (Shakespeare) 23, 24, 126, 150, 153, 164
Russell, Willy see *Educating Rita*

S

School for Scandal, The (Sheridan) 93, 97-109
Scott, Sir Walter 141
semantics **163**
setting of novels 49-50, 55, 150
Shakespeare, William 115-30
   characters 23-4, 119, 120-6, 149, 153
   essay plan on 156-7
   exam questions 153
   Hamlet 23, 123
   Henry IV Part One 126-8, 129, 130
   and historical events 34-5, 125
   Julius Caesar 145, 146-8, 161
   language 127-30, 161
   Macbeth see *Macbeth*
   Merchant of Venice, The 25, 26, 123
   minor characters and sub-plots 119, 120, 122-6
   Much Ado About Nothing 123-5, 126-7
   plots 119-20, 149
   Romeo and Juliet 23, 24, 126, 150, 153, 164
   Shall I compare thee to a summer's day? 140-1, 144
   sonnet form 140
   themes 126-7, 130, 149

Twelfth Night 119, 120, 122
   understanding text 115-19
   versions 128
Shall I compare thee to a summer's day? (Shakespeare) 140-1
Sheridan, Richard Brinsley: *School for Scandal, The* 93, 97-103
short stories 56-63
   in 20th century 61-3
   before 1900 57-60
simile 18, **163**
social background see historical
Soil (Thomas) 135
soliloquy **163**
sonnet 140-1, 144, **164**
Son's Veto, The (Hardy) 37-9
stanza 142, **164**
Steinbeck, John see *Of Mice and Men*
Stevenson, Robert Louis: *Dr Jekyll and Mr Hyde* 155-6
Stop All the Clocks, Cut Off the Telephone (Auden) 137
stories see novels; short stories
structure and form of novels 50-1, 55
style **164**
   drama 110-14
   novels 50-1, 55
sub-plots see minor characters and sub-plots
Swindells, Robert: *Daz 4 Zoe* 41

T

Taste of Honey, A (Delaney) 64-5
   characters 81
   ending 74-6
   exam question 85
   language 84-5
   opening 68-9
   plot 82
   themes 24
Taylor, Mildred: *Roll of Thunder, Hear My Cry* 36, 49-50
Tennyson, Alfred Lord 22, 141
themes **164**
   comparisons 24-6
   drama 23-4, 25-6, 82, 94, 126-7, 130, 149
   novels 24-5, 31-2, 36, 48, 51-3, 55, 150
   poetry 19-22, 136-9
There Was a Boy (Wordsworth) 134
Thomas, R.S.: *Cynddylan* and *Soil* 135
Tickets, Please (Lawrence) 56, 61-2
To a Butterfly (Wordsworth) 134
To His Coy Mistress (Marvell) 19, 20
To Kill a Mockingbird (Lee)
   exam question 153-4
   narrator 50, 52
   response to 53
   themes 25-6, 48, 51-3
tragedy **164**
Trollope, Anthony 32
Twain, Mark 35
Twelfth Night (Shakespeare) 119, 120, 122

V

verse 142, **164**
vocabulary 18
voice **164**

W

war poetry 20-2, 36, 137-9, 149, 154;
    see also Owen
Westall, Robert: *Supertrack 5* 37
When I consider how my light is spent (Milton) 140-1
Wilde, Oscar see *Importance of Being Earnest, The*
Willing Mistress, The (Behn) 20
Withered Arm, The (Hardy) 154
Wordsworth, William 132-4
    I Wandered Lonely As a Cloud 23, 131, 133
    Prelude 132-3, 141
    sonnet style 140
    There Was a Boy 134
    To a Butterfly 134

Z

Zoo Story, The (Albee) 85-92

Acknowledgements

The authors and publishers gratefully acknowledge the following:

'Naming of Parts' reprinted from Henry Reed: *Collected Poems* edited by Jon Stallworthy (1991) by permission of Oxford University Press (p. 22); extract from St Matthew's Gospel, taken from the *Jerusalem Bible*, published and copyright 1966, 1967 and 1968 by Darton Longman and Todd Ltd and Doubleday & Co Inc, and used by permission of the publishers (p.27); extract from 'The Son's Veto' from *The Collected Short Stories* (pp.37-8), extract from *The Mayor of Casterbridge* (pp.42-4), 'Men Who Marched Away' from *The Complete Poems* (p.138), all by Thomas Hardy, published by Papermac; extract from *Roll of Thunder, Hear My Cry* by Mildred Taylor, published by Victor Gollancz and reproduced by courtesy of Penguin Books Ltd (pp.49-50); extract from *To Kill a Mockingbird* by Harper Lee, published by William Heinemann Ltd (pp.51-2); extracts from *An Inspector Calls*, reprinted by permission of The Peters Fraser and Dunlop Group Limited on behalf of J. B. Priestley © 1945, first published by William Heinemann Ltd 1950 (pp.65-7, 72-4, 79, 80, 83-4); extracts from *A Taste of Honey* by Shelagh Delaney, published by Methuen London (pp.68-9, 74-6, 84); extracts from *Educating Rita* by Willy Russell, published by Methuen London (pp.70-1, 76-8, 83); extracts from *The Zoo Story* by Edward Albee, published by Jonathan Cape (pp.86-7, 87-91, 91-2); 'He's Behind Yer' from *Strictly Private*, reprinted by permission of The Peters Fraser and Dunlop Group on behalf of Roger McGough (p.131); 'Cynddylan on a Tractor' from *Collected Poems 1945–1990* by R. S. Thomas, reprinted by permission of J. M. Dent, and 'Soil', reprinted by permission of R. S. Thomas (p.135); 'Even Tho' from *Fat Black Women's Poems* by Grace Nichols, published by Virago Press (p.136); 'Stop All the Clocks, Cut Off the Telephone' from 'Twelve Songs' in *Collected Poems* by W. H. Auden, published by Faber and Faber Ltd (p.137); extract from *Of Mice and Men* by John Steinbeck, published by William Heinemann Ltd (p.155).

The authors gratefully acknowledge the Midland Examining Group, the Southern Examining Group, the Welsh Joint Education Committee and the Northern Examinations and Assessment Board for permission to use examination questions.

Any approaches suggested for answering questions are solely the responsibility of the authors and have not been provided or approved by the examination boards.